CW00447148

Postmodernism in Music

Postmodernism is a term that has been used extensively to describe general trends and specific works in many different cultural contexts, including literature, cinema, architecture and the visual arts. This *Introduction* clarifies the term, and explores its relevance for music through discussion of specific musical examples from the 1950s to the present day, providing an engagement between theory and practice. Overall, the book equips readers with a thorough understanding of this complex but important topic in music studies.

- Outlines and addresses the problems of defining what we mean by postmodernism
- Explores when postmodernism begins
- Engages with a broad range of literature and sources, inviting wider reading and thinking
- Uses specific musical examples to present ways of interpreting music that can be defined as postmodernist.

KENNETH GLOAG is Reader in Musicology at Cardiff University.

Cambridge Introductions to Music

Postmodernism in Music

KENNETH GLOAG

CAMBRIDGE
UNIVERSITY PRESS

CAMBRIDGE UNIVERSITY PRESS
Cambridge, New York, Melbourne, Madrid, Cape Town,
Singapore, São Paulo, Delhi, Mexico City

Cambridge University Press
The Edinburgh Building, Cambridge CB2 8RU, UK

Published in the United States of America by Cambridge University Press, New York

www.cambridge.org
Information on this title: www.cambridge.org/9780521151573

© Kenneth Gloag 2012

This publication is in copyright. Subject to statutory exception
and to the provisions of relevant collective licensing agreements,
no reproduction of any part may take place without the written
permission of Cambridge University Press.

First published 2012

Printed in the United Kingdom at the University Press, Cambridge

A catalogue record for this publication is available from the British Library

Library of Congress Cataloguing in Publication data
Gloag, Kenneth.
Postmodernism in music / Kenneth Gloag.
   p.   cm. – (Cambridge introductions to music)
Includes bibliographical references and index.
ISBN 978-0-521-15157-3
1. Music – 20th century – Philosophy and aesthetics.   2. Postmodernism.   I. Title.
ML3800.G53   2012
780.9′04–dc23

                                                    2011049115

ISBN 978-0-521-76671-5 Hardback
ISBN 978-0-521-15157-3 Paperback

Cambridge University Press has no responsibility for the persistence or
accuracy of URLs for external or third-party internet websites referred to
in this publication, and does not guarantee that any content on such
websites is, or will remain, accurate or appropriate.

In memory of my father

Contents

Contents

Music examples

Preface

This book is an introduction to postmodernism in music. It aims to provide an introduction to what we understand by postmodernism in general and to further explore some music that can be heard as appropriate examples of it. However, this exercise is not as straightforward as this statement may suggest. Postmodernism is an illusive term and, as will be discussed in chapter 1, it remains highly resistant to definition. The application of postmodernism to music, both through the identification of specific musical practices as postmodernist and as a broad framework of interpretation, would seem to only offer new problems. This book will not always necessarily solve such problems but it will provide some directions and seek to put in place a context for further debate and discussion. The approach will often be knowingly provisional, posited at the level of suggestion, which invites the reader to do their own interpretive work in order to begin to shape their own responses and inform their own conclusions.

Postmodernism is often claimed to be about plurality, fragmentation, difference. All of which means that there is a great deal of music that could feature in this book. There is a degree of diversity to the music that is discussed here, beginning with John Cage in the 1950s and ending much more recently with DJ Spooky. Between these two points many different musical contexts and practices are highlighted. Some of the music selected for discussion reflects my own personal tastes and interests while in some instances, such as the case studies of George Rochberg and John Zorn, their inclusion is based on the existing literature that situates the music in relation to postmodernism, with the wish to build dialogues with what has already been written forming a central strategy in the book. But this book does not offer a comprehensive account, no book could, and there is much that is not featured. One notable exception is the phenomenon of world music and its reflection of a global culture and economy, which for some is an extension of postmodernism. I think this particular set of issues demands an introduction of its own.

Reading

Clearly postmodernism implies some form of relationship to modernism, and it is important to have some understanding of that earlier context and concept before moving fully to confront postmodernism. However, although this book does touch upon some key aspects of modernism it cannot offer a full account. Inexperienced readers will therefore find it useful to engage with some background reading and listening in relation to modernism. I suggest Leon Botstein's excellent survey of modernism in *New Grove* as a starting point.[1]

One of the key books regularly referenced here is *The Condition of Postmodernity* by David Harvey. It also provides a quite brilliant synopsis of modernism and I think that this forms an important background, particularly as it comes within the context of a book on postmodernism.[2] A general awareness of the main developments in twentieth-century music will also help to provide an initial orientation. Arnold Whittall's *Exploring Twentieth-Century Music* presents an overview that can act as an invaluable guide to the music of the period.[3]

All the literature that is cited in the book, and some others that have exerted an influence on the writing of it, is presented again at the end in the form of a bibliography. There is no list of recommended reading as such. Throughout this book there are many quotations, at times quite extensive, from other books and articles. This book is in part a text about other texts. Postmodernism is always in some way a discourse, a debate about what we think it means and to which it might be applied. It is therefore essential that we engage with what has already been written on the subject. Chapter 1 provides an overview of some of the general, theoretical literature on postmodernism. This is highly selective, but many of the key thinkers and key texts that are featured do remain central to postmodernism. It is hoped that readers will not only use this overview as foundational to what follows in this book, but will also pursue some of the ideas that are presented here through the reading of the selected quotations back into the context from which they came. Often there will be suggestions for further reading and development in the form of references given in the notes. It is not expected that every reader will engage with every suggestion, but it is hoped that some will choose to follow certain directions and ask their own questions.

Given the initial complexity that seems to often envelop discussions of post-modernism some readers may find it useful to look at some other concise surveys by way of introductory co-reading. I still find Jann Pasler's discussion of postmodernism in *New Grove* to be a highly effective summary,[4] and Derek Scott's 'Postmodernism and Music' is an admirably concise outline of postmodernism and its relevance for music.[5] I also think that the early stages of David Bennett's *Sounding Postmodernism* provide a highly valuable account of postmodernism and music.[6]

At various points in the book specific concepts and contexts are mentioned – feminism, intertextuality, subjectivity, among many others. In some cases clarification of a concept and some background will be given but it is not always possible to stop the flow of the discussion to fully explain such terminology, but nor is it considered necessary to provide a glossary. Rather I think it would be more productive for readers to seek clarification when required through reference to other texts. Andrew Edgar and Peter Sedgwick's *Cultural Theory: The Key Concepts* provides helpful accounts of many concepts, including postmodernism,[7] and *Musicology: The Key Concepts* by David Beard and myself is directed specifically to the exploration of such concepts from a musicological perspective.[8] I think many readers would benefit from easy access to both books.

Listening

It is hoped that the descriptions of music given at various stages of the book will encourage readers to seek out the relevant recordings and scores, and form their own impressions of both the music and the interpretation of it that is presented. The list of recordings provided only brings together those recordings that have been featured in the discussion. It does not, for example, include recommended recordings of works as such, particularly those only mentioned in passing. Given the nature of the issues that this book engages with I think it would be highly appropriate for readers to respond through their own listening preferences. I am always surprised and stimulated when I ask students to bring recordings of what they hear as post-modernism in music to the discussion, and I hope readers will pursue that speculative but thought-provoking process for themselves.

Dates are provided for specific works, recordings, composers and musicians that are considered to be central to the main direction of the discussion but not when mentioned only as passing references and suggested points of comparison.

Acknowledgements

David Harvey mentions in the preface to his book *The Condition of Postmodernity* that he cannot recall when or how he first became aware of the term postmodernism. I share that sense of uncertainty as to how or when I first encountered it, although I do know that reading Harvey's book was a pathway to a better understanding of the seemingly complex nature of postmodernism. But, if I cannot reconstruct exactly the first encounter, then certainly the memory of one of the first direct engagements is based on my own undergraduate student experience at Surrey University in the late 1980s and being asked by George Mowat-Brown to write an essay that critiqued Christopher Butler's book *After the Wake* (thanks, George!). That essay, and the supervision of it, pointed me in the direction of postmodernism, which has remained an area of interest since that time.

Postmodernism has featured extensively in my teaching at Cardiff University over many years and in many different contexts, and I would like to thank all those students, undergraduate and postgraduate, who participated in many relevant discussions. In particular I would like to acknowledge the contribution of Alexis Paterson, whose doctoral research on minimalism and postmodernism overlapped with the planning of this book.

I would also like to thank several friends and colleagues at Cardiff University – David Beard, Keith Chapin, Sarah Hill, Nicholas Jones, Clair Rowden, Peter Sedgwick and Charles Wilson – for their interest and support. I would also like to thank the music library staff at Cardiff University for their help and assistance in many ways.

I also extend thanks to Vicki Cooper and her colleagues at Cambridge University Press for their help and support for this book, and I would like to thank, once again, Nicholas Jones for his work in preparing the music examples.

Chapter 1

Introducing postmodernism

Postmodernism is a word that has been applied to many different forms of cultural activity from the 1960s onwards. For some time there has been an ongoing debate about postmodernism through which many attempts have been made to give more precise definition to what we might understand by it and the contexts – such as architecture, literature and film, for example – to which it has been applied. The use of the term has also at times shifted from academic disciplines such as philosophy, literary theory and cultural studies into more general usage through its application to particular styles and trends in a variety of different contexts and situations. For example, in *The Guardian* newspaper on Friday 29 July 2011, film critic Peter Bradshaw described the latest Hollywood production *Captain America: The First Avenger* as having a 'clever postmodern twist',[1] while in the book review section of the same newspaper the following day a new novel from Hari Kunzru, *Gods Without Men*, is claimed as an example of 'ironic postmodern sophistication'.[2] It is not necessary to explain why these examples are described in this way, rather it is sufficient at this stage simply to note the reference to post-modernism in relation to both film and literature within a current journalistic but still critical discourse.

Within this chapter, and at later stages of the book, reference will be made to some definitions and applications of postmodernism as it emerged through wide intellectual contexts. The attempt to create an understanding of the 'resolutely contradictory' phenomenon that is postmodernism and the outlining of some starting points that follows will be taken from philosophy and other related disciplines, such as literary theory. This will involve summary of some key thinkers and ideas and go some way towards anticipating their potential relevance to music. However, the primary purpose of this stage of the discussion will be, through continuing to pose the question of what postmodernism is, to put in place some substantial theoretical and contextual points of reference that will be returned to throughout the subsequent stages of this book, in dialogue with a more direct turn towards exploring what postmodernism in music might actually sound like.

What is postmodernism?

Although this question in itself seems straightforward, providing an adequate answer is far from easy. It can be assumed that postmodernism is a word, a concept, that has been developed in order to define culture after modernism, with the prefix 'post' simply indicating the going beyond of modernism. But how that culture is identified, defined and discussed remains open to interpretation. For some, the direction of the debate, and the answer to the question of what postmodernism is, will be that there is no such thing while, for others, the relevance of the term will be recognized but still left in a rather problematic, unresolved state.[3] Of those who take a positive view of postmodernism there may be a suggestion of a certain consensus; there are certainly a number of recurring factors in most discussions of postmodernism – fragmentation, pluralism, difference – but there will still be divergences, variations of subject matter and interpretation.

One recurrent factor in most attempts to provide some kind of answer to the question of 'what is postmodernism?' is the initial complexity and resistance to definition that seems to be inherent within the term. For example, Hans Bertens, writing at the start of a book that claims to be a history of the idea of the postmodern, can state that

> Postmodernism is an exasperating term, and so are postmodern, postmodernist, postmodernity, and whatever else one might come across in the way of derivation.[4]

Utilizing a similar starting point, Linda Hutcheon, in the context of an introduction to a highly stimulating study of postmodernism in literature titled *A Poetics of Postmodernism*, claims:

> Of all the terms bandied about in both current cultural theory and contemporary writing on the arts, postmodernism must be the most over- and under-defined.[5]

And, in a closely related book, *The Politics of Postmodernism*, first published in 1989, Hutcheon similarly begins:

> Few words are more used and abused in discussions of contemporary culture than the word 'postmodernism.' As a result, any attempt to define the word will necessarily and simultaneously have both positive and negative dimensions.[6]

There must be something quite paradoxical and perplexing about a term that invites use, perhaps overuse, but which remains 'exasperating', 'under-defined', 'abused' and has simultaneously both 'positive and negative dimensions'. The section that follows will begin with an attempt to define postmodernism from one specific perspective and will then explore further some of the reasons why postmodernism appears 'exasperating', 'under-defined' and so on. We might not always resolve these problems, to expect to do so might be a rather un-postmodernist way of thinking, but we can begin to understand how and why postmodernism might remain, perhaps must remain, both paradoxical and resistant, with the resistance to easy definition forming part of what postmodernism both means and represents. Accepting that resistance, and embracing the contradictions while suppressing any desire to seek an easy resolution, will go some way towards beginning to understand postmodernism. As Hutcheon suggests, 'postmodernism is a phenomenon whose mode is resolutely contradictory'.[7]

Lyotard – metanarrative – modernism

The most widely cited attempt to effectively pose the question of what postmodernism is was provided by the French philosopher Jean-François Lyotard, and his position has been restated in many general texts on postmodernism. Lyotard began his intellectual development through a positive engagement with Marxism, the ideological project whose origins and development were closely intertwined with a modernist perspective. However, Lyotard, like many intellectuals of the post-1945 world, rather self-consciously distanced himself from that particular context.

Lyotard's most direct attempt to define and delineate postmodernism comes in a book titled *The Postmodern Condition*, first published in French in 1979 and then translated into English in 1984.[8] However, although this is the text within which Lyotard outlines his highly influential account of postmodernism, the book is primarily about the condition and value of knowledge. As Stuart Sim, in summarizing Lyotard's position, states, 'knowledge is now the world's most significant commodity'.[9] It could be argued that the commodity status of knowledge has now been further intensified through the development of some aspects of the Internet and related electronic media. Lyotard's discussion is positioned in relation to a scientific rather than cultural discourse, with science being framed by its own systems of knowledge and forms of legitimacy. These concerns are reflected in the quasi-scientific aura of the book's subtitle, 'A Report on Knowledge'.

Lyotard begins with a seemingly succinct definition of the modern:

> I will use the term *modern* to designate any science that legitimates itself with reference to a metadiscourse of this kind making an explicit appeal to some grand narrative, such as the dialectics of Spirit, the hermeneutics of meaning, the emancipation of the rational or working subject, or the creation of wealth.[10]

Clearly if we wish to understand postmodernism, which implies a going beyond of modernism, then we need to understand modernism as the point of departure, or rejection, a suggestion to which we will return. However, what Lyotard seems to posit as the modern here seems rather different from what we may understand by both modern and modernism, particularly in relation to music. For Lyotard, as suggested above, this argument seems to be about science rather than culture, but if we interpret Lyotard's science as a generally rigorous thought process rather than a specific scientific practice it can be transferred into other contexts, primarily cultural, a shift that has been made in a great deal of literature on Lyotard and postmodernism. Through the cultural implications of Lyotard's description of the modern we can see that what is being argued for here is the claim that such modern thinking defines itself, or justifies itself, through reference to something called a 'metadiscourse' which then appeals to 'some grand narrative'. It is clear that both sets of terminologies, 'meta-discourse' and 'grand narrative', have something in common in that both suggest the large scale – the meta of metadiscourse, the debate about the debate – and the narrative, the story that is being told, is grand. Therefore the modern, for Lyotard, appeals to, or is told via, the big, 'grand', narrative. In other words, there are large-scale stories that have been constructed by, and act as representations of, a modernist mindset. The examples Lyotard gives of such grand narratives may now appear to be rather obscure. But they look towards, for example, the Enlightenment, through the reference to 'the emancipation of the rational or working subject'. The eighteenth-century project of Enlightenment stands for the rejection of out-dated superstitions and the beginning of a modern awareness of knowledge through the projection of highly ambitious, perhaps utopian, aspirations of enlightened progress. The large-scale, universal nature of such claims and ambitions could therefore be read, through a process of generalization, in terms of Lyotard's metadiscourse and, with reference to its scale, the grand narrative. Other examples of such metanarratives, as the grand narrative is more routinely termed, would include the already mentioned ideology of Marxism, which aspired to conditions of universality and sought to project a powerful aura of historical progress as both radical and inevitable.

Although Lyotard's description of the modern now seems more accessible, it is notable that, as already highlighted, he does not use the more culturally specific term of modernism. Modernism represents the radical redefinition of art and culture in the early twentieth century and beyond. In terms of music, modernism is seen to define, for example, the music of both Schoenberg and Stravinsky, and subsequently later composers who continue a modernist legacy. In translating Lyotard's version of the modern, by implication modernism, into the context of music we can see that, for example, Schoenberg's 'emancipation of the dissonance', which distanced music from the conventions and traditions of tonality, followed by the development of serialism, which sought to rationalize musical content as defined by pitch, *could* be argued to represent musical versions of the attempted construction of modern metanarratives in that they are intentionally big ideas about the nature of music with large-scale historical, formal and stylistic implications.

Lyotard – micronarrative – postmodernism

Although it is clearly important to understand modernism in order to then interpret postmodernism, this understanding does not in itself provide a definition of postmodernism. But, having situated modernism in relation to such metanarratives, Lyotard moves towards defining postmodernism:

> Simplifying to the extreme, I define *postmodern* as incredulity toward metanarratives.[11]

This really is 'simplifying to the extreme', and Lyotard's use of deliberately direct language is an intentional point of contrast to the complexity of the surrounding context and related issues. However, the key point in this stage of the argument is the assertion that we become postmodern because we cannot believe in the large-scale stories, the metanarratives, both about modernism and told by modernism. We are now simply incredulous towards such ambitions and therefore cannot invest belief in them. On the basis of this incredulity we are rejecting a certain modern consciousness and ideology and in that moment of rejection we effectively become postmodern.

It would seem that if we seek a Lyotardian answer to the question of what is postmodernism then the answer might be that it is essentially a highly sceptical, critical attitude towards modernism, a move that is often represented as an 'anti-modernism'. And yet this seems rather negative. To define postmodernism in this way seems only to say nothing more than that we are no longer modernists. At a later stage of *The Postmodern Condition*, Lyotard effectively restates this argument:

> We no longer have recourse to the grand narratives – we can resort neither to the dialectic of Spirit nor even to the emancipation of humanity as a validation for postmodern scientific discourse.[12]

Again science is invoked, but now with the assertion that the grand, metanarratives of, by implication, modernism, no longer have the value that was previously attached to them. In other words, in a postmodern context such narratives cannot act as a source of validation or legitimation. Lyotard continues:

> But as we have seen, the little narrative remains the quintessential form of imaginative invention ...[13]

In other words, Lyotard is now arguing that if we cannot invest belief in the big ideas of modernism, the meta or grand narratives, what remains, in contrast to the large, is the small: the 'little narrative' (micronarrative) is now the primary form of 'imaginative invention'. The focus is now shifted from the large to the small, and in making this move there is also a resulting shift from the singular (there cannot be that many potential metanarratives) to the plural. If the 'little narrative' is now primary there can of course be many such little narratives. This means, in effect, that there are now many stories to be told, and many different voices with which to tell them. These multiple stories, and voices, now suggest a culture made up of many different things: a plural and fragmented cultural, social and political landscape, with each fragmentary 'little narrative' potentially claiming its own identity and value without at any point coalescing into a larger totality. In other words, each 'little narrative' constructs its own sense of a self-contained legitimacy and place within a broad spectrum defined as postmodernism. The image of a shift in scale from the large to the small is also articulated in the work of another key thinker of postmodernism, Jean Baudrillard, who in his central book on postmodernism, *Fatal Strategies*, originally published in 1983, states that 'we are no longer in the age of grandiose collapses and resurrections ... but of little fractal events'.[14]

Following the above outline of what Lyotard leads us towards as an understanding of postmodernism we can now begin to at least address the question of what postmodernism is with the possible answer that postmodernism now provides us with a meaningful way of describing the loss of belief in the essential characteristics of modernism, becoming an important terminology that can envelop and reflect multiple voices and stories. In doing so it celebrates plurality, fragmentation and difference, and situates the self-contained legitimacy of many contrasting cultural ideas and practices. However, this 'answer' is framed only as a 'possible answer' because in a postmodernist context the provisional and the undecided will come to be interpreted as positive attributes in contrast to the allegedly rigid certainties and orthodoxies of the past as defined by modernism. For Victor Burgin the postmodern can only be understood as 'a complex of heterogeneous but interrelated questions which will not be silenced by any spuriously *unitary* answer'.[15]

The discussion thus far has addressed the question of what postmodernism is through reference to some key ideas from Lyotard's characterization of a post-modern condition. It has not provided a direct answer as such, but it has outlined the issues that inevitably come to the surface through the asking of the question. In conjunction with the problem of defining postmodernism comes the related question of when this proposed shift from modernism to postmodernism might have happened, or, at least, became evident.

When was postmodernism?

Lyotard's understanding of postmodernism also involves a critical retrospective reflection on the Enlightenment and modernism, both of which are now redefined as metanarratives, a move that positions both concepts as what had once been large-scale constructions but which have now lost their value. This reflection on both concepts suggests a degree of historical distance through an effective rejection of the validity of these earlier concepts, a process of rejection that seems to push them ever further into the past. However, Lyotard does not really fix his argument with any real sense of historical precision or detail. Although he refers to broad concepts such as the modern and the Enlightenment that can be placed in a historical context, he does not search for supporting evidence in the specific details that can be contained within, and contribute to, these concepts. But clearly changes occur at certain moments and have either inspired or reflected the debates about the identification and nature of such broad categories. Postmodernism is also reflected through, and identified with, specific developments in the cultural, and other, spheres. These happened in real time and suggest the possibility that postmodernism not only reflects and articulates certain historical transformations but also has now become subject to historical change.

The proposed situating of postmodernism in broadly historical terms can be strongly reinforced by the realization that since the late 1970s and early 1980s the world has experienced some profound changes – the fall of Communism, the Internet, 9/11, among others – all of which could now have further implications for defining the condition of knowledge, culture and experience after modernism. The seemingly endless theorizing around the term and the fact that the key texts on postmodernism, not just that of Lyotard, were all written some time ago now reinforces this suggestion. Linda Hutcheon, in a revised version of *The Politics of Postmodernism* published in 2002, states that postmodernism is now 'a thing of the past', becoming 'fully institutionalized, it has its canonized texts, its anthologies, primers and readers, its dictionaries and its histories'.[16] If this was the case in 2002 it is even more evidently so now. Postmodernism not only creates a distance to the past through its rejection of modernism, but is now itself already historical, with Lyotard's *Postmodern Condition* being a canonical text within that history.

Reference has already been made to Hans Bertens's book and its intriguing title of *The Idea of the Postmodern: A History*, a title that suggests an appropriate sense of historical distance to the emergence and development of the idea of postmodernism. It implies that the relationship between postmodernism and the culture defined and described by that idea can be considered through certain historical perspectives. Bertens provides a chronology of the debates about postmodernism and in effect positions a series of historical moments in relation to postmodernism. In doing so he also makes direct reference to various cultural contexts. For example, following a summary of some interesting early usages of postmodernism, Bertens goes on to position the music of John Cage, along with work of the painter Robert Rauschenberg and the dancer Merce Cunningham, as part of an 'anti-modernist cultural revolt that gradually gained momentum in the 1950s'.[17] This proposal not only situates the implied postmodernism of the suggested 'anti-modernist cultural revolt' but directly and usefully connects the historical moment with a distinct set of cultural practices within the broader context and concept of an emergent post-modernism. Just as the actual practices and practitioners of modernism – Joyce, Picasso, Schoenberg, Stravinsky, among others – inform how we construct our retrospective, historical view of modernism, it is also the case that a similar process is necessary in understanding postmodernism. This encounter with specific cultural practices, in this case music, will underpin much of this book.

As well as looking for relevant historical and cultural signposts, it is also possible to position postmodernism as a new site of historical awareness, a possibility that is rigorously pursued by Fredric Jameson, most distinctly and significantly in a book titled *Postmodernism, or, the Cultural Logic of Late Capitalism*, first published in 1991.[18] Jameson's distinctive contribution to the postmodernism debate is to project an essentially Marxist understanding of the world, through reference to capitalism and globalization, in postmodernist terms. This grounds the debate in a certain social and historical reality, arguing for postmodernism as the cultural dominant in a late capitalist world, with the use of 'late' also suggesting a certain historical periodization. However, Jameson extends this historical perspective into an under-standing of postmodernism that also involves thinking the present (postmodern-ism) in historical terms. He begins with the bold statement:

> It is safest to grasp the concept of the postmodern as an attempt to think the present historically in an age that has forgotten how to think historically in the first place.[19]

This statement may remind us of the power of history, the situation of the past in the present, but it also highlights how that historical consciousness impacts on our sense of place within a rapidly changing world. It also begins to provide a fitting reflection of a number of examples of postmodernist architecture, literature, film and music within which an awareness of the past is defined through, for example, quotation of, and allusion to, styles and materials from many different, previous eras. Such creative practices and processes open windows on the past while simultaneously disrupting expectations of historical and, as will become evident, musical time. This reflection upon, and interaction with, the past is also distinct from what was perceived as a 'year-degree zero' mentality in some forms of modernism through the aura of a de-contextualized autonomy in which the individual work was perceived to exist in isolation. As will be explored in chapter 3, this version of modernism was highly influential in the post-war world of the late 1940s and early 1950s. The new postmodern form of 'thinking the present historically' and its realization within various different musical contexts will be explored further in subsequent chapters of this book.

In a move that is similar to Bertens's identification of a specific historical moment as defined through a set of specific cultural practices, Jameson goes on to provide a fascinating account of what he sees as the 'radical break' with modernism from which a postmodernism can retrospectively be seen to emerge:

> The case for its [postmodernism's] existence depends on the hypothesis of some radical break or *coupure*, generally traced back to the end of the 1950s or the early 1960s.[20]

As was also argued for by Bertens the 1950s becomes significant, but for Jameson it is specifically the end of the decade, the point at which it slips into the 1960s, which is identified as this moment of great change. It is clear that a great deal begins to happen into the 1960s that is fundamentally different from what has come before, and positioning this difference within and through postmodernism becomes an interesting strategy.

If Jameson's account of the culture that emerges after, or through, the 'radical break' shifts the focus towards the 1960s and suggests a degree of historical specificity then a similar focus is also evident in the work of David Harvey. Writing from the perspective of an economic-based urban geography, Harvey begins his study of *The Condition of Postmodernity* with the outlining of his 'argument', the basic premise of the book, which begins with yet another bold statement:

> There has been a sea-change in cultural as well as in political-economic practices since around 1972.[21]

This 'sea-change' will be defined via 'the emergence of new dominant ways in which we experience space and time'.[22] Much of Harvey's project will involve often quite detailed discussions of changing experiences of space and time from the Enlightenment to what is termed 'time-space compression' in both modernism and postmodernism. This argument, as Harvey fashions it, involves a highly sophisticated theoretical understanding of changing economic conditions that are beyond the scope of this introduction. However, I will make regular reference back to Harvey's key points as outlined above, but such references will take the form of what I freely admit to be a loose, un-theorized translation into the context of music, in which much, if not all, of the music discussed in this book can be understood as in some way reflecting new experiences of space and time, even if our use of these terms might be rather different from how Harvey originally positioned them.

What is most immediately graspable about Harvey's statement in the immediate context of this chapter is its remarkable degree of historical precision. Marked by the onset of a world economic downturn instigated by rapid rises in oil prices, 1973 can be seen as the moment at which the utopian optimism of the 1960s finally disappeared and was replaced by new levels of pessimism within which, for example, nostalgia for a romanticized past becomes a new cultural mode. For Harvey, the 'sea-change' as defined by 1972 becomes the historical marker for postmodernism. At the end of a chapter titled 'Modernity and Modernism', a highly stimulating and effective outline of modernism, Harvey concludes:

> Though a failure, at least judged in its own terms, the movement of 1968 has to be viewed, however, as the cultural and political harbinger of the subsequent turn to postmodernism. Somewhere between 1968 and 1972, therefore, we see postmodernism emerge as a full-blown though still incoherent movement out of the chrysalis of the anti-modern movement of the 1960s.[23]

The image of 'revolution' conjured by the events of 1968 in Paris, and other major cities, in which students and others confronted what was perceived to be a hostile, conservative establishment, ended inevitably in failure. This sense of failure not only provides a symbolic end to the 1960s but also had a direct impact on many intellectuals, including Lyotard and Baudrillard. From this moment, on the basis of Harvey's interpretation, postmodernism emerges from a moment of 'anti-modernism' into a 'full-blown though still incoherent movement' in the early 1970s. Harvey's use of 'movement' poses some difficult questions from within the context of postmodernism: does 'the movement of 1968' imply a level of intent? Does the 'anti-modern movement of the 1960s' suggest a coherence, even allowing for his qualification that the movement is still incoherent, that may actually be rather inconsistent with most characterizations of the fragmentary nature of postmodernism? However, what we most need to retain from Harvey's account in this context is the sense of a distinct historical moment.

Interestingly this moment, and its proposed 'anti-modernism', seems quite different from that of Bertens's suggestion of an anti-modernist revolt of the 1950s. For Jameson, the 'radical break' comes around the late 1950s into the 1960s, and that feels rather different from Harvey's suggested historical space of 'somewhere between 1968 and 1972'. While these subtle variations in chronology reflect both the fluidity of the shifting landscape of the period in general and the diversity and differences inherent within the debates and discussions around postmodernism, it is possible to bring these chronologies closer together into some form of coherent picture and suggest the following outline:

1950s: 'anti-modernism' (Bertens) – rejection of modernism

From which emerges

Late 1950s–early 1960s: 'radical break' (Jameson) – rupture between modernism and postmodernism

After which

1968–1972: 'we see postmodernism emerge as a full-blown though still incoherent movement' (Harvey)

On the basis of this outline we can see a sequence of moments that begins with the rejection of modernism, which creates the potential for rupture from which postmodernism emerges. It also neatly contains the three stages, or moments, within a compact time frame that contained many significant cultural changes: the rise of a popular culture, various experimental art forms, and the events of 1968, among others. However, there are some clearly defined problems with this outline. For example, there are two different anti-modernist moments, Bertens's 1950s and Harvey's suggestion of the 1960s. This could be explained by the proposal that postmodernism is always in some sense a form of 'anti-modernism' and from the initial point of emergence in the 1950s it becomes a process that, in Bertens's words, 'developed momentum in the course of the 1960s'.[24] But there are still some basic methodological concerns. Constructing an outline in this way reduces the complexity of the issues into a format that is perhaps too neat. If postmodernism is defined via its ruptures and fragments then it cannot be so easily contained within a smooth linear historical model that somehow imposes a definition of postmodernism on everything that happens after a certain point, which is a strategy that is often used. For example, Paul Hoover, writing within the context of an introduction to an anthology of American poetry, states: 'As used here, "postmodern" means the historical period following World War II.'[25] Such an all-encompassing strategy presents problems that David Brackett, among others, is highly sensitive to: 'if used simply as a periodizing label across categories, [postmodernism] threatens to be totalizing in the same way as a term such as "modernism".'[26] The pursuit of such an understanding of postmodernism not only has the potential to become a totality in the way that Brackett suggests, but it could also be seen as an attempt to artificially resolve the 'resolutely contradictory' nature of postmodernism and, following Burgin, impose a 'spuriously *unitary* answer' of postmodernism as a discrete historical phase or epoch. However, if we follow the arguments of Fredric Jameson, and view the postmodern as a 'periodizing hypothesis' that is defined as a 'cultural dominant', then what becomes dominant is exactly the spread of diverse factors – Lyotard's micronarratives – without a point of unity or synthesis. This 'hypothesis' allows 'for the presence and coexistence of a range of very different' features to saturate the cultural field and, as described above, there must be definable moments at which these 'very different' features become evident.[27]

For the pragmatic purposes of introducing postmodernism, the historical outline given above does also serve to provide a helpful framework for, in the first instance, highlighting important perspectives and issues drawn from some of the key texts on postmodernism. It can now also provide an initial chronology onto which specific musical practices and contexts can potentially be mapped. Much of the music discussed in this book will begin from within this chronology but will not be restricted to it. Although there have been attempts to provide various periods and divisions of a postmodern era they will not feature in this discussion. Following this initial periodization it will be assumed that what follows is always somehow reflected through postmodernism. However, while Jameson refers to the 'postmodern present',[28] if postmodernism, as suggested above, is both about history and subject to it, then presumably at some point the critical relevance of postmodernism must begin to dissolve. Some of the issues that emerge from this possibility will be highlighted in the postscript.

Postmodernism – style

Following the proposal of postmodernism as a historical condition it is important to acknowledge the distinction that can be drawn between postmodernism as history and postmodernism as a style. According to Jameson:

> The conception of postmodernism … is a historical rather than a merely stylistic one. I cannot stress too greatly the radical distinction between a view for which the postmodern is one (optional) style among many others available and one which seeks to grasp it as the cultural dominant of the logic of late capitalism.[29]

In other words, although there may indeed be specific qualities that allow certain music, or any other art form, to be defined as postmodern, the conception of postmodernism is not merely that of a stylistic option – we cannot simply decide to be postmodern and there is no one postmodern style that merely coexists with other non-postmodern styles, such as those that may be associated with the continuing legacy and influence of modernism.[30] Rather, as anticipated at the conclusion of the previous section, it is the coexistence of many different styles defined as micronarratives ('little narratives'), potentially endless, some of which may still reflect aspects of modernism while others may be more obviously postmodern, that becomes the identifying characteristic of postmodernism.

However, there are clearly some specific qualities and characteristics which reflect postmodernism more than others and which therefore deserve to be brought more directly to the surface in any discussion about postmodernism. It is notable that Jameson, following his identification of a 'radical break' between modernism and postmodernism, moves directly to the identification of individual artists and writers and the specific characterization of their work in relation to either side of the proposed 'radical break' of the late 1950s and early 60s, the second stage of our historical outline. This is a long list, but it is worth quoting in full:

> As the word [postmodernism] itself suggests, this break is most often related to notions of the waning or extinction of the hundred-year-old modern movement

(or to its ideological or aesthetic repudiation). Thus abstract expressionism in painting, existentialism in philosophy, the final forms of representation in the novel, the films of the great *auteurs*, or the modernist school of poetry (as institutionalized and canonized in the works of Wallace Stevens) all are now seen as the final, extraordinary flowering of a high-modernist impulse which is spent and exhausted with them. The enumeration of what follows, then, at once becomes empirical, chaotic, and heterogeneous: Andy Warhol and pop art, but also photorealism, and beyond it, the 'new expressionism'; the moment, in music, of John Cage, but also the synthesis of classical and 'popular' styles found in composers like Phil Glass and Terry Riley, and also punk and new wave rock (the Beatles and the Stones now standing as the high-modernist moment of that more recent and rapidly evolving tradition); in film, Godard, post-Godard, and experimental cinema and video, but also a whole type of commercial film ... Burroughs, Pynchon, or Ishmael Reed, on the one hand, and the French *nouveau roman* and its succession, on the other, along with alarming new kinds of literary criticism based on some new aesthetic of textuality or *écriture* ... The list might be extended indefinitely; but does it imply any more fundamental change or break than the periodic style and fashion changes determined by an older high-modernist imperative of stylistic innovation?[31]

This statement ends with a question about whether the proposed 'break' between modernism and postmodernism is really any different from previous stylistic changes, as identified through modernism's preoccupation with innovation that powerfully drove the desire for such change. Clearly for Jameson the answer to the question that he poses would be that there is a difference, that rather than experiencing just another change in style postmodernism suggests something much more fundamental in terms of how culture is constructed, interpreted and valued. Much of his book will in effect be a response to this question.

In the long list provided by Jameson in the above quotation there is much that deserves further comment. It enshrines a sense of break, or rupture, between 'the waning or extinction' of modernism ('the hundred-year-old modern movement') and what follows in the form of postmodernism, now characterized as 'empirical, chaotic, and heterogeneous'. On the one side, that of the modern, Jameson positions works such as that of the 'great *auteurs*' of cinema. Auteur theory developed during the 1950s by French film critics and theorists can be defined as the interpretation of film through the unifying vision and perspective of the director as 'author'. François Truffaut, among others, developed this unified conception of cinematic authorship in both theory and practice. On this late modernist side of the 'radical break', Jameson also highlights, among other examples, abstract expressionist art, defined by the work of American painters such as Jackson Pollock and Willem de Kooning during the late 1940s and 50s, within which highly intense painting that was somehow both expressive and abstract captured something of a modernist autonomy in both the work itself and its reception by critics such as Clement Greenberg. Such work for Jameson belongs to the great but final endgame of modernism, with art historian T. J. Clark viewing abstract expressionist art as part of a 'farewell to an idea', the idea of modernism.[32]

Following the farewell to this 'final, extraordinary flowering of a high-modernist impulse', we now encounter what Jameson outlines as the 'empirical, chaotic, and heterogeneous' qualities of postmodernism. What we are presented with is a quite basic juxtaposition of work that is seen to define the late stage of modernism, the work of the cinematic auteurs and abstract expressionist art, with that of a post-modernism as defined through various developments of the 1960s. The visual art of Andy Warhol, with its playful engagement with popular culture and celebration of commercialism, now provides a sharp contrast to the intensity of a Pollock or de Kooning. Jameson also highlights the films of Godard as postmodernist, with the increasingly experimental, at times chaotic, aspects of his work fitting well into this context. But it is also worth noting the music that appears in Jameson's list of emergent postmodernists. The music of John Cage, the minimalism of Philip Glass and Terry Riley, and the assertion of a synthesis of classical and popular styles, all of which will receive further comment at later stages of this book. Popular music is highlighted through Jameson's description of the Beatles and the Rolling Stones as 'now standing as the high-modernist moment' in contrast to punk and new wave, with these later developments now positioned as postmodernist. It is intensely frustrating that Jameson does not develop these musical references, choosing instead to focus on architecture, literature, film and video, but they do at least provide one direct point of entry into talking about postmodernism in music.

However, the most immediately significant aspect of Jameson's long list is its degree of specificity, identifying individual artists and works that capture something of the end of modernism and others which can be seen as emblematic reflections of a newly emergent postmodernism. While some of Jameson's examples may remain open to interpretation – Godard could be positioned as both a modernist 'auteur' and a somewhat 'chaotic' postmodernist, and much abstract expressionist art could be explained in similar terms – what this process of selection and identification suggests is that although Lyotard's generalization of a postmodern condition must remain central, as does Jameson's claim of history over style, there are also specific details within such larger perspectives that can form part of the attempted answers to questions of what is, and when was, postmodernism. In participating in the construction of postmodernism such specific details and examples also begin to form reflections of the larger context and shape how it might be interpreted. There is now a great deal of cultural work – literature, art, cinema, architecture, music – that must be understood via Lyotard's little narratives through a self-defining sense of identity and legitimacy, but in this condition of self-definition may retrospectively become symbolic examples of a postmodernism: the experimental music of John Cage, the minimalism of Philip Glass, the visual imagery of Andy Warhol, among endless others.

Other theorists of postmodernism have pursued the possibility of highlighting some specific qualities that could help to define postmodernism as reflected both in and through specific cultural practices. The most notable and widely discussed attempt has been that of Ihab Hassan. In an essay titled 'Toward a Concept of Postmodernism', first published in 1982 and therefore broadly contemporary with Lyotard's *Postmodern Condition* and anticipating the work of Jameson, Hassan outlines 'certain schematic differences' between postmodernism and modernism. He does so through two lists, one of which identifies some key characteristics of modernism while the other does the same for postmodernism, suggesting a set of binary oppositions. This is an adapted selection of some of the terms Hassan juxtaposes:[33]

Modernism	Postmodernism
Purpose	Play
Design	Chance
Hierarchy	Anarchy
Synthesis	Antithesis
Presence	Absence

While Hassan uses several more words in the process of juxtaposition, the few selected above indicate a consistent process that may be described as the uncertainty of postmodernism set against the certainty of modernism. The use of 'Purpose' to suggest modernism implies a sense of direction and intent while 'Design' implies a known structure that is constructed. 'Synthesis' articulates modernism's desire to bring its own fragments together into a coherent unity and 'Presence' may, among other things, imply the controlling figure of the author. Against these modernist certainties the words Hassan uses to characterize postmodernism all suggest an opposing sense of uncertainty: the instability of 'Play', the randomness of 'Chance', the contradictory force of the 'Antithesis' and the 'Absence' of a controlling presence. The inherently unstable nature of Hassan's keywords of postmodernism acts as another reminder of the 'exasperating', 'resolutely contradictory' nature of postmodernism with which we began.

Chapter 2

Postmodern musicology – postmodern music

The previous chapter presented a summary of how postmodernism might begin to be defined and described through consideration of Lyotard's philosophy. The question of definition was further positioned in relation to some ideas about when postmodernism emerges (Bertens, Jameson, Harvey) and highlighted several distinctive characteristics of postmodernism (Jameson, Hassan). Having covered this territory and given some direction as to how questions about postmodernism might begin to be addressed, it is now possible to look more directly towards the encounter with some approaches to music that may be reflective of postmodernism.

In a collection of essays titled *The Cambridge Companion to Postmodernism*, published by Cambridge University Press in 2004, we find essays on postmodernism and film, literature, art, performance, space, science, post-religion, ethics and justice. In other words, the book contains discussions about postmodernism in relation to just about everything other than music. This exclusion seems rather striking given that, as will be explored in subsequent chapters, a great deal of music from the 1950s and 1960s onwards *could* to varying degrees be considered in relation to, and defined by, postmodernism. Also, there is a significant developing body of literature on music that, either in terms of subject matter or methodology, can be read as having some form of relationship to postmodernism. However, the editor of *The Cambridge Companion to Postmodernism*, Steven Connor, a noted commentator on postmodernism, justifies this exclusion:

> Given the conspicuous role that music had in the formation of modernism, one might have expected a stronger conception of postmodernism to have taken root in music studies. The relative conservatism and autonomy of the world of academic music study may account for its long resistance to postmodernist formulations and arguments. Even where there is a willingness to explore the applicability of postmodernist concepts to concert music, it has taken a conservative turn.[1]

Connor is arguing that what he describes as 'academic music study', by implication musicology, has not yet addressed postmodernism or become open to its influence. It may be that we experience a delay effect, with music and musicology lagging behind other disciplines, such as literary theory and film studies, both of which have fully encountered postmodernism.[2] And yet, there is also a view that, from certain perspectives, musicology has been excessively bound by a modernist agenda that conceives and constricts the musical work as an essentially autonomous object and which therefore removes musical experience from any real sense of context. When viewed from this perspective music can be mistakenly interpreted as highly resistant to the widely conceived forms of critical engagement and interpretation that are symptomatic of postmodernism.

New (postmodern) musicologies

The critique of this understanding of music effectively begins from within musicology through Joseph Kerman's highly influential survey of the discipline in a book titled *Musicology*, published in 1985. In this book Kerman highlighted the fact that criticism, defined as 'the study of the meaning and value of art works', did not 'figure in the explicit programmes of musicology or theory'.[3] This meant, in effect, that thinking about music had lost any real sense of an evaluative, interpretive response. Of course, what is known broadly as hermeneutics, and more generally interpretation, had always been a strong presence in critical writings about music, particularly in the nineteenth century. However, a series of interrelated and recurring concerns of musicology, which included the preoccupation with historical fact, the focus on canonical composers and works, the concept of the musical work as autonomous, and the self-contained analytical response, could all be seen as parts of what Connor describes as 'academic music study' that may have contributed at times to a discipline that was defined by a 'relative conservatism and autonomy'.[4] Kerman also noted that 'post-structuralism, deconstruction, and serious feminism have yet to make their debuts in musicology or music theory'.[5] These concepts are not automatically synonymous with postmodernism, but they do share something in common in terms of a chronological overlap; they also have some shared concerns, and many key texts have been situated in relation to, or interpreted via, more than one such concept.[6] After this point in the mid-1980s such concepts would come to have a significant impact in relation to musicology. Writing from the vantage point of the late 1990s, Nicholas Cook and Mark Everist, in the preface to a multi-authored book titled *Rethinking Music*, describe a 'before Kerman/after Kerman paradigm' that may be a myth, but, 'as myths go, this is quite a helpful one'.[7]

Clearly we cannot over-interpret the impact of Kerman's text, but it does provide a useful point of division, a helpful 'myth', after which it is possible to trace new formations of thought that are distinctly different to some of what had come before. It is certainly notable that the aftermath of Kerman's book coincided with the emergence of new ways of thinking about music that became loosely defined in very broad terms as a new musicology. This new musicology positively embraced the dimensions of music and musical experience previously sidelined by some of the now outdated agendas of musicology as outlined above. In *Musicology: The Key Concepts*, David Beard and I provided the following synoptic definition of the new musicology which, although originally published in 2005, I still find to be an adequate account and therefore worth quoting at length:

> There can be no sense in which the new musicology ever existed as an integrated movement. It would be more accurate to describe it as a loose amalgam of individuals and ideas, dating from the mid-1980s, nearly exclusively based in America, whose work has largely been absorbed into the common practice. However, these individuals bring to their own particular fields of expertise a number of shared concerns and focus on recurring issues and problems that reflect a wider postmodern move to displace positivism and the concept of the autonomous musical work. This is manifested in a will to engage with disciplines outside musicology, in particular those in the humanities and social sciences, and a desire to alter the framework of musicological discussion.[8]

On the basis of the above account we can see the emergence of a new kind of musicological thought that was inherently interdisciplinary through the encounter with the kind of concepts that Kerman had noted as then not yet having made their debuts in musicology. The outcome of this process is the construction of new modes of interpretation from outside conventional musicological frameworks that results in a focus on music that is intentionally broad while also often involving quite specific references and responses to individual musical moments and works. One of the central protagonists in what has become known as the new musicology has been Lawrence Kramer. In a book titled *Interpreting Music* Kramer isolates the above account from *Musicology: The Key Concepts* and gives his own response to it:

> As one of the individuals involved, I find this fair enough. For me, and I believe for several of the other usual suspects such as Susan McClary and Richard Leppert, the aim of the reorientation described by Beard and Gloag is really quite modest. The idea is to combine aesthetic insight into music with a fuller understanding of its cultural, social, historical, and political dimensions than was customary for most of the twentieth century. The means is the (open) interpretation of (nonautonomous) music in its worldly contexts. The end is to understand the meanings of music as cultural practice.[9]

One of the key points in this summary is that of context – social, historical, political, cultural, interpretive – the locations which shape the construction of music and condition its interpretation. Kramer's suggestion of context as 'worldly' points to an understanding of music as not only best situated within its contexts but also effectively marked by them. That understanding of music as being marked by its contexts needs to be fully recognized and in that moment of recognition any attempt to isolate a specific musical work, or any discrete part of it, becomes problematic and therefore argues against the possibility of the musical work being conceived as an autonomous entity. This understanding of music in its nonautonomous condition within its worldly contexts is accessed through what is described as open interpretation. This proposed open interpretation can be positioned as the process of understanding music through interpreting specific musical works and related issues as an ongoing process that is not restricted by concept, methodology or predetermined conclusion, so that there is no one 'correct' interpretation. In other words, the interpretation of music is always open to new possibilities and challenges. In this context we are using interpretation to reflect how we understand music – how we listen to it, how we read texts about it – which may seem distinct from musical interpretation through the act of performance. However, there are still strong convergences between how we interpret music through performance and wider, more general strategies. We might all follow the composer's instructions in the score but the outcome will always be subtly different, and this sense of difference is also an active presence in how we interpret music more generally – how we value it, how we ascribe meaning to it, what we hear as significant within it; the list of such possibilities goes on.

Questions of interpretation are pursued directly and expansively in Kramer's own work, and also that of Richard Leppert and Susan McClary as outlined by Kramer. In the case of Leppert the representation of music, and its relationship to the body, is explored.[10] In the work of McClary, the interpretation of music from feminist perspectives, and the encounter with a broad range of different musics, creates an understanding of music in terms of certain social, human realities. Of course, such concerns do not necessarily mean that such work automatically forms a postmodern musicology, but the sense of plurality, the openness of interpretation, and the importance of context, all provide certain convergences between such work and wider conceptions of postmodernism. In specific texts both Lawrence Kramer and Susan McClary draw attention to these convergences.

In a book with the highly thought-provoking title of *Classical Music and Postmodern Knowledge*, Kramer, in an initial chapter titled 'Prospects: Postmodernism and Musicology', presents his own version of the engagement between postmodernism and musicology. Kramer's theoretical starting point for this text are the ideas of Lyotard, with which we now have some familiarity from chapter 1:

> As I use it, loosely following Jean-François Lyotard, the term [postmodernism] designates a conceptual order in which grand, synthesizing schemes of explanation have lost their place and in which the traditional bases of rational

understanding – unity, coherence, generality, totality, structure – have lost their authority if not their pertinence.[11]

This use of the term effectively restates Lyotard's 'incredulity toward metanarratives', with the metanarrative described using somewhat different language as 'grand, synthesizing schemes of explanation' that are no longer valid. In Kramer's terms they 'have lost their place', with this sense of loss effectively restating Lyotard's 'incredulity'. In contrast, 'postmodernist strategies of understanding are incorrigibly interdisciplinary and irreducibly plural. Like the theories that ground them, they make up not a system but an ethos'.[12] Again, through the description of the 'irreducibly plural' we see a meaningful reflection of Lyotard's micronarratives, of which there are many – hence the focus on the plural. Kramer's characterization of postmodernism also looks to 'strategies of understanding' that are 'incorrigibly interdisciplinary'. This statement provides another articulation of the importance of a broadening sense of context as outlined above, but it also argues for the necessity of an engagement with different methodologies and models of interpretation. The pursuit of this necessity takes the form of a wide range of references to texts and concepts, including those mentioned by Kerman, but this does not amount to a system. Any attempt to construct such a system would run against the true nature of postmodernism. In place of system we are given what Kramer defines as an 'ethos', which can be understood as an attitude towards such issues that shapes the questions that are asked.

However, it is notable that the musical dimension to which Kramer's 'incorrigibly interdisciplinary and irreducibly plural' postmodernist strategies are related is that of 'classical music'. Kramer's project in general is essentially an attempt to provide new ways of thinking about old music – that of the classical tradition. The composers discussed in *Postmodern Knowledge and Classical Music* – Haydn, Mendelssohn, Ives, Ravel – obviously do not belong either historically or stylistically to postmodernism, although the music of Ives generates some interesting interpretive issues from this perspective through its often disruptive surfaces and relationship to other music, which could be argued to anticipate features that will come to be associated with postmodernism in music.[13]

The attention given to old music does not in any way invalidate Kramer's project; in fact, by projecting a new focus on, and generating new interpretations of, old music, it is doing important work that highlights how postmodernist strategies can open up new ways of thinking about music that are dramatically distinct from earlier forms of musicology.[14] But it still leaves open the question of how postmodern theory might be used to explain postmodern music.[15]

The work of Susan McClary also reflects strategies of interpretation that can be seen at times to converge with what we might now understand as postmodernism as defined in Kramer's terms of the 'incorrigibly interdisciplinary and irreducibly plural'. Although her work has many different starting points, its theoretical, interdisciplinary perspective is that of feminism, and through that perspective issues of gender, sexuality, meaning and subjectivity come to the surface. Like Kramer, her work engages with old music, in particular the Renaissance madrigal.[16] However, McClary's musical references are truly 'irreducibly plural'. Within one book, *Feminine Endings*, first published in 1991, we encounter references to, and interpretations of, the music of Bartók, Monteverdi, Bizet, Tchaikovsky, Donizetti, Vandervelde, Laurie Anderson and Madonna, among others. This is a richly diverse list of musical practices, ranging from the operatic (Monteverdi) to the symphonic (Tchaikovsky) and embracing the contemporary (Vandervelde) and the popular (Madonna).[17] Such diversity in itself does not make the project postmodernist, but, as Judy Lochead describes it, this 'ground-breaking book', is 'one of the first instances of music scholarship in the 1990s that explicitly engages postmodern thought'.[18] I agree with Lochead's evaluation of this book, but I do not read its engagement with postmodernism as explicit. It is not a book about postmodern theory as such; it does not seek to theorize, or define, postmodernism. However, clearly a deep awareness of such work both informs and illuminates the encounters with so many musical contexts and related issues, which generates a general spirit, a feeling perhaps, that positions this book, in its musical plurality and open interpretations, as a new musicology that is conceived against, and articulated through, the context of postmodernism.

In other texts McClary makes this postmodern context and perspective more explicit. For example, a chapter titled 'Reveling in the Rubble: The Postmodern Condition', which forms the concluding stage of *Conventional Wisdom*, a book first published in 2000, provides a meaningful encounter with the very different but still postmodern musics of Philip Glass, John Zorn, Prince, k.d. lang and Public Enemy. All of these musicians are seen as being 'concerned with performing some active negotiation with the cultural past for the sake of here and now'.[19] This process of 'negotiation' takes the form of a celebration ('reveling') of the fragments of culture ('rubble'), processes that draw attention to postmodernism as a concern with the fragment. The historical nature of such fragments ('the cultural past') was implicit in Jameson's articulation of a certain postmodern historical awareness that was explored in the previous chapter and will be revisited as this discussion unfolds.

The reflections of the theories and practices of postmodernism that have emerged from the new musicology as identified through the work of both Kramer and McClary, much of which has now been in place for some time, suggest some ways in which postmodern ideas about music can have a real critical force. However, we now return to Connor's introduction to *The Cambridge Companion to Postmodernism* and note his conclusion that:

The strange absence of a mature postmodernist discourse within music studies, rather than the absence of potential fields in which it might be brought to bear, is the reason that musical postmodernism is not one of the areas reported on in this current collection.[20]

Given the changes in thinking about music outlined above, and the prevalence of specifically postmodernist musical practices, Connor's conclusion seems rather problematic. But there is a sense in which he is correct in that, although some texts about music clearly adopt a postmodernist approach and method or address a postmodern music, there is no real sense of an accumulated body of literature that fully works through the consequences of postmodernism for music in the way that, for example, the work of Linda Hutcheon, Brian McHale and Connor himself, among others, has done for literature.[21]

Postmodern music

If Connor's claim about the absence of a discourse of postmodernism in the study of music carries some validity, there have been some notable reflections on music from within postmodern theory, including the music mentioned by Jameson in his proposed 'radical break' as discussed in the previous chapter, and other theorists, including Lyotard, have made some direct references to music.[22] Linda Hutcheon in *The Politics of Postmodernism* also provides some commentary on music and notes the relative absence of postmodernism in what she describes as 'music criticism', which here can be taken to extend to musicology as an academic discipline:

> 'Postmodern' is a term that is not used very often in music criticism, yet there are analogies between postmodern architecture or dance and contemporary music: in music too we find a stress on communication with the audience through simple repetitive harmonies (offered in complex rhythmic forms) in the work of Phil Glass or through a parodic return to tonality and to the past of music, not as a source of embarrassment or inspiration, but with ironic distance, as in the work of Lukas Foss or Luciano Berio. What I shall argue to be typically postmodern genre-boundary crossings can also be found in music: Phil Glass's *The Photographer* is a dramatic musical piece on the life and work of photographer Eadweard Muybridge. And, going in another direction, his 'cross-over' *Songs from Liquid Days* is both a song cycle and a pop album. Much of what might be called postmodern music requires of its listeners a certain theoretical sophistication and historical memory.[23]

Of course, Hutcheon's claim that postmodernism 'is a term that is not used very often in music criticism' can be understood retrospectively, as the book was originally published in 1989 and much has changed since then, although not if we agree with Connor's diagnosis.

For Hutcheon there are some specific qualities in music that allow for an understanding of it as postmodernist. The first such quality she identifies is enclosed within the claim that a postmodernist music will be communicative, making direct connections with an audience. This statement highlights the fact that certain composers, and other musicians, have produced music that has an access to an audience through the use of already familiar sounds. In some cases, this familiarity takes the form of direct quotation of, or allusion to, other, often historical music. Alternatively, it may involve a more generalized return to recognizable forms, genres and materials of the past. Such musical processes are reflected in McClary's proposal of the 'active negotiation with the cultural past for the sake of here and now'.[24] This accessibility may be intentionally contrasted with the alleged celebration of complexity and difficulty in some modernist music.

It is also notable that Hutcheon positions this accessibility in relation to the music of Philip Glass, which is described as forming 'postmodern genre-boundary crossings'. Glass was also mentioned in Jameson's delineation of emergent postmodernist practices and discussed in McClary's 'Reveling in the Rubble'. It is clear that Glass's minimalism enjoys a higher profile than some forms of contemporary music and that the often basic harmonic language in dialogue with an often direct, yet complex, rhythmic energy gives this music a sense of immediacy. While the question of whether such qualities become 'genre-boundary crossings' or constitute a 'crossover' with popular music will be explored in greater detail in a later chapter, the stress on communication that Hutcheon indicates gives one generalized aspect of postmodernism in music – but there will be others. The search for some of these other aspects takes us back once again to Connor and his comments on 'the strange absence of a mature postmodernist discourse within music studies'.[25]

Between the two passages cited above, Connor does refer directly to some specific writing on postmodernism and music, a collection of essays titled *Postmodern Music/Postmodern Thought*, edited by Judy Lochead and Joseph Auner and published in 2002.[26] For Connor, this collection, one of the first books to concern itself directly with postmodernism in music, is seen as representing 'the most conservative kind of extension of postmodernism's range'.[27] For Connor, the 'conservative' nature of the engagement between postmodern theory and specific musical contexts and practices arises through the concern to 'establish analogies and continuities between postmodern discourse and the discussion of concert music'.[28] This concern with 'concert music' suggests a degree of conservatism in that it implies a relationship to specific musical practices based on composition and conceived within some form of relationship to the tradition of Western classical music. In focusing on this musical context, however broadly conceived, the essays contained within *Postmodern Music/Postmodern Thought* could be perceived as perpetuating that tradition. In doing so, there is little

> acknowledgment of the difference made by the enormous reconfiguration not only of the sphere of music in general, but even of the terms and conditions of concert music. It would be possible to characterize the postmodernism of music not in terms of the stylistic changes and changes to musical language that take place in scores and in concert halls, but in terms of the explosion of collaborations and fusions, and the many ways in which the gap between classical and popular music has been narrowed.[29]

Connor is arguing for an account of postmodernism in music that might be based upon the changing nature of how we receive music, and the impact of new technologies would become highly relevant to an understanding of such changes. Of more immediate relevance, however, might be the suggested need to highlight new collaborative ventures and fusions between different musics. This possibility will be revisited at later stages of this book, as will Connor's claim that 'the gap between classical and popular music has been narrowed', a claim which effectively echoes Hutcheon's highlighting of 'genre-boundary crossings' and 'cross-overs' as well as Jameson's proposed 'synthesis of classical and popular styles'.[30] Connor may be correct to highlight the absence of certain contexts and practices from *Postmodern Music/Postmodern Thought* but much of what is contained in this book does provide some useful connections between postmodern modes of thought and the actual sounds of postmodernism in music.

We have seen that the search for specific stylistic markers has a certain presence in the existing literature about postmodernism in general, and this search must feature extensively in how we hear postmodernism in music. One of the first and most notable general examples of this perspective comes in the work of Jonathan Kramer.[31] In a chapter titled 'The Nature and Origins of Musical Postmodernism', included in *Postmodern Music/Postmodern Thought*, Jonathan Kramer explores the 'postmodern attitude' and outlines a series of possible characteristics of postmodernism in music. These characteristics are presented in the form of a list and, in some places, reflect some of the issues that we have already encountered but from a slightly different perspective. For example, the eighth characteristic that Jonathan Kramer defines is that which 'considers music not as autonomous but as relevant to cultural, social, and political contexts'.[32] This characteristic would seem to move the focus back to the discussion of the new musicology in which context was seen to be an important factor through which music could not then be understood as autonomous. However, Jonathan Kramer does not spell out how this characteristic relates to specific musical practices. What is proposed here could suggest an attitude towards any music, and may be reflected in how we place any earlier era or style of music in context. For example, we need to recognize the basic fact that modernism was also a context, one that through its often-dissonant, fractured music provided a meaningful reflection of the wider social and cultural tensions of the early twentieth century. The importance of context does not in itself necessarily define music, or musicological work, as postmodern. We might extend the enquiry further and ask how the 'cultural, social, and political contexts' become relevant; do they only influence how we hear the music or are such contexts somehow ingrained within the specific details of the musical materials and forms, and, if they are, how, and why, do they become audible?

However, some of the other characteristics that Jonathan Kramer outlines become more relevant to the actual sounds of postmodernism in music. What follows is an engagement with a carefully chosen selection drawn from Jonathan Kramer's long list (sixteen in total). The first such characteristic is one that claims that postmodern music

> is not simply a repudiation of modernism or its continuation, but has aspects of both a break and an extension.[33]

This proposal seems to contradict some of the bigger ideas explored in the first chapter, which juxtaposed modernism and postmodernism, and considered some of the names that could be positioned on either side of what Jameson defines as the 'radical break'. In contrast to such proposals Jonathan Kramer seems to be suggesting something perhaps more subtle and flexible. Even if we accept, on the basis of Lyotard's incredulity, that the big ideas of modernism, the metanarratives, no longer hold legitimacy, some of the actual details of specific materials and practices of music cannot always be reduced to a neat opposition between modernism and postmodernism, with the potential for points of contact between them being implicit in the development of Lyotard's descriptions of postmodernism. We may hear a sharp contrast between, for example, the stylistic continuity of modernism in the music of a composer such as Brian Ferneyhough and the obviously postmodern music of Michael Daugherty, but there are other musical contexts within which such clearly defined distinctions may be significantly less evident, a point that has already been made in relation to the music of Ives.

In the first chapter passing reference was made to the music of Schoenberg and Stravinsky, both of whom belong historically and stylistically to modernism. However, while Schoenberg's music may sit easily within the broad context of modernism, the music of Stravinsky presents a more complex picture. While Stravinsky (1882–1971), in works such as *The Rite of Spring* (1913), *Symphonies of Wind Instruments* (1920) and *Les Noces* (1923), presented a music that articulated a radical modernist aesthetic, by 1920 Stravinsky's music was already taking a rather different direction through what has been defined as neoclassicism. This term reflects the return to, or acknowledgement of, older, 'classical', musical forms and materials.[34] In *Pulcinella* (1920), Stravinsky's neoclassicism took the form of an almost pastiche realization of eighteenth-century music based on Pergolesi. This retrospective direction is clearly some way from the innovations of *The Rite of Spring* and *Symphonies of Wind Instruments*. In making this historical gesture in this work, and much of his music from the 1920s onwards, perhaps Stravinsky is reflecting something of the historical awareness that Jameson identifies within postmodernism. This possibility leads Jameson to assert that 'Stravinsky is the true precursor of postmodern cultural production'.[35] Jameson does not support this claim with any direct reference to Stravinsky's music, that is not the real purpose of his book, but it does highlight the possibility of certain continuities between modernism and postmodernism. In the case of Stravinsky we can hear how the moments of rhythmic consistency in some of his music may be reflected in the minimalism of Philip Glass and Steve Reich. It may also be the case that Stravinsky's reinvention of tonal materials as early as *Petrushka* (1911) can be heard to be repeated in the postmodern, post-minimalist music of Michael Torke, among many other possible reflections. Such instances would seem to illustrate Jonathan Kramer's suggestion of an 'extension', while the fact that the music of Michael Torke, for example, sounds very different from that of Stravinsky also articulates the possibility that such extensions coexist with the proposed 'break' between modernism and postmodernism.

If the music of Stravinsky, which may act as a precursor for postmodernism, is relevant in relation to this, the first of Jonathan Kramer's characteristics, then it could also come into play with reference to the sequence of four characteristics that follow, which claim that postmodern music:

(2) is, on some level and in some way, ironic;
(3) does not respect boundaries between sonorities and procedures of the past and the present;
(4) challenges barriers between 'high' and 'low' styles;
(5) shows disdain for the often unquestioned value of structural unity.[36]

Stravinsky's music has often been described in terms of its 'irony', which is partly reflected through the use of 'sonorities and procedures of the past'. It also, in some specific works, if not actually challenging the 'barriers between "high" and "low" styles', then at least looked towards the popular 'low' for ideas and materials.[37] In addition works such as *The Rite of Spring* and *Symphonies of Wind Instruments* avoided, if not actually showed disdain for, the assumed value of a unified structure. The fact that Stravinsky, as a modernist composer, would seem to exhibit several of Jonathan Kramer's characteristics of postmodern music could be taken to undermine the relevance or appropriateness of these specific characteristics for an understanding of postmodernism in music. It may also suggest that any attempt to produce such a list will always be full of pitfalls, which Jonathan Kramer is sensitive to. One notable consequence of such an approach might be that it begins to impose a level of order and control on what in Jameson's terms are the 'empirical, chaotic, and heterogeneous' aspects of postmodernism.[38] In doing so it also effectively seeks to stabilize the inherently and intentionally unstable status of Hassan's keywords of postmodernism[39] that were highlighted in the previous chapter, and consequently undermine what for Hutcheon is the 'resolutely contradictory' nature of postmodernism.[40]

However, once we become aware of what the problems might be of constructing such a list, and sensitive to the limitations of the approach, then it becomes possible to proceed with a degree of caution. In relation to the above selection from Jonathan Kramer's long list of characteristics of postmodern music it could be argued that, while they all may relate to the music of Stravinsky, this is quite exceptional and it may be that because they become recurrent, perhaps even 'dominant', within post-modernism that they have a higher level of relevance in the new context. This heightened sense of relevance becomes evident through further consideration of Jonathan Kramer's second characteristic, which states that a postmodern music 'is, on some level and in some way, ironic'. Irony was a quality identified by Linda Hutcheon to reflect a certain distancing that takes place in some music, and other contexts, with irony emerging as a recurring theme in a great deal of general literature on postmodernism.[41]

Dead Elvis

I do not think that all music that can be described as postmodernist is 'ironic', but some of it is. The music of American composer Michael Daugherty (b.1954) has been routinely identified as postmodernist. It also regularly engages with popular culture and can often be described as ironic. One direct example of irony, among many, can be found in Daugherty's work titled *Dead Elvis* (1993). The title is an obvious reference to Elvis Presley, whose death carried great importance for gen-erations of fans, as did the discourse and symbolism that evolved around his passing. The applications and appropriations of this symbolism extend to Lawrence Kramer's engagement between postmodern knowledge and classical music, within which he declares that 'the Autonomous Artwork is dead as Elvis'.[42]

The iconic status of Presley is further emphasized by the fact that the recording of *Dead Elvis* appears on a CD of Daugherty's music titled *American Icons*, which also features works that contain references to other iconic figures from popular culture, including the actor James Cagney (*Snap!* (1987)), Barbie and Ken dolls (*What's That Spell?* (1995)), the pianist and entertainer Liberace (*Le Tombeau de Liberace* (1996)) and the sound of Motown (*Motown Metal* (1994)).[43]

In *Dead Elvis* the irony is partially constructed by the conditions of performance, within which the solo bassoonist is dressed as Elvis in his late, Las Vegas, persona. The musical material that is the focal point of the work is the *Dies Irae* – the Latin chant for the Day of Judgement – which reinforces the aura of death in relation to Elvis.

Example 2.1 reproduces the opening moments of *Dead Elvis*. The work begins with the insistent rhythmic pattern of the bass line, over which the solo bassoon (identified as 'Elvis') makes what could be conceived as a 'vocal' gesture. At Fig. C the violin then trombone articulate the recognizable melodic shape of the *Dies Irae* chant (C–B–C–A–B–G–A).

In utilizing such historically profound material Daugherty is making an ironic gesture through shifting the potential meaning of this material from one context into another. It could also suggest a commentary on other usages and appropriations. For example, Daugherty's use of the *Dies Irae* in this instrumental work might bring to mind Berlioz's use of the same material in his *Symphonie fantastique* as well as the many other instances of its appropriation in many different contexts such as film music, with one example being the use of Berlioz's realization in the film *Sleeping with the Enemy* (1991), in which it is obviously used to signify a sinister, threatening presence.

As well as the use of the *Dies Irae* there are further layers of ironic reflection in *Dead Elvis*. The work is scored for the same instrumental ensemble as Stravinsky's *The Soldier's Tale* (1918), which Daugherty describes as 'more than a coincidence'.[44] *The Soldier's Tale* involves a soldier selling his violin, and his soul, which is now translated into a rock star selling 'out to Hollywood, Colonel Parker, and Las Vegas for wealth and fame'.[45] Not only does this suggest something in common in terms of subject matter, the sound of the ensemble immediately brings to mind the actual sound of Stravinsky's music. This similarity is extended through the use of repeated ostinato figures, which are a telling feature of Stravinsky's music and with which the work begins (see Ex. 2.1). However, while such a texture is suggestive of aspects of Stravinsky's music there is another musical reference that is significant. In the words of Daugherty, we 'hear fast and slow fifties rock and roll ostinato in the double bass, violin, and bongos, while the bassoonist gyrates, double-tongues, and croons his way through variations of the *Dies Irae*'.[46] In the light of what Daugherty tells us we can hear the repeated rhythmic pattern as a gesture towards the historical context of 1950s popular music, while his use of 'gyrates' and 'croons' makes knowing references to Presley as both body and voice.

On the basis of the above description it is clear that Daugherty's *Dead Elvis* makes a clear correspondence to Jonathan Kramer's identification of irony as a characteristic of postmodern music. It also, on the basis of Daugherty's own description, fits neatly into the suggestion that such music 'challenges barriers between "high" and "low" styles' in that it clearly adopts sounds and images from the world of a now

Example 2.1 Michael Daugherty, *Dead Elvis*, opening to Fig. E

Example 2.1   (cont.)

historical popular music, that of 1950s rock 'n' roll. In doing so this music 'does not respect boundaries between sonorities and procedures of the past and the present'. *Dead Elvis* can also be heard as showing 'disdain for the often unquestioned value of structural unity' through its sudden stops, which break the consistency of the rhythmic direction, after which it then seems to suddenly begin again. Figure G (see Ex. 2.2) is a striking example of this, but it happens again with some degree of regularity (Figs. J, K, L, M).

The inclusion, perhaps intrusion, of 'other' material is extended through a version of the song 'It's Now or Never'. This was a song recorded by Presley in 1960 and which is based on the standard Italian song 'O sole mio'. Not only is the insertion of this song into *Dead Elvis* disruptive, but it also serves to heighten the popular culture dimension while adding further layers to what the work might 'mean'. The insertion of this material poses questions about 'structural unity' in that it seems to come from nowhere with no real audible connection to what has already been heard. The projection of the melody as a high bassoon line is required to be expressed in the style of Las Vegas, a reference to Presley's late period, and it certainly 'croons' (see Ex. 2.3, Fig. M).

It is clear from this brief account of Daugherty's *Dead Elvis* that it could be positioned as a definitive example of postmodernism in music, illustrating as it does several of Jonathan Kramer's key characteristics. In particular, its references to popular culture would seem to exemplify the points made by Connor, Hutcheon and Jameson, among others, on the ways in which postmodernism in general engages in the subversion of the perceived barriers between 'high' and 'low' culture. This possibility will be explored further in chapter 7.

While we remain aware that the identification of any individual music as post-modern is always loaded with problems and questions, in this instance the fact that this music, and its composer, seems so obviously postmodernist suggests that we might now be left with the question of why we need theories of postmodernism in order to interpret it. The responses to this question take us back to the importance of context, which was emphasized through reference to Lawrence Kramer's placement of 'nonautonomous' music in its 'worldly contexts', and also featured as one of Jonathan Kramer's specific characteristics of postmodern music. To construct a context for *Dead Elvis* may require acknowledgement that the time in which the music was composed, the early 1990s, and the era to which it ironically refers – the 1950s in terms of the iconic image of Presley, the 1970s in terms of the ironic parody of that iconic image – are part of the historical time frame of postmodernism that was established in the previous chapter. In the case of the 1950s it was a moment of 'anti-modernism', while somewhere between the late 1960s (1968) and early 1970s (1972), for Harvey, saw 'postmodernism emerge as a full-blown though still inco-herent movement'.[47] When Daugherty's references to popular culture are placed in

Example 2.2 Michael Daugherty, *Dead Elvis*, from Fig. G to Fig. M

Example 2.2 (cont.)

Example 2.2   (cont.)

Example 2.3   Michael Daugherty, *Dead Elvis*, from Fig. M to Fig. N

this historical context, that of postmodernism, we already begin to see that this music could never be conceived as a self-contained autonomous work. Positioned in relation to, and interpreted through, postmodernism, it now invites further reflection, the first stage of which is to situate it in relationship to the ideas of Lyotard that we are now familiar with. Within Lyotard's description of postmodernism, we encountered the micronarrative, of which there are many. Perhaps Daugherty's music is one such, very small, narrative. It has its own individual identity and it would be difficult to produce points of comparison that could be used as sources of legitimacy through which this music could be evaluated. This situation does not, in its moment of self-definition, remove this music from context as such; rather, it is now positioned in a context that is defined by the coexistence of many different musical practices, of which this is merely one possibility.

Intertextuality: from *Dead Elvis* to 'death of the author'

The individuality of *Dead Elvis*, and Daugherty's music more generally, is, as has already been described, largely formed upon 'other', already existing music – the *Dies Irae*, 'It's Now or Never', defining features of 1950s rock 'n' roll. It is also possible that reference to 'other' material is also active in other ways. When I hear *Dead Elvis* I do not only hear Daugherty's music and what it appropriates in terms of the chant or the song, but I also somehow 'see' the postmodern visual imagery produced by artist Andy Warhol. Warhol was positioned on the postmodern, early 1960s, side of the 'radical break' proposed by Jameson and discussed at some length in the previous chapter.[48] Warhol's work was defined initially during the early 1960s by images of objects from everyday life, such as Coca-Cola bottles, Campbell's soup cans and Brillo boxes, all of which can be interpreted as the blurring of the boundaries between art and life, 'high' and 'low' cultures. However, Warhol also produced, in fact reproduced, images of iconic figures from popular culture, including Marilyn Monroe, Elizabeth Taylor and, most importantly in the context of this discussion, Elvis Presley. In works such as *Red Elvis* (1962), *Double Elvis* (1963) and *Elvis I and II* (1964) Warhol both replicates and reinvents the iconic image of Presley. Of course, these are not late images of Presley, Elvis is not yet 'dead' in these works, rather they are reflections of how he once might have been. But now that Elvis is 'Dead', as is Warhol, they form part of a memorial trace. In suggesting that I somehow 'see' these images when I 'hear' Daugherty's *Dead Elvis* I cannot support such an interpretation in terms of documentation that may prove how the composer might have been in some sense influenced by Warhol. But I can offer it as, in terms of what has been described through reference to Lawrence Kramer's work, an open interpretation. It is an interpretation that is open to further reflection and the generation of yet more possibilities and questions.

This open interpretation could also be defined and extended further through the concept of intertextuality, which is implicitly present in a number of Jonathan Kramer's specific characteristics of postmodern music and which will reappear throughout this book. Intertextuality is a concept that developed through literary theory, and is broadly identified with the work of Julia Kristeva, the term being defined by Kristeva in her essay 'Word, Dialogue and Novel', written in 1966 and published in 1969.[49] The work of literary and cultural theorist Roland Barthes is also relevant. Barthes's seminal text 'The Death of the Author', another 'death' reference, was originally published in 1968. Although Barthes did not speak directly about postmodernism, nor can he be claimed as a theorist of it, his work did make contact with aspects of postmodernism, and issues of popular culture, within the historical time frame established in this book. In 'Death of the Author' Barthes shifts the focus of attention from the author to the reader as the location of meaning for a text. According to Barthes, the literary text does not have a single source of meaning as identified through a concept of authorship:

> We know now that a text is not a line of words releasing a single 'theological' meaning (the 'message' of the Author-God) but a multi-dimensional space in which a variety of writings, none of them original, blend and clash. The text is a tissue of quotations drawn from the innumerable centres of culture.[50]

For Barthes, then, we move away from the certainty provided by the assumed presence of the author to something which is a remarkably radical proposal that not only displaces the author but also any understanding of a text as original – everything is in effect a quotation of something else. On this account all texts ('a multi-dimensional space') are defined through their relationships with other texts, which 'blend and clash'. This space that Barthes opens up leads to the presence of the reader as the focal point:

> The reader is the space on which all quotations that make up a writing are inscribed without any of them being lost; a text's unity lies not in its origin but in its destination.[51]

Now it is the reader, and the act of reading, that gives meaning to the words on the page, not the intentions of the author. Barthes's argument here is intentionally provocative. This is a polemical essay that dramatizes the opposition to more conventional ways of understanding questions of authorship, largely through the biography of the author, and assumptions of originality. But, if taken literally, it becomes rather problematic. How might we read Barthes's own work and his status as its author? How does this argument relate to specific examples of literature other than that cited by Barthes?

But Barthes's underlying point about texts being defined through their relationships to other texts remains compelling, and the concept of intertextuality that emerges from this, and other, work is highly useful even if it is not without problems and limits. Intertextuality can be defined broadly as a way of conceiving of texts as somehow dependent upon, or suggestive of, other texts. In other words, one text always makes us think of another text, or, in the example of music, some music always suggests some other music. However, not all music that could be described as intertextual is necessarily postmodern, with many examples of borrowing evident in earlier music, as is the presence of audible traces and reflections of other music.

In some cases intertextuality may be an intentional strategy. In the example of Daugherty's *Dead Elvis* the use of both the *Dies Irae* chant and 'It's Now or Never' is clearly an intentionally intertextual strategy on the part of the composer that directs our response towards these specific sources. On the other hand, if I suggest that Daugherty's use of the *Dies Irae* chant forms an intertextual relationship to Berlioz's use of the same material in his *Symphony fantastique* or the film *Sleeping With the Enemy*, or that *Dead Elvis* somehow suggests Warhol's *Double Elvis*, I cannot claim that this is intentional on the composer's part, but I can propose it as an interesting way of interpreting the work that creates a web of potential meanings for it. When placed within this web it also becomes possible to hear *Dead Elvis* within a context of how other specific musical examples use, or suggest, such relationships to produce sounds that become open to such processes of interpretation.

This proliferation of interpretation and meaning flows from the desire to place *Dead Elvis* within the context of postmodernism, and to apply certain strategies and ask questions that relate to, or emerge from, that context. When we pursue such strategies and ask these questions, Elvis sounds very much alive.

In the discussion of postmodernism in music in the chapters that follow the aim will be to explain some interesting examples of specific musics that are open to being situated in, and interpreted through, the context of postmodernism. These examples are not comprehensive, they are a selection that, in some cases, reflects my own personal interests, while, in others, their inclusion has been influenced by claims made in the existing literature. They will not necessarily always be explained through a methodology that can in itself be defined as postmodern nor will all the issues explored in this and the previous chapter always remain consistently in focus. But relevant musical details will be highlighted and related directly to questions of why, and how, they can be heard as postmodern.

Chapter 3

From anti-modernism to postmodern nostalgia

In the first chapter we encountered Hans Bertens's description of the 1950s as a moment of 'anti-modernism' and Jameson's identification of the end of the 1950s as part of the 'radical break' between modernism and postmodernism. Both of these proposals were featured in the historical outline of chapter 1 to suggest a moment of emergence in the 1950s, defined through the rejection of modernism, that then opens up the space through which postmodernist practices can begin to reveal themselves into the 1960s. This chapter will involve exploring some music, and related issues, from this first moment in the 1950s. However, by way of contrast, how this moment may be interpreted retrospectively from the vantage point of a more fully recognizable postmodernism in the early 1970s will form a significant part of this chapter. This later moment was the point at which, for Harvey, postmodernism emerged as a 'full-blown though still incoherent movement'[1] and which constituted the third stage of the historical outline. The focus on both of these moments within this chapter is intended to capture something of the mobility within, and plurality of, postmodernism. But it also highlights the realization that while postmodernism may reflect a new historical awareness after modernism it does not easily lend itself to being represented through a clearly defined historical narrative.

High modernism

Any consideration of the 1950s must begin by recognizing the impact of the ending of World War II in 1945 and the emerging new reality as defined by the Cold War. The cultural impact and legacy of the war could be conceived as a clear break with the immediate past, and we have already encountered this possibility in the first chapter. The most significant articulation of this view comes from Christopher Butler in a book titled *After the Wake*, which is presented as an essay on the contemporary avant-garde.[2] The wake that Butler highlights is James Joyce's *Finnegans Wake*, a book published in 1939 by an author often described as modernist, but whose work, particularly in this book, prefigures postmodernism. For Butler there 'is a confirmation of a new "postmodern" artistic epoch in the 1950s'.[3] Butler gives a list of examples of such work, which in terms of music include the identification of postmodernism in the 'post-1945 rediscovery of the Second Viennese School and particularly of Webern … the critical work of René Leibowitz, and the teaching of Messiaen, and the music of Nono, Boulez, Henze, and Stockhausen'.[4] Anyone familiar with the music of these composers from this period might be rather surprised by this identification of it as postmodernist. This music, in most cases, is generally seen as a heightening, an intensification, of modernism. The rediscovery of second-Viennese-school modernism, as defined primarily through Webern's serialism, led to the further extension of serial techniques from within the context of a pre-war modernism into the post-war period through the music of Boulez and Stockhausen, among others identified with the Darmstadt summer school in the early 1950s. This extension took the form of applying serial techniques to parameters of music other than just pitch, including rhythm, duration, timbre and dynamics. The effect of these extensions is often described as total or integral serialism.[5]

Rather than directly initiating a clean break between modernism and postmodernism as Butler suggests, the post-war period witnessed the emergence of this, in David Bernstein's words, 'new "radicalized" or "high" modernism in the arts'.[6] For Bernstein high modernism represented a certain departure within modernism. He continues:

> The modernism of the previous half-century had lost its credibility as a revolutionary movement. It was replaced by a technocratic, positivistic, and rationalistic high modernism, which was, above all, de-politicized. High-modernist art was autonomous, formalist and anti-representational, as exemplified by the purist high-modernist architecture of Le Corbusier.[7]

Bernstein's account of modernism in its high phase highlights the claim, often made, that some of the music produced at this time was defined by both its autonomous and formalist characteristics. Autonomy, the claim that the artwork exists in isolation, was mentioned in the second chapter in relation to the changing nature of musicology and the criticism of such an understanding of music. Formalism suggests something similar to autonomy in that it is claimed to consider the understanding of the form of an artwork as an end in itself. The fascination with the technical and formal parameters of some music in the 1950s does intersect with this understanding of a high modernism as outlined by Bernstein, although perhaps not to the extent that some commentaries on this music suggest. Bernstein's highlighting of the 'technocratic, positivistic, and rationalistic' features of high modernism draws attention to the aura of scientific progress and technological change that accrued to this specific cultural context and towards which postmodernism would become incredulous. It is also notable that this statement from Bernstein includes reference to the architecture of Le Corbusier, whose high modernist style, defined by its 'purity' and systematic simplicity, was characterized as producing a 'machine for modern living'. This 'machine' is part of the highly rationalistic sense of order and the prioritizing of the technocratic that Bernstein effectively emphasizes. If this reference to the architecture of Le Corbusier is worthy of note so too is the claim by Charles Jencks that, as described by David Harvey, it is possible to date 'the symbolic end of modernism and the passage to the postmodern as 3.32 p.m. on 15 July 1972, when the Pruitt–Igoe housing development in St Louis (a prize-winning version of Le Corbusier's "machine for modern living") was dynamited as an uninhabitable environment for the low-income people it housed'.[8] Clearly Jencks is doing something rather 'ironic' in attaching such symbolism to the destruction of one example of high-modernist architecture, built in the mid-1950s, but such gestures do come to symbolize a sense of passing, and in this instance it presents a dramatically physical removal of a once dominant high-modernist presence within the time frame of the early 1970s.

Rather than becoming a postmodern moment or style, as Butler implies, high-modernist music of the 1950s begins to coexist with the emergence of other musical contexts and practices that run in very different directions. One such very powerful direction is that which is often described as experimental and, in contrast to European modernism, emerges from the USA. Georgina Born, in a chapter that considers both modernism and postmodernism in relation to music, highlights this experimentalism as an alternative direction to that of a high modernism as defined in musical terms by the extensions of serialism:

> But, serialism, though dominant, was not the only development within the musical avant-garde after the war. In this period also, its fortunes developed in counterpoint with those of rival movements. The main alternative from the 1950s on was the tradition of experimental music that focused on the American composer and guru John Cage and his followers, including composers Morton Feldman, Christian Wolff, Earle Brown, and later La Monte Young and Cornelius Cardew. This is often considered the centrepiece of musical postmodernism. For decades these composers remained less well known, less powerful and less legitimate than the serialists; they were the 'unserious' dissidents of the avant-garde.[9]

This statement by Born emphasizes the importance of John Cage in this context and his influence at this time on a group of primarily, although not exclusively, American composers. Born is arguing that the direction taken by such composers was overshadowed by the dominance of European serially based high-modernist music which had very quickly become the 'official' version of modernism in music at this time. Although there is historical evidence to support this claim, it is also worth remembering that Cage's music was well known in new music circles in Europe, and for a time there was a degree of contact and interaction between Cage and Boulez, who was seen as the leading figure of a European high modernism.[10]

I think any binary opposition between high modernism and postmodernism as defined by 'the tradition of experimental music' would be both uninteresting and untenable. But there is clearly a tension between these two musical directions that is productive in that the distance and difference between them begin to indicate something of the emergent pluralities of the period. It may be difficult to isolate John Cage and those he influenced as 'the centrepiece of musical postmodernism', with the suggestion of a centre seeming to suggest a point of unity or focus that runs against the more general claims about postmodernism made elsewhere. But, if there is no centrepiece as such, John Cage is as good a place as any, and better than most, to begin to look more directly at specific musical practices at this point of post-modern emergence in the early 1950s.

John Cage – 'the first postmodernist'

John Cage (1912–92) was a radical experimental American composer who also wrote extensively about music, often in a highly imaginative and experimental way, and whose work often intersected with other art forms, primarily dance and the visual arts.

The identification of John Cage as an 'early' postmodernist is, as suggested by Born, often articulated in some specific literature on music, with Paul Griffiths, for example, speculating that 'Cage, in seeking an escape from the arbitrary arbitrations of taste in the early 1950s, was probably the first to recognise the postmodern condition'.[11] In contrast to the passing commentary of Griffiths, Alastair Williams provides an extended overview of the potential interactions between Cage and postmodernism, stating that from 'his earliest days ... Cage exhibited traits that would now be described as postmodernist'.[12] This statement accurately positions Cage in terms of an emergence that can only be conceptualized through post-modernism retrospectively. While Michael Nyman mentions Cage as 'the first postmodernist',[13] Charles Hamm makes a most overt connection between Cage and postmodernism:

> around 1950 he [Cage] began creating works that broke radically with modernism in their anticipation of stylistic and conceptual matters later associated with postmodernism: fragmentation of style and structure within the art object; the abandonment of narrative linearity; questioning the role of intentionality in the creation of art and challenging the hegemony of Western culture; redefining the role of the listener/observer in the perception, reception and use of the art object.[14]

Cage had been composing music since the 1930s, but in the early 1950s, as Hamm suggests, a new direction emerges that challenges many preconceptions about music in terms of the role of the composer, performer and, most importantly, listener. Hamm's highlighting of 'fragmentation', for example, draws a meaningful parallel between Cage and a recurring characteristic of most discussions and descriptions of postmodernism, including Jonathan Kramer's long list of characteristics of postmodern music that we engaged with in the previous chapter. Hamm also draws attention to Cage's 'challenging the hegemony of Western culture'. Cage drew a great deal of inspiration and ideas from various non-Western ideas and practices. This in itself may not amount to a profound challenge, but it did produce a meaningful sense of 'otherness' to Cage's music through helping to construct a plurality of different musical materials and sounds.[15]

For Hans Bertens, Cage's compositional practices of the early 1950s are part of an 'anti-modernism' that is initially identified through the work and presence of poet Charles Olson, who 'picks up the term' postmodernism 'from the early 1950s onwards' and relates it to 'an anti-modernist strain in contemporary poetry'.[16] In 1951, Olson became a visiting professor at Black Mountain College in North Carolina, and in this location experiments involving artists, poets and musicians took place during this time:

> Olson was right from the start involved in the anti-modernist cultural revolt that gradually gained momentum in the 1950s. The most famous of all the early anti-modern manifestations, staged by John Cage, took place in the summer of 1952 at Olson's Black Mountain College. Cage, Olson, the painter Robert Rauschenberg, the dancer Merce Cunningham, and some lesser-known artists, performed in an event that experimented with chance and improvisation. Its course was determined by the throwing of I Ching coins, while the participants were unaware of each other's intentions.[17]

In this statement Bertens draws attention to Cage's interaction with other artists, including the dancer Merce Cunningham, who would become a regular collaborator. The painter Robert Rauschenberg is also mentioned in this context, with an example of his work being described by David Harvey as a 'pioneering postmodernist work'.[18] Bertens also recognizes the development of chance and improvisational procedures at this point. For Cage the random indeterminate outcome of such processes would be highly attractive. This approach also displaces the dominance of intentionality in art, which assumes that the outcome is already determined in the creative process. Chance operations come into Cage's music in the later stages of the Concerto for Prepared Piano and Orchestra (1950–1).[19] As highlighted by Bertens, Cage had discovered the *I Ching*, an ancient Chinese text that uses randomly selected images derived by the throwing of sticks or coins. Cage utilized this as a means of randomly generating sounds and thus abandoned authorial control over the outcome.[20] Other radical, experimental works by Cage include the encounter of music as silence, most demonstrably in the experience of 4′33″ in 1952 and the further exploration of the possibilities of chance procedures in other works of the early 1950s such as *Music of Changes* and *Imaginary Landscape No. 4 for 12 radios* (both from 1951), which exploited the random nature of sound.

These experimentations may add to the construction of a certain image of an avant-garde art that is searching for new ideas that 'progress' the art form, and Cage was always searching for new ideas, sounds and forms. But the role that Cage was playing at this time, through his interaction with other arts and artists, and the nature of the sounds he produced, subverted the modernist desire for aesthetic and formal autonomy as defined through the highly determinate nature of serialism and its extension into high modernism. He also shifted the focus from the musical work as a concept in itself towards an essentially performative, and therefore highly subjective, experience. John Cage may, or may not, have been the 'first postmodernist' composer, but he did, in both specifically musical terms and in broad cultural ways, articulate incredulity towards the assumptions of modernism. Cage's music and ideas from the early 1950s fit well into the list of words that Hassan used to describe postmodernism as cited on p. 15; which highlighted the instability of play, the randomness of chance, and the absence of authorial control. In being seen to fit into this context the music of John Cage can begin to be interpreted as the telling of many interesting little narratives about music and its place within the wider world.

'The moment of pop culture'

If the 1950s was a time of both a high modernism and experimentalism it was also a time of popular culture, a moment that Richard Middleton characterizes as one of 'situational change' that begins 'sometime after the Second World War – most strikingly with the advent of rock 'n' roll – and can be termed the moment of "pop culture"'.[21] It is perhaps accidental, and also somewhat ironic, that this moment of popular culture occurs in the same historical space as that of a high-modernist music defined by the extensions of serialism and the Darmstadt experience.[22] The coinciding of these two very different musical contexts highlights the fundamental yet potentially superficial division of the cultural field. Although radically different, within the critical framework of the present discussion both musical contexts do have something in common – the disruption of a linear account of historical change through the assertion of a new music. In both cases the moment emerges as if from nowhere, not as an inevitable consequence of previous developments but as effective rupture. Of course, in retrospect, the emergence of rock 'n' roll in the 1950s was highly dependent on existing musics – blues, country and western – but the appearance of the new music, even if it was swiftly absorbed into the culture industry, was remarkably rapid and intense.[23] This was also the case with the emergence of the high modernism of the post-war period, with its aura of the 'blank page' and the obliteration of the past generating a new sense of immediacy. Again, the retrospective view will suggest underlying continuities and precedents, although in this case the most obvious, Webern, was remarkably recent, but in the moment itself the construction of difference was everything. Both contexts then challenge assumptions about history, historical change and progress. One notable difference may be the essentially commercial orientation of the emergent new popular music of the 1950s, but, in counterpoint with that process, high modernism was assimilated with remarkable speed into the institutions, and institutionalization, of culture.[24]

'Tell Tchaikovsky the news ...'

The attempt to position the stylistic developments of rock 'n' roll in the 1950s as a part of an emergent postmodernism is far from easy. In the context of the tradition of Western classical music we can see how some work provides a point of rejection or departure over a long span of historical time, even if this process of identification is not always straightforward. In the context of popular music, however, it is much more difficult to construct a recognizable historical narrative through which this music can be represented. Clearly folk music traditions existed in many geographical regions, and at specific points in time it is possible to identify popular cultural practices. But in terms of how we now experience popular music, and what we understand by the term, we are dealing with a relatively limited period of historical time that, while it may be strongly anticipated in some contexts, is compressed into a moment that begins in the immediate post-war period, the early 1950s, and extends to the present. This compressed historical framework of popular music makes it difficult to identify a moment of modernism that postmodernism might react to or depart from. According to David Brackett: 'In order to discuss postmodernism in popular music, one must first determine what "modernist" popular music is/was.'[25] For Brackett a modernist popular music can be conceived through 'certain forms of popular music' that can be 'understood as having values opposed to commercialism',[26] a proposal that looks towards the increasing complexity and experimentalism in some 1960s rock music as a modernist resistance to the commercialism of the popular music produced by the culture industry. Fredric Jameson looks in a similar direction. Within the long list of cultural practices identified on one side or the other of the 'radical break' between modernism and postmodernism that was featured in chapter 1, the Beatles and Rolling Stones are positioned as 'the high-modernist moment' of a 'recent and rapidly evolving tradition'.[27] This seems to suggest that popular music before the explosion of rock in the 1960s was premodern and what will come after it is postmodern, with the new more complex nature of the music from the mid-1960s suggesting a certain parallel with aspects of high modernism that had been evident in other contexts.

However, it is also possible to look to 1950s rock 'n' roll for possible characteristics of postmodernism. Bruce Tucker pursues this possibility in some detail in an article titled 'Tell Tchaikovsky the News', a reference to Chuck Berry's 'Roll Over Beethoven' (1956), an ironic rock 'n' roll commentary on what was perceived to be the outdated identity of classical music.[28] For Tucker, 1950s rock 'n' roll can be seen as a celebration of otherness, it brings questions of race, social class and sexuality to the surface and it was a 'frontal attack on high culture'.[29] I do not think that this music was really a 'frontal attack' on anything, but in its own time it was perceived as carrying a cultural threat as evident by the at times hostile reaction which articulated the impact of generational change and conflict that had fractured the hegemony of a mass culture audience as formed in the pre-1945 period. This music was in part based on the mixing of previously distinct stylistic and cultural identities as defined by race. The music of Chuck Berry, a black musician and songwriter who recorded for the blues-based Chess records in Chicago, is evidence of this through his appropriation of a white country sound, most notably on his hit 'Maybellene' (1955). Elvis Presley, a white singer with origins in country music who initially produced music identified with a black culture, provides another telling instance of the blurring of race-based musical identities at this time. This music also featured a heightening of sexual energy and identity, which provided another strong sense of threat to a perceived cultural and social mainstream. As Tucker documents, Elvis Presley, Little Richard and Jerry Lee Lewis all played with highly charged sexual identities. In the case of Presley the exaggeration of male sexuality is now one of the iconic images of the period. None of this necessarily makes 1950s rock 'n' roll postmodern as such, but it does at least highlight the fact that such music was new and different, and, through the construction of new stylistic and cultural hybrids, was posing new questions of identity for a cultural mainstream from within the broad context of popular culture. In doing so it also provided anticipations of some of the new critical directions popular music, and its discourse, would take in the 1960s.

'I remember when rock was young …'

Tucker's positioning of the emergence of rock 'n' roll in relation to postmodernism highlights the importance of developments in the 1950s.[30] However, how that decade, its cultural contexts and specific musical practices have been viewed from later perspectives further extends the debate about postmodernism in music. In this section of this chapter we will contrast music from the 1950s with how that era, and its culture, was viewed through some specific work from the early 1970s. In doing so we return to David Harvey's identification of a moment, between 1968 and 1972, at which postmodernism emerges as 'a full-blown though still incoherent movement',[31] which was positioned as a suggested third stage in the emergence of postmodernism in chapter 1. That moment, for Harvey, was further defined through 'new dominant ways in which we experience space and time'.[32] In what follows, how popular culture of the early 1970s interpreted that of the 1950s will be seen to articulate such experiences.

Within the context of popular music this moment, the early 1970s, was about many things, with one powerful aspect being the attempt to convey an aura of progression, as defined by the progressive rock of bands such as Emerson, Lake and Palmer, and Yes. But it also witnessed the escapist fantasy of glam-rock that appropriated images of the future, and also projected new issues of sexual identity and the blurring of gendered images. However, this music also articulated retrospective musical gestures towards 1950s rock 'n' roll.[33] Many different popular musical practices and contexts of the early 1970s actively engaged in similar retrospective processes, including cover versions – David Bowie's *Pin Ups* and Bryan Ferry's *These Foolish Things* albums from 1973 are good examples of this[34] – and reunions, as exemplified by Dion and the Belmonts' *Reunion: Live at Madison Square Garden* album from 1972, a recording which evocatively articulates a generalized nostalgia for the 1950s through the resurrection of iconic artists and sounds of that earlier moment.

Elton John's 'Crocodile Rock' was a hit single in 1972. This is a recording which is formed through its recollection and re-imagining of the past as defined by its opening words – 'I remember when rock was young' – which suggest a relationship to 1950s rock 'n' roll, the time and style to which Daugherty's *Dead Elvis* was seen, in part, to make intertextual references. In this stage of the discussion 'Crocodile Rock' will provide a starting point for an exploration of the historical awareness active in the nostalgia of the early 1970s, a time when rock was already growing old, for the 1950s, a time when 'rock was young'. We will also consider how this moment creates a space for the emergence of a historicization of popular music and its relationship to other historical formations and cultural contexts within a broad conception of postmodernism.

'Crocodile Rock' touches upon many of the archetypal popular culture images of the 1950s, including two primary symbols: the car ('had an old gold chevy') and the girl who just happens to be called Suzie ('me and Suzie had so much fun'), thus instantly invoking memories of various recordings from the 1950s: Little Richard's 'Tutti Frutti' (1955), the Everly Brother's 'Wake Up Little Susie' (1957) and Dion's

'Runaround Sue' (1961). But, while the narrator may 'remember when rock was young' and invokes these quite specific cultural memories, in musical terms this recording does not present a stylistic reconstruction of 1950s rock 'n' roll. While the guitar riff when it enters sounds reminiscent of the Rolling Stones and their own reconstruction of the past, much of the song sounds quite distinct from rock 'n' roll as it sounded during its formative stages of the mid-1950s – as defined by, for example, early Elvis Presley, Chuck Berry and Little Richard – as described and discussed by Tucker. The specific musical details of 'Crocodile Rock' look in other directions. The introduction and verses bring to mind the pop-orientated sounds of the later 1950s and early 60s; while the fake falsetto line possibly evokes the doo-wop vocal group style of the 1950s it more specifically cites Pat Boone's 'Speedy Gonzales' from 1962, a reference which shifts the focus to an already highly synthetic pop prevalent in the early 1960s. In other words, 'Crocodile Rock' forms a network of meanings and relationships that signify past popular musics, but it does not restate that past as it sounded at what might have been remembered as its moment of origin. It may claim to 'remember when rock was young' (the mid-1950s) but in doing so what it actually remembers (perhaps parodies) is the sounds of the later 1950s and early 60s; a time when rock (rock 'n' roll) was no longer young, before any potential boundary between rock and pop had been meaningfully con-structed. It therefore creates a degree of confusion over historical time and stylistic space around this period of the later 1950s and early 60s, a moment that was featured as the second stage of the historical outline presented in chapter 1 through Jameson's proposal of a 'radical break' at this time.

According to some recurrent historical narratives, the late 1950s and early 60s was the moment at which popular music first experienced a significant rupture in terms of identity and direction and became synonymous with the celebration of the superficial. Paul Longhurst articulates this view in his book *Popular Music and Society*:

> The conventional account of the development of rock and pop sees a bland period between the late 1950s and 1963. This is the period where, according to Gillett, the excitement of rock 'n' roll is replaced by standardized music industry products such as Fabian in the United States and Cliff Richard in Britain.[35]

Of course, this view only serves to marginalize many popular music practices of the period and projects a rock-based historical narrative that prepares the ground for the emergence of the Beatles in 1963 and their subsequent canonization.[36] It also conveniently avoids the operations of the culture industry prior to this point, a gesture that is intended to preserve the nostalgic idealization of a notional point of origin, the time when 'rock was young'.

This historical narrative is, as indicated by Longhurst, largely dependent upon the work of Gillett. Charlie Gillett's *The Sound of the City* was first published in 1970 and has been one of the standard histories of popular music since then; it therefore provides a central reference point for a historiography of popular music. Not only does it construct and project this historical narrative, situating the 1950s at its centre, it also effectively intersects with much of the general historical awareness evident in much of the popular music mentioned above.[37]

In retrospect, the early 1970s could appear as an end of an era in popular music, the moment at which the optimism and imagination of the 1960s disappears, symbolized by the break-up of the Beatles and the death of Hendrix, and the ending of a historical trajectory that began with rock 'n' roll in the 1950s. As 'Crocodile Rock' laments, 'the years went by and the rock just died'. For Gillett this sense of closure is symbolized through Don McLean's 'American Pie', a recording in the singer-songwriter tradition that was a surprise hit in 1972. Gillett, in a later edition of his book, states:

> 'American Pie' came to be the epitaph for the fifteen-year era just ended ... For an audience which found itself offended by the bubblegum trivia being passed off as pop music, and which found the sheer volume of the stadium-based rock-blues groups hard to handle, here was the perfect embodiment of their mounting nostalgia for the irretrievably lost era.[38]

In other words, for those not interested in Elton John's play with the surfaces of past popular musics, there was always the alleged authenticity of the singer-songwriter in the easy listening shape of Don McLean. But what is most relevant in this context is Gillett's suggestion of a 'mounting nostalgia for the irretrievably lost era', a suggestion which evocatively captures a sense of desire for an era of innocence and certainty, which, in the American context, is a nostalgic desire for a time before Vietnam, a nostalgia which was to be further intensified through the reality of the Watergate experience, while in Britain it perhaps reflected the loss of a collective identity that had been forged through wartime and post-war experiences.

For Fredric Jameson, this nostalgia situates the 1950s as the 'privileged lost object of desire',[39] a suggestion which in its own way echoes Gillett's 'irretrievably lost era' and is made in relation to the film *American Graffiti*. From this perspective the early 1970s, the third stage of our historical outline, looks back to the 1950s, the first stage. In doing so the later stage privileges the music of that earlier moment and its aura of innocence, but it also knowingly articulates a desire for this time and its popular culture that can never be fulfilled.

American Graffiti

Cinema participated in the construction of meaningful, in fact definitive, reflections of this musical retrospection and cultural desire for the 1950s during the early 1970s.

Two films, *That'll Be the Day* and the already mentioned *American Graffiti*, both from 1973, capture this historical gesture, but in different ways. *That'll Be the Day*, which takes its title from the Buddy Holly song of 1957, is set in 1950s Britain, reflecting the British post-war experience and the assimilation of American popular culture. The central character in the film is played by David Essex, then a current British pop star, as an innocent, idealistic young man dreaming of the rock 'n' roll life and an escape from a set of expectations that were seemingly restricted by a class-based social context. Within the film we hear various instances of 1950s music, including, for example, an early scene set in a cafe (coffee bar) and which features 'Born too Late' by the Poni-Tails (1958) and a later fairground scene which uses 'Red River Rock' by Johnny and the Hurricanes (1959). But these specific instances are used only to ground the film in the period; although audible to the characters on screen, they do not directly become part of its narrative or discourse.

That'll Be the Day may form part of a new historical awareness through which some of us began to discover that popular music had a past as well as a present, but it does not really do anything more than that. It is *American Graffiti*, directed by George Lucas (before Star Wars) that further extends this musical dimension, with the soundtrack initially appearing to define the context of the film. It is also a film that has attracted much attention from film scholars, including Colin MacCabe, David Shumway and Jeff Smith.[40]

Set in a small Californian town, the film reflects a group of young people, their relationships and their musical preferences. The film's content unfolds through one night, the night before some of the main characters are due to depart for college. The opening moments of the film seem clearly to situate it within 1950s America as defined by the sound of Bill Haley's 'Rock Around the Clock' (1954–5), a hit recording from the period and generally considered to be one of the definitive sounds of rock 'n' roll music. Its positioning as the first sounds heard in the film appears to render the period reference explicit, as do the evocative visual images of highly stylized cars and other related symbols.[41]

However, the soundtrack of *American Graffiti* shifts from the mid-1950s and Bill Haley's 'Rock Around the Clock' to the mid-1960s as defined by the Beach Boys' 'All Summer Long' (1964). This ten-year sweep of popular music history encloses both the emergence of rock 'n' roll and what may be part of its legacy in the form of the Beach Boys' surf sound within a single compressed narrative. It is this extensive range of musical repertoire that lends a sense of history to the film and accentuates the passing of time, even though very little real time passes in the film. It therefore also, like 'Crocodile Rock', intentionally confuses and disrupts both historical time and stylistic space.

The extended use of and reference to popular music also creates a sense of loss. One character, in response to hearing the Beach Boys on the car radio, laments: 'Rock 'n' roll's been goin' down hill ever since Buddy Holly died', which echoes the claim of 'Crocodile Rock' that 'the rock just died' as well as Don McLean's 'the day the music died' from 'American Pie'. The retrospective reference to Holly's death, which occurred in 1959, is one of the few moments which suggest the film is actually located not in the 1950s but the early 1960s (1962), a fact that is confused by the Beach Boys reference. Interestingly, the only other moment that fully reveals the film's true historical location is a passing reference to President Kennedy (pre-assassination), again a nostalgic glance backwards to what was now perceived as a more innocent, perhaps idealistic, time.[42]

In retrospect, *American Graffiti*, as well as being a vivid representation of the 1970s fascination with the 1950s, is seen to form an important statement in the development of cinema and its interaction with popular music. According to Stephen Paul Miller:

> By 1973 there is a heightened nostalgia for the sounds of the early sixties and late fifties. *American Graffiti* (1973) is the first film fully to realize the value of using former hits on movie soundtracks ... Lucas's *American Graffiti* is a groundbreaking project in the 'representation' of a recent past in a symbiotic relationship with the present. The film renders a Northern California town of a mere ten years earlier as an antiquated reality, but nevertheless a reality that we now seem to know we cannot escape.[43]

Reality is now antiquated, but we cannot escape from the legacy of the past or our desire for it. In effect, through this film, and its soundtrack, we experience the representation of the end of one moment (the early 1970s as the end of the 1960s) looking back nostalgically at the end of a previous moment (the early 1960s as the end of the 1950s). Jameson, as part of his discussion around the 'privileged lost object of desire', extends this trope of nostalgia further, suggesting that it operates at the level of genre, that of the nostalgia film, and reflects much wider historical and cultural tendencies:

> Nostalgia films restructure the whole issue of pastiche and project it onto a collective and social level, where the desperate attempt to appropriate a missing past is now refracted through the iron law of fashion change and the emergent ideology of the generation. The inaugural film of this new aesthetic discourse, George Lucas's *American Graffiti* (1973), set out to recapture, as so many films have attempted since, the henceforth mesmerizing lost reality of the Eisenhower era; and one tends to feel, that for Americans at least, the 1950s remain the privileged lost object of desire.[44]

In Jameson's terms, we can generalize the experience of *American Graffiti*, viewing it as part of a collective process that is definitive of wider cultural and historical conditions. While 'Crocodile Rock' plays with the surfaces of past musics (Jameson's pastiche) and 'American Pie' laments the passing of an era, *American Graffiti* uses music to portray personal identity and historical resonance. But there are similar processes at work. 'Crocodile Rock' may confuse 'when rock was young' in terms of style and history, but *American Graffiti* explores a similar historical dislocation, with a film made in 1973, set in 1962 and evoking the music of the 1950s. Its movement across these differing historical stages is further extended through the insertion of my own subjective experiences of viewing the film in 1974 (and many times since), and buying and living with the soundtrack album.

The images of retrospection and nostalgic desire active in *American Graffiti*, Gillett's *Sound of the City* and Elton John's 'Crocodile Rock' provide symbolic cultural reflections of wider processes; they reflect, in Harvey's terms, new post-modern ways of experiencing the space and time of a certain past. In doing so they tell us more about postmodernism in the early 1970s than they ever could about the reality of the 1950s.

Chapter 4

The challenge of the past

> I think of the postmodern attitude as that of a man who loves a very cultivated woman and knows he cannot say to her, 'I love you madly,' because he knows that she knows (and that she knows that he knows) that these words have already been written by Barbara Cartland. Still, there is a solution. He can say, 'As Barbara Cartland would put it, I love you madly.' At this point, having avoided false innocence, having said clearly that it is no longer possible to speak innocently, he will nevertheless have said what he wanted to say to the woman: that he loves her, but he loves her in an age of lost innocence. If the woman goes along with this, she will have received a declaration of love all the same. Neither of the two speakers will feel innocent, both will have accepted the challenge of the past, of the already said, which cannot be eliminated; both will consciously and with pleasure play the game of irony … But both will have succeeded, once again, in speaking of love.[1]

The above statement comes from the Italian novelist, critic and literary theorist Umberto Eco in a text titled *Postscript to the Name of the Rose*. This text, as the title suggests, is a series of reflections on Eco's own commercially and critically successful novel *The Name of the Rose*, which was first published in the early 1980s.[2] This is a novel that is loaded with historical preoccupations, reflecting upon the detective novel as a historical genre and making intertextual references to specific precursors. As Brian McHale explains: 'Its principal intertextual model, as the name of its hero, William of Baskerville, proclaims, is Conan Doyle's *The Hound of the Baskervilles*', with the earlier text standing as both precursor to, and target for, the later text.[3] We have confronted intertextual relationships already within the context of music through reference to Michael Daugherty's *Dead Elvis* and this chapter will pursue such relationships more generally, using references to literature, film and ideas from literary theory as ways of situating and interpreting this particular representation of postmodernism in music.

Eco's description of postmodernism given above reflects something of his practice as a novelist as defined by *The Name of the Rose*, with the process of writing a postscript forming part of a highly self-conscious critical gesture that highlights the engagement between theory and practice that is often indicative of postmodernism. In both the practice of the novel and the theory of the postscript Eco is saying something distinctive yet also by now rather familiar about postmodernism. Both are in effect engagements with the past. In his outlining of 'the postmodern attitude' this is articulated as the acceptance of the challenge of the past. But this challenge occurs in what Eco describes as an age of 'lost innocence'. Eco may be suggesting that this is, or was, a time in which, through the accumulation of information, and a heightened sense of scepticism – perhaps some might say cynicism – we have lost the sense of innocence that conditioned responses to art in earlier times. The proposed age of 'lost innocence' also suggests a general retreat from belief in the effective transformation of the economic, political and cultural spheres. The sense of loss that Eco articulates here comes close to what is implied by Lyotard's 'incredulity toward metanarratives', with the inability to invest belief in the big stories of modernism reflecting the loss of the innocence that was once required in order to make such an investment.[4]

We could interpret much of the music we have already encountered as statements about the challenge that Eco poses. The discussions of *Dead Elvis*, 'Crocodile Rock' and *American Graffiti* in previous chapters could now be restated using Eco's words. His account of postmodernism also, like *Dead Elvis*, clearly uses a degree of irony to articulate the challenge of saying again what has already been said, but which can only be said in the form of quotation – I cannot say I love you, I can only say 'I love you'. This challenge as Eco fashions it seems to effectively displace the assumption of originality that was central to modernism and, before that, romanticism. But, while Eco's *The Name of the Rose* may be dependent upon its intertextual relationship to the historical genre of the detective novel, I think any reader would find it impossible to claim that it was therefore unoriginal, and, as we have already discovered, there is nothing that sounds quite like Michael Daugherty's *Dead Elvis*.

It will now be useful to explore further this 'postmodern attitude' as described by Eco and look at some ways in which the acceptance of the challenge of the past, of the already said, can be heard in music. In pursuing this possibility we are effectively making contact again with Fredric Jameson's representation of postmodernism as an attempt 'to think the present historically in an age that has forgotten how to think historically in the first place'.[5] The seemingly paradoxical process of thinking the present historically can also reflect David Harvey's 'new dominant ways in which we experience space and time'.[6] Music that accepts the challenge that Eco describes not only confuses our sense of the present but also often presents interesting new ways of hearing the past. In doing so it once again articulates postmodernism's historical awareness after modernism.

Berio – *Sinfonia*

One common factor in the various attempts to construct a historical framework for the emergence of postmodernism was the 1960s, the time in which so much seemed to be changing in both the cultural and political spheres. In particular the events around 1968 now in retrospect assume a certain symbolic importance; as we now recall, they formed a historical marker in Harvey's proposal that we can observe postmodernism emerging 'somewhere between 1968 and 1972'.[7] A great deal of the music that appears in this historical space reflects the claims made by both Jameson and Harvey in relation to a certain historical awareness which makes us rethink assumptions of how we experience space and time. This new experience is partly reflected through much of the rock music of the period, particularly around 1968, which celebrated an extension of the temporal dimensions of the music, often in the form of extended improvisations and expanded structures. But other musical practices begin to occur around this time, which rather than extending the linear temporality of music now articulates a disruptive relationship between the present and the past and in doing so begins to suggest other ways in which postmodernism in music can be defined through new experiences of time. These new experiences can be understood in terms of both historical perspective and musical temporality, which therefore opens up new stylistic spaces through the repositioning of specific music from the past within a new context. Such processes occur in Luciano Berio's *Sinfonia* (1968–9), a work that has been extensively discussed from many different perspectives, including that of a postmodern intertextuality, and which will form the next stage of the discussion.

Luciano Berio (1925–2003) was initially aligned with the post-1945 generation identified with Darmstadt and the technical and aesthetic parameters of serialism. However, Berio's adoption of serial techniques was rather brief and mostly restricted to his early music of the 1950s.[8] With *Sinfonia* Berio asserted a dramatic difference to the legacy of high modernism.

Sinfonia is a five-movement work for voices and orchestra. The second movement is a rethinking of another Berio work *O King* (1967–8). This reworking and repositioning is part of Berio's process of commentary, with the new context in effect commenting on the old. What we hear in this movement is a very gentle reiteration of the name of Martin Luther King, which situates the music in relationship to the wider political context of the late 1960s. The effect of this music is both subdued and static. This is sharply contrasted by the intense activity of the central third movement, which, as is widely known, is based directly upon the scherzo third movement from Mahler's second symphony as its 'core "text"' and has many layers of other texts, both musical and literary, placed over it.[9] The additional musical materials involve reference to a wide range of music, including Beethoven's sixth symphony (the 'Pastoral'), Berlioz's *Symphonie fantastique*, Debussy's *La Mer*, Ravel's *La Valse* and Strauss's *Der Rosenkavalier*, among many others. The literary references are also highly plural, but Samuel Beckett's *The Unnamable* provides the core along with many other fragments of other texts that come in and out of focus. This extensive use of many different sources suggests that this movement is in effect a collage made of many things.

The use of collage to describe this music seems appropriate; it captures the sense of juxtaposition of textures and materials as originally identified through the importance of such processes in the visual arts. It also suggests some resemblance to other musical works that can be described in this way, from the radical juxtapositions in the music of Ives, which predates postmodernism, to the music of Bernd Alois Zimmermann (1918–70), which is broadly contemporary with that of Berio. Zimmermann's opera *Die Soldaten* (1957–65) uses a wide range of recognizable musical materials, while his *Requiem for a Young Poet* (1969) makes use of many literary sources as part of a broad historical view of twentieth-century Europe, including authors such as Joyce, Pound, Camus and Wittgenstein, and fragments of political texts by Hitler, Goebbels, Chamberlain, Nagy and Mao Zedong. The music is also based on the collage-effect of many sources, including historical – such as Beethoven's ninth symphony, the 'Ode to Joy' – and contemporary – as defined by the Beatles' 'Hey Jude', which situates the work in the wider cultural context of the late 1960s. However, Berio himself was rather resistant to *Sinfonia* being described as collage; there is nothing accidental or spontaneous in the particular intertextual web constructed by Berio: the score is both carefully composed and highly structured.[10]

For Jane Piper Clendinning the intertextuality of *Sinfonia* positions it as 'an early example of a postmodern composition'.[11] Many other commentators look in the same direction. For example, Jonathan Kramer in his overview of postmodern music positions *Sinfonia* in a long list of works which 'do not so much conserve as radically transform the past as – each in its own way – they simultaneously embrace and repudiate history'.[12] This is a meaningful description in that it acknowledges that the relationship articulated by Berio through the use of the Mahler material is not a conservative gesture. Now the past as defined by Mahler is viewed in new ways that may subject it to displacement through the rupturing of any notional historical continuity. The removal of the 'original' from its context could also be interpreted as simultaneously repudiating history. However, such postmodern processes also, unlike modernism, recognize that the past must somehow be acknowledged even when it is subject to disruption and displacement. In doing so it effectively breaks through any notional autonomy or formal self-dependency, producing a sound that is both multi-dimensional and multi-temporal.

If Berio's use of the Mahler scherzo, and other material, does not seek to conserve the past it is still notable that it allows for the past as defined by tonality to come into a then contemporary soundworld, with tonality being the musical resource most dramatically displaced by modernism. In chapter 2 we considered Linda Hutcheon's descriptions of what postmodernism in music sounds like as defined 'through a parodic return to tonality and to the past of music, not as a source of embarrassment or inspiration, but with ironic distance, as in the work of … Luciano Berio'.[13] In this statement Hutcheon does not comment directly on *Sinfonia*, or any other specific work by Berio, but it is worth speculating that it does somehow refer to this music. There is a sense of distance to how we hear the tonality of Mahler's scherzo as redefined by Berio, but it is difficult to connect that sense of distance with a concept of irony or how the specifics of this movement are part of 'a parodic return to tonality'. It is also the case that much of Berio's other music, although distanced from a high modernist serialism, cannot easily be defined as a return to tonality as such.

Although we now hear this third movement of *Sinfonia* within the context of postmodernism, and it does fit neatly into the chronology established earlier in this book, it is a very specific example. While in this instance Berio is clearly looking in this particular direction, and both collage and intertextuality can be used to describe the interconnections and dependencies of the multiple texts that are in play in this movement, this is a highly individual moment and one that does not necessarily lend itself easily to generalization. In terms of Berio's own music it does open a certain path that will revisit material from earlier composers, including *Rendering* (1989), an orchestral work that is based upon fragments of Schubert. However, this direction is coexistent with other aspects of Berio's work, including the reworking and redefinition of his own music through the process of commentary, and it is not therefore in itself necessarily definitive of Berio's music in general.

If we want to create a context within which the individuality of this moment in *Sinfonia* can be situated then, rather than looking for how it might fit in relation to other music by Berio, it will be much more productive to consider other works, including literature and cinema as well as music, that employ similar intertextual strategies and present new ways of reading and hearing the past.

Historiographic metafiction

Within the context of post-1945 literature the novelist John Updike was one of the great literary chroniclers of the post-war world, particularly the American experience of that world. In his work recurrent themes of alienation and identity are redefined and repositioned. This is not necessarily to claim Updike for postmodernism; in fact the male neurosis, anxiety and alienation that Updike documents in, for example, the Rabbit books carry strong resonances of modernism.[14] However, in the novel titled *Memories of the Ford Administration* (1993), which is not directly intertextual in relation to specific texts, Updike tells a story about the blurring of the boundaries between past and present, and between fact and fiction.[15] John Duvall tells an interesting story about Updike's story. He begins with the following summary:

This novel's blurring of the boundary between history and fiction occurs through the self-conscious academic voice of a history professor, Alfred Clayton. The fictive premise is that Clayton is responding to a request from a history journal, *Retrospect*, that he provide impressions of Gerald Ford's administration. Clayton instead comments on his adulterous personal life during the Ford years, layering in his unpublished research on the administration of President James Buchanan.[16]

From this summary it is clear that in this particular novel a number of boundaries, or divisions, are effectively erased: professional (history) and personal (sex), fact (Ford) and fiction (Clayton). This in itself presents a multi-layering of shifting temporalities that are further intensified through the reader's reception of, and response to, such a text. Any such response may be conditioned by factors such as, for example, personal memory of the time of the Ford administration (1974–6), the time and place within which the act of reading occurred, and the memories, or impressions, that may be triggered by both the historical and fictional details of the text. Duvall links his summary of the Updike novel through its unique interplay of fact and fiction to the theoretical work of Linda Hutcheon, which we have already encountered in this chapter and at earlier stages of this book.

Hutcheon, in the preliminary moments of her *Poetics of Postmodernism*, makes a direct reference to Terry Gilliam's film *Brazil* (1985), which is described through a 'postmodern ironic rethinking of history' that is 'textualized in the many general parodic references to other movies' and more 'specific parodic recalls'.[17] On the basis of this description this film stands as a brilliant example of a postmodern work, one that is defined through already existing images, which are treated in a manner of parody and, due to the historical nature of the sources that are referred to, views the past through a somewhat ironic lens. Such processes lead to 'typically postmodern contradictions', including, most notably, 'the co-existence of heterogeneous filmic genres'.[18] Hutcheon's summary of this particular film is, I think, accurate and, in its play with many different sources, suggests some points of comparison with other work that may contain a similar multiplicity of levels. While I think it is difficult to hear the third movement of Berio's *Sinfonia* in a way that is similar to how Hutcheon views *Brazil*, this music, as already demonstrated, does evince a play of historical materials, even if its contradictions are not necessarily defined via the coexistence of heterogeneous genres as such (the musical references are too specific to be truly generic), and processes of irony and parody remain problematic in the particular example of *Sinfonia*.

The brief references to the film of Terry Gilliam, the music of Luciano Berio and the fiction of Umberto Eco in this chapter already look towards the wider usage of such strategies as reflected in the claim that all forms and contexts of culture offer examples of this kind of postmodern intertextuality. However, while our attention will become drawn exclusively to music that positively explores such implications, Hutcheon's concern is primarily with 'the novel genre' and a particular form, or perhaps a genre, she terms 'historiographic metafiction':

> By this I mean those well known and popular novels which are both intensely self-reflexive and yet paradoxically also lay claim to historical events and personages: *The French Lieutenant's Woman, Midnight's Children, Ragtime, Legs, G., Famous Last Words.*[19]

And to this list, along with many other novels, can be added both Eco's *The Name of the Rose* and Updike's *Memories of the Ford Administration* as situated by John Duvall through his reference to Hutcheon's conception of historiographic metafiction. Among such works Hutcheon highlights an intense self-reflexivity – that is, as I interpret it, a preoccupation with the text's own condition of language and its relationship to stylistic and generic frameworks. Yet this essentially internal focus coexists with an often historical subject matter and manner of representation that dramatically extends the parameters of the text beyond its own immediate internal properties and characteristics. Historiographic metafiction is always somehow engaged with history while simultaneously being self-consciously fictional. It may take the form of intertextual engagement but, as in the case of Updike's *Memories of the Ford Administration*, this is not the only way in which a text may become both historiographic and metafictional. Of the novels mentioned by Hutcheon, John Fowles's *The French Lieutenant's Woman* is a quite brilliant example of a text that celebrates such processes. This book was first published in 1969 and is therefore situated within Harvey's proposed chronology of postmodernism. It utilizes a deliberately 'old-fashioned' stylistic language to represent an historical time, bringing to mind, for this reader, the novels of Thomas Hardy, although not necessarily in an ironic or parodistic way.[20] It also references other texts and in doing so creates a context for its own interpretation. We read a novel written in the late 1960s as a reflection of a past as defined through its construction and representation by earlier novelists and other writers. The richness of this encounter is further enhanced by knowledge of the film version of this novel. Directed by Karel Reisz in 1981 the film reflects the literary playfulness of the book through the cinematic convention of the film within a film. We see the leading performers, Jeremy Irons and Meryl Streep, both in and out of character. This effect of telling parallel stories, the relationship between the two principal characters of the story, and the relationship between the two individuals who perform the roles, provides a contemporary frame around the historical. Hutcheon continues:

> In most of the critical work on postmodernism, it is narrative – be it in literature, history, or theory – that has usually been the major focus of attention.

> Historiographic metafiction incorporates all three of these domains: that is,
> its theoretical self-awareness of history and fiction as human constructs
> (historio*graphic meta*fiction) is made the grounds for its rethinking and
> reworking of the forms and contents of the past.[21]

This theoretical self-awareness of history, prising open the constructedness of what
actually constitutes the past through the reworking of its forms and contents, is, as
Hutcheon demonstrates, a real presence in the domain of fiction as defined through
the genre of the novel and, as we have seen, in film as defined by *American Graffiti*,
Brazil and, in a rather different way, *The French Lieutenant's Woman*. There are
many more such examples from both literature and cinema that could be cited here
but it is now time to return the focus back towards music that, in confronting Eco's
challenge of the past, without directly engaging in detailed comparison, suggests
general but effective parallels with Hutcheon's historiographic metafiction.

New romanticisms

Without claiming it as emblematic or definitive statements of postmodernism in music
as such, the music of Nicholas Maw (1935–2009) and Robin Holloway (b.1943), both
British composers who formed distinctive musical voices in the 1960s and into the
early 1970s, will be central to this stage of the discussion.[22] Both composers emerged
from the shadow of a perceived Darmstadt-dominated high modernism of the 1950s
and went on to articulate a critical distance to that moment, what in an initial sense
might again be defined as an 'anti-modernism'. For Maw, this process of rejection was
highly self-conscious and deliberate:

> The particular style that prevailed when I was beginning in the 1950s – the
> Darmstadt version of the post-Viennese school – was one that rejected too much
> of the past for my temperament.[23]

It is notable that the point of rejection in relation to the Darmstadt experience of
what we have come to understand as high modernism is formed around the musical
past, with the 'Darmstadt version' of modernism perceived as an attempt to oblit-
erate that past. In contrast a history of music was quickly reconstructed by Maw as a
residual source of musical ideas and materials. For Maw, 'we can plug in anywhere
we like in order to nourish our own music: in my own case it was somewhere
between about 1860 and 1914'.[24] In other words, Maw as a postmodern composer
chooses to look towards the music of late romanticism and early modernism, not
as the result of a historically driven imperative but as the consequence of a highly
subjective preference. The process may appear to be somewhat similar to Stravinsky's

neoclassical appropriation of the past, but the actual location is very different. The focus on this particular location is aurally evident in all of Maw's music, from the 'watershed' of *Scenes and Arias* (1962–6), which resonates with echoes of Strauss and early Schoenberg, through large-scale works such as the massive orchestral work *Odyssey* (1972–87) and the opera *Sophie's Choice* (1990–2002), which are characterized through large, sweeping thematic gestures and rich tonally based harmonies.

This retrospective gesture towards romanticism suggests that Maw's music may align itself with other similar music within what has often been labelled a 'neo' or 'new' romanticism. This particular stylistic label emerged in the 1980s as identified by a festival hosted by the New York Philharmonic at Lincoln Center in 1983: 'Horizons '83: Since 1968, A New Romanticism'. Designed by then composer in residence Jacob Druckman, the festival featured a wide range of composers, some of whom, such as Peter Maxwell Davies, do not fit all that neatly into this context, but also composers such as David Del Tredici, Fred Lerdahl and Druckman himself, whose work involved a return to tonality, although not quite in the way that Hutcheon outlined, perhaps rather misleadingly, in relation to Berio.[25] This return may have at times an element of parody through pastiche, a factor we will encounter in relation to George Rochberg's music in the next chapter, but it does not necessarily have to be ironic. However, if Maw's music does form a certain new (or neo-) romantic stylistic orientation then it is worth emphasizing the fact that Maw was looking in this direction in the early 1960s, long before the rather self-conscious construction of this particular terminology in the 1980s, and his music is very different from that of other composers routinely mentioned in this context.

The works of Maw highlighted above suggest a certain historical reference but they do not lend themselves to the identification of specific precursors through processes of intertextual citation. If we hear the presence of the past in a work such as Maw's *Odyssey*, for example, it does not come to us via such direct references but through a more generalized aura. Much of the critical reception of this work involved the identification of precursors through description of the work's textures, forms and scale as 'Brucknerian' and/or 'Mahlerian', but there is some distance between describing a work as, for example, 'Brucknerian' and finding direct intertextual engagements between the music of two different composers, Maw and Bruckner, from two different eras, postmodernism and romanticism.[26]

Music of Memory

In a work evocatively titled *Music of Memory* for solo guitar (1989) Maw makes what is for him a quite exceptionally explicit reference to already-existing music, in this case from Mendelssohn's String Quartet in A minor Op. 13, with Mendelssohn's own version of romanticism perhaps providing a sense of distance to the intensely expressive nature of the late romanticism and early modernism with which Maw had most often readily identified. The source already sounds somehow archaic, distant, and the construction of memory is multiplied through the indebtedness of the Mendelssohn source to its own past, its own construction of history.

Example 4.1 reproduces the first few pages of *Music of Memory*. We hear Maw's own music as leading towards the first presentation of the Mendelssohn material, which is clearly indicated and acknowledged in the score. This small example highlights, rather than a basic juxtaposition, the attempted integration between two distinct musical contexts. As the work unfolds it also becomes evident that there is a variation process in play that is based on the Mendelssohn theme, but this is effectively distributed throughout and embedded within the work. This variation process, and the careful avoiding of theme followed by variation, accentuates the role of 'memory' within the work through the recollection of fragments of recognizable material. Such processes already highlight the distance between Maw's *Music of Memory* and other music that may be described through a postmodern intertextuality. It sounds obviously different from Daugherty's *Dead Elvis*, and its treatment of the Mendelssohn theme is very different from the layering effect of the Mahler scherzo in Berio's *Sinfonia*. In comparison to that example, Maw's *Music of Memory* is essentially linear, it unfolds through a sequence of connected events, while in *Sinfonia* the effect is effectively layered, with material placed *on* or *over* the 'core' text of the Mahler scherzo. This could partially be explained by the basic fact that Maw's *Music of Memory* is composed for a solo instrument and therefore less likely to lend itself to such layering effects, but the linear unfolding is intentional and the result is goal orientated in that the work concludes with the return to the Mendelssohn theme and its A minor tonality. This brief comparison of two very different musical works, by two very different composers, already suggests that although a significant amount of music that is open to a definition of postmodernism can often be described through intertextuality, not all such music situates and articulates such relationships in the same way.

Scenes from Schumann

If Maw's appropriation of Mendelssohn in *Music of Memory* is an exceptional moment in his oeuvre, in contrast the music of Robin Holloway has often looked more directly to a process of citation of music from the past. Like Maw, Holloway's first works reflect the mastering of serial techniques. In several works from the mid-1960s, such as the Concertino No. 1 (1964, rev. 1968–9), Holloway announced himself as a composer competent in, and confident of, serialism. But by the early 1970s Holloway was already looking in a quite different direction, as defined by his

[‿ = left hand legato or slur; all fingering, string and fret markings have been omitted]

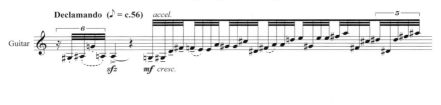

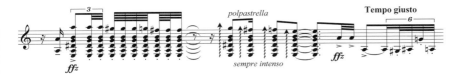

Example 4.1 Nicholas Maw, *Music of Memory*, opening

* Mendelssohn, String Quartet Op. 13 (*Allegretto con moto* in original)

Example 4.1 (cont.)

Example 4.1 (cont.)

breakthrough work *Scenes from Schumann* (1970, rev. 1986). For Julian Anderson, this work 'seemed to represent a complete rupture with the diktats of modernism'.[27] It makes this break, as the title suggests, through looking to the romantic music of Schumann as a source of compositional material. Each movement, by implication scene, is based on an individual Schumann song, which is indicated in the title of each movement. Holloway provides his own effective description in the preface to the published score:

> Each movement is based upon the Schumann song of the same title. The originals have been recomposed in a manner for which Stravinsky's treatment of Tchaikovsky in *Le Baiser de la Fée* [1928] is the nearest precedent. I have attempted to get 'inside' the songs and from inside to send them in different directions. Though there is hardly a bar left which could have been written by Schumann, the intention is not to distort but rather to amplify and intensify the originals. Images and feelings from the poems as well as from the music have been allowed to ramify in free-association; the resulting work is an affectionate homage to the spirit and style of a favourite phase of German romanticism.[28]

Again Holloway draws attention to Stravinsky's appropriation of past materials, in this case that of Tchaikovsky, as a precedent for the re-composition of existing musical materials. It is significant that in the above description Holloway does not really say anything that could be interpreted as suggestive of collage and/or intertextuality. In trying to 'get inside' selected Schumann songs and 'send them in different directions' Holloway is effectively trying to do something that could be perceived as potentially more integrative than collage or the direct presentation of an intertextual relationship.

Scenes from Schumann consists of seven movements, each of which is, as already suggested, based directly on an individual Schumann song taken from different sources. It is scored for a conventional orchestra. The third movement, titled 'Dream Vision' and based on the song 'Allnächtlich im Traume' from Schumann's *Dichterliebe* cycle (Op. 48, No. 14), gives a good example of Holloway's relationship to the original material. Example 4.2a reproduces the opening passage of the score, in which the Schumann melody is stated intact by the flutes and supported by the B major harmonic context that is also consistent with the original (see Ex. 4.2b, which reproduces the opening moments of the Schumann song). Any listener already familiar with the original source would readily recognize its repositioning in the new context. However, as the movement unfolds, the treatment of the theme becomes more expansive and developed, but in this instance the representation of the Schumann source remains quite literal. In contrast, Schumann's 'Allnächtlich im Traume' is used again as the basis of the fifth movement, titled 'Dream Visitation'. Now the treatment of the source is rather different. Its transformation is already in place with obvious signs of Holloway getting 'inside' the Schumann song and

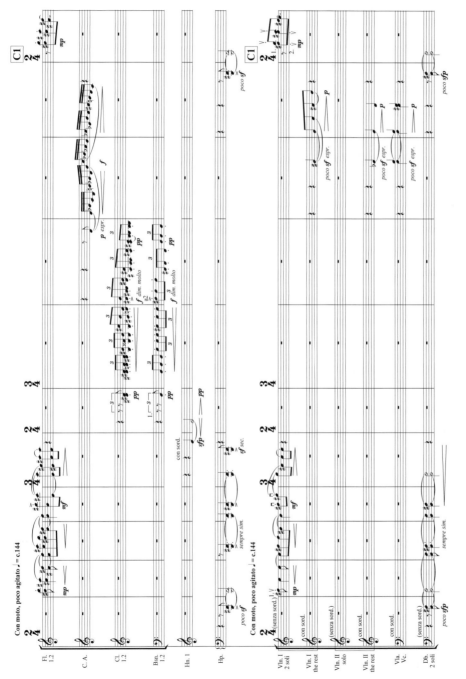

Example 4.2a Robin Holloway, *Scenes from Schumann*, 3. 'Dream Vision' ('Allnächtlich im Traume' Op. 48, No. 14), opening

Example 4.2b Robert Schumann, *Dichterliebe* Op. 48, No. 14 ('Allnächtlich im Traume')

of it going in different directions. Example 4.2c presents the opening of this movement. The orchestral texture is now more expansive, deeper, and the tonality,
although obscured, is shifted from the original B major to Db major as defined by
the sustained pedal note, which is present throughout the movement. However,
there are still clearly recognizable traces of the Schumann song, with its original
melodic gesture of B–A♯–F♯ now simply transposed to Db–C–Ab. These two appropriations of the same song from *Dichterliebe* act as a frame to the central fourth
movement of the work: a substantial reinterpretation of 'Auf einer Burg' from
Schumann's *Liederkreis* (Op. 39, No. 7).

This reference to the music of Schumann is also evident in other works by
Holloway, including *Fantasy-Pieces* (1971). This instrumental work for chamber
ensemble is based directly on material from *Liederkreis* (Op. 24), a song cycle based
on the poetry of Heine. Holloway's *Fantasy-Pieces* consist of five titled pieces:
Praeludium, Half Asleep, Adagio, Scherzo ostinato, Finale: Roses – thorns and
flowers. Holloway has sanctioned a performance of *Liederkreis* between the
Praeludium and Half Asleep. This is how it appears on the recording.[29] Hearing
the complete Schumann cycle inserted into the context of Holloway's work will
clearly have a radical impact on how we hear the music of both composers. If
listened to in this way, following the initial Praeludium and then the Schumann
cycle, the next stage of *Fantasy-Pieces* is Half Asleep. In this movement, songs 1, 2

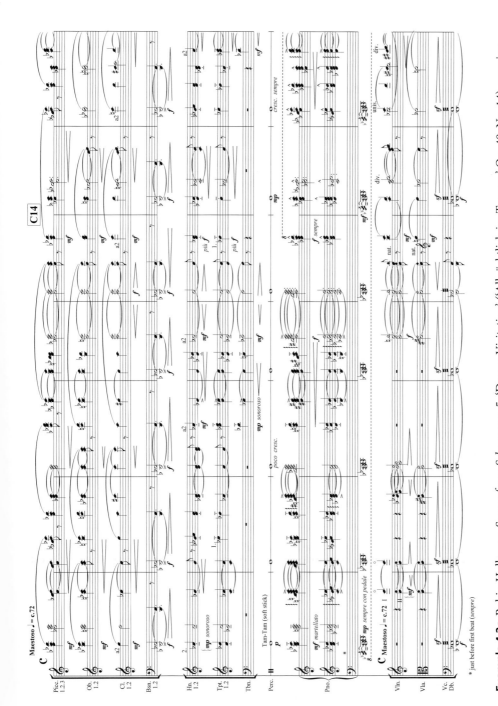

Example 4.2c Robin Holloway, *Scenes from Schumann*, 5. 'Dream Visitation' ('Allnächtlich im Traume' Op. 48, No. 14), opening

* just before first beat (*sempre*)

and 4 of the Schumann source are used in a multi-layering of harmonic and instrumental textures.

Example 4.3a represents the opening moments of Half Asleep. In this example we hear the appropriation of the piano accompaniment to the first song of *Liederkreis* (see Ex. 4.3b). Holloway's usage of this material is fairly obvious, but there are subtle differences. For example, the move between D and C♯ in the piano part is now repeated before the descent from B to E. But such differences are slight; they do not in themselves really transform how we might hear the Schumann material. However, the layering effect on top of the piano part does begin to have such an effect.

The melody projected at Fig. 4 by the flutes and violin is clearly based on the melody of the fourth song from *Leiderkreis*. In between this melody and accompaniment, the middle layer (clarinet, bassoon and viola) reflects the second *Liederkreis* song as defined by its B–A♯–B gesture. These are small details but they are part of a larger picture.

The music of both Maw and Holloway suggests different answers to the question of what it means to compose, and listen to, a postmodern music, to construct music in the aftermath of modernism, and to generate new ideas through the refashioning of a premodern musical language. Both emerge through a historical space, from the 1960s to early 1970s, and make contact with the theoretical ground covered in this book. These examples reflect Jameson's assertion of the need to think the present historically and clearly provide musical representations of Harvey's new ways of experiencing space and time; in this instance it is the distant time and critical space of romanticism that is revisited and filtered through a contemporary experience. In doing so they produce music, quite unintentionally, that begins to suggest certain parallels with some of the literature described by Hutcheon as examples of historiographic metafiction: music about other music that again brings the past into the present, not as historical fact but as a musical fiction.

It is notable that it is the music of romanticism that is identified as the source for postmodern music in these examples. It may be possible to tentatively suggest a postmodern music as one that escapes modernism in order to construct itself in relation to the premodernist moment that was romanticism. It may also be possible to suggest that, in invoking the cultural memories of romanticism, that which postmodernism finds so seductively attractive in this particular past is its heightened subjectivity and intensity of expression in contrast to the now displaced 'technocratic, positivistic, and rationalist' aspects of high modernism.[30]

Clearly the desire to continually look in this direction may be limited in terms of composition, which is reflected by Holloway's playful admission that 'one can't spend the rest of one's life recomposing Schumann!'[31] However, many composers have looked in the direction of nineteenth-century romanticism, and often specifically to Schumann, as a source. Further examples of the presence of Schumann in this context

Example 4.3a Robin Holloway, *Fantasy-Pieces*, 1. 'Half Asleep', bars 1–12

Example 4.3a (cont.)

Example 4.3b Robert Schumann, *Liederkreis* Op. 24, No. 1 ('Morgens steh' ich auf')

include György Kurtág's *Hommage à R. Sch.* (1990), *Fremde Szenen* I–III (1982–3) by Wolfgang Rihm, and Karl Aage Rasmussen's own *Liederkreis* (1986). Other specific examples based on relationships to nineteenth-century music other than that of Schumann are also evident. The music of Schubert as a source for Berio's *Rendering* has already been mentioned. To this example can be added works such as Aribert Reimann's *Metamorphosen* on a minuet by Schubert (1997) and Kurt Schwertsik's *Epilogue to Rosamunde* (1978). In the case of the Reimann work we are presented with the first few bars of Schubert's Minuet in C♯ minor D600, which is then followed by a sudden change of direction into a seemingly other soundworld but which is still marked by traces of familiarity and is defined by returns to the original material. In contrast, Schwertsik's *Epilogue* articulates a more obviously recognizable nostalgic desire for the music of Schubert's time. Perhaps the most striking reinvention of Schubert comes in Hans Zender's version of Schubert's *Winterreise* (1993). Subtitled as 'A Composed Interpretation', this work is effectively an orchestration of Schubert's famous song cycle, originally for voice and piano. Although the orchestral sonorities render the original material as different, there is still a strong recognizable presence of the original music and text.

'Modernism and After in Music'

Robin Holloway is notable for being a composer prepared to comment directly on the discourses and contexts of modernism and postmodernism. In a provocative essay titled 'Modernism and After in Music', published in 1989, he makes his own contribution to the debate.[32] This is a highly individual text, which begins with a historical survey of modernism in music before going on to define postmodernism. In this survey Holloway returns to the importance of Stravinsky's neoclassicism and positions it as part of a series of '"post-modern" reactions by the principal modernists themselves'.[33] Holloway also goes on to assert his own distaste for, and distance from, the high modernism of the immediate post-war years:

> And the next wave of modernists was far from sympathetic. For their spokesman Boulez (aged 20 in 1945) this broadly speaking neoclassical turn on the part of the great pioneers was not so much a retrenchment as a betrayal. Boulez's notoriously unforgiving attacks are the negative aspect of a new, fighting, hard-line that takes as its starting-point the late work of Webern … These composers (including Stockhausen and Nono, with Boulez the erstwhile 'Holy Trinity' of the European avant-garde) set up as heirs to the revolution, returning to the straight and narrow in 'correction' of the great pioneers' 'backsliding'. The only permissible past is an invented trajectory of perpetual progress, arrogantly prescribing that every work must be a completely new start.[34]

In this extended quotation Holloway takes us back to that moment in the 1950s that was explored in the previous chapter and makes a strong denunciation of the ideology of a high modernist music. For Holloway, there was clearly something quite meaningful in Stravinskian neoclassicism that was unfairly dismissed by the then new generation. As is now expected, what Holloway is drawn to in neoclassicism is precisely its engagement with past musics. But it is this historical perspective that, according to Holloway, composers such as Boulez reacted to in such a negative way, replacing it with what is described as the 'invented trajectory of perpetual progress'. This trajectory could only look forward in a straight line. For Holloway, and others, this singular approach would be unacceptable. In response Holloway identifies sightings of thaws 'within the citadel itself' and mentions the music of Ligeti in the early 1960s as one such example, and highlights John Cage as another.[35] Attention is also drawn to Berio's *Sinfonia*, which is described through its 'multilingual layers of intertextual song and speech'.[36] By way of a postmodern response, Holloway draws attention to George Rochberg, David Del Tredici and the 'antimodernist reaction of ... American minimalism'.[37]

In this text, which has not received the critical scrutiny it deserves, Holloway has many interesting things to say about both modernism and postmodernism, even if his perspective is too closely aligned with his own compositional practice to offer a wider theoretical and contextual focus. However, there are some issues that deserve further comment. For Holloway, in contrast to much postmodern thought, postmodernism in music 'is putting the pieces together again',[38] and he concludes that, 'as time passes, there is a strong sense that the fragments want to join up again to form a coherent face'.[39] Holloway is in effect now arguing that musical history and culture were ruptured by the later manifestations of modernism and postmodernism in an attempt to reconnect with what had been lost. Much of the music considered in this chapter does seek to do that in practice. But there is a great deal of music that could be described as postmodernist which does not choose to look towards music before modernism as a source. It would be difficult to see and hear how music could provide that source of healing that Holloway implies, or why it might be necessary to expect that it can. Following the ideas of Lyotard that we encountered in the first chapter, we might now be incredulous towards such a desire. On the basis of that theoretical context it would be more logical to accept that the pieces cannot be put back together again and there cannot again be a 'coherent face'. Postmodernism, in both theory and practice, is comfortable with the fragmentary. Rather than projecting a new coherence Holloway is telling one further 'little narrative' about the postmodern challenge of the past.

Chapter 5

The music of George Rochberg: from modern serialism to postmodern pastiche

This chapter will focus on the music of American composer George Rochberg (1918–2005) as a case study that connects with, and extends, postmodern constructions such as Eco's challenge of the past and Hutcheon's historiographic metafiction. Rochberg as a composer shifted from being a modernist who utilized serial techniques to a postmodern composer whose music articulated the encounter with the past through first citation and then pastiche. At each stage of this long journey the music that Rochberg produced remains of interest, but the reception of his music also provokes further questions about postmodernism in music.

12 Bagatelles – Symphony No. 2 – String Quartet No. 2

Rochberg's early music was influenced by the modernism of composers such as Stravinsky, Bartók and Hindemith, and reflected the energy and rhythmic drive associated with that music. In the 1950s Rochberg discovered the music of Schoenberg, Berg and Webern and became heavily influenced by, and identified with, serialism. However, this engagement with serialism would also reflect an awareness of Stravinsky's somewhat surprising turn in this direction in the early 1950s, which had a notable impact on several American composers. Works by Rochberg that are often mentioned in this context include the Chamber Symphony (1952), 12 Bagatelles for piano (1952), *David the Psalmist* (1954) and the second symphony (1955–6). The piano Bagatelles form part of what, for Alexander Ringer, from the perspective of an overview of Rochberg's music up to the mid-1960s, was a key moment in Rochberg's career: 'with the Bagatelles he established himself unequivocally as a composer speaking to the 20th century at the halfway mark from the perspective of the generation born during the last years of World War 1'.[1] The Bagatelles in their short aphoristic forms bring to mind Schoenberg's Op. 19 piano pieces, but here the musical language, and the generation of materials, is strictly controlled by a highly rigorous serial technique. Rochberg also become a theorist of serialism, publishing a short book on its technical characteristics and potential in 1955,[2] and was fully convinced of the wider historical significance of this compositional method:

> The method of 'composition with 12 tones related only to one another,' as Arnold Schoenberg called it, seems at last to have established itself unquestionably as the most positive contribution of general significance to music in the twentieth century.[3]

The second symphony, composed between 1955 and 1956 and first performed by George Szell and the Cleveland Orchestra in 1959, is one of Rochberg's most impressive achievements from this stage of his career. It demonstrates again Rochberg's engagement with serialism, but also highlights the individual nature of that engagement.

The symphony is in one continuous movement that is divided into a series of readily identifiable sections. The composer described it as 'essentially four move-ments linked by brief interludes into a thirty-minute uninterrupted musical whole'.[4] In using the single-movement model it looks back to Schoenberg's Chamber Symphony and its radical, early twentieth-century realization of that model. But in doing so it also recalls Schoenberg's own nineteenth-century precursors, most notably Liszt's B minor Piano Sonata. This symphony may be, as Christopher Lyndon-Gee describes it, a 'fully-fledged twelve-tone work',[5] but there is little aural reflection of the second Viennese school as identified with Schoenberg, and there is no parallel to the high modernism of the period as defined by Boulez, among others. The music may be strikingly modernist and dramatically dissonant, but there is still a strong trace of Stravinskian neoclassicism in this work, with its dramatic opening gesture (see Ex. 5.1) providing a reflection of the Beethovenian symphonic archetype, and the reinvention of that archetype in Stravinsky's *Symphony in Three Movements* (1942–5).

This opening gesture reflects a meaningful trace of tonality, with the shift from the initial A-centred thematic statement to the E major reference, as defined by the descending major third of G♯ to E that concludes the first phrase, providing points of tonal reference. These references do not in anyway make the music sound tonal as such, but they do highlight the difference between this and other music of the period that is constructed through the deployment of serial techniques. This difference is also evident in the conclusion to the work, at which point the bass articulates a cadential gesture that moves from C to F. While this move is not necessarily reflected in the wider harmonic context, it does provide a reflection of tonality that again suggests Stravinskian neoclassicism as a meaningful point of departure (Ex. 5.2).

Rochberg's use of serial techniques coexisted with, and formed an integral part of, his interest in the 'spatialization of music'. This interest was based around questions of how music exists in, and moves through, time. Rochberg would come to an

* Dynamic markings apply to all instruments. All transposing instruments written in C.

Example 5.1   George Rochberg, Symphony No. 2, opening, bars 1–4

Example 5.2   George Rochberg, Symphony No. 2, ending, Fig. 790

understanding of music that moved away from a view of it as unfolding through time in a linear sequence; as defined by, for example, Schoenberg's concept of 'developing variation', in which the transformation of a basic idea, or shape, is subject to ongoing developments and transformations.[6] This account was based on an understanding of the primacy of such processes from Beethoven onwards. Rochberg's exploration of the potential of new ideas about temporality and spatialization in music, in contrast, was influenced by the music of Varèse, and resulted in the juxtaposition of relatively discrete and static blocks of musical material. This approach also had something in common with the Stravinsky of *The Rite of Spring* and *Symphonies of Wind Instruments*. Although such disruptions of the expected linear progress of music occurred within the broad contexts of modernism, Rochberg's relationship to these new possibilities may begin to reflect the claims made by Harvey in relation to 'new dominant ways in which we experience space and time' within postmodernism as highlighted in previous chapters.[7]

Rochberg's ideas about the spatialization of music are given practical application in his second string quartet. Composed in 1961 this string quartet also features a solo soprano voice and sets the poetry of Rilke as its text. The inclusion of voice and text suggests a meaningful awareness of Schoenberg's own second string quartet in which the female voice, and the text that is sung, becomes a significant stage in Schoenberg's own move into atonality.

The presentation of the score looks different and reflects Rochberg's new concern with the spatial distribution of sound. The visual presentation of the musical materials, more generally, and basically, makes the music look modern as well as sound modern. In doing so it provides a certain reflection of works such as Stravinsky's then recent *Movements* for piano and orchestra. In this quartet the complex serial structure of the music is partially reflected in how the score is arranged on the page through the separation of each part, which is intended to highlight their independence from each other within the new spatial arrangement.

Example 5.3, which presents the opening moments of the quartet, draws attention to the essentially linear nature of this music. Although the serial construction of this music enshrines a sense of internal continuity, the disruption of texture is already evident at the end of the first page of the score, marked by the pause which seems to make the music stop and which therefore must in effect begin again. Joseph Straus in his brief analysis of this work, which is featured in his survey of American twelve-tone (serial) music, discusses a passage from approximately the midpoint of the quartet (pp. 24–5 of the score), the moment at which the voice enters (see Ex. 5.4). Straus draws attention to the layout of this section of the score as a representation of Rochberg's interest in 'the spatialization of music' and the independence of parts. Straus's analysis extends this independence to how the series is used: 'From a twelve-tone [serial] point of view, each of the parts projects its own forms of the series, usually melodically, one note at a time. The series are never shared between the parts, and the parts state only one series at a time (with the rather frequent possibility of omitting notes of the series).'[8] As a consequence of this deployment, and the spatial distribution of sound, Rochberg produced some of his most self-consciously radical music yet, and certainly in terms of its complexity it marked an 'advance' on works such as the second symphony. It would be difficult to hear in this quartet any significant anticipation of the direction that Rochberg's music would soon take.

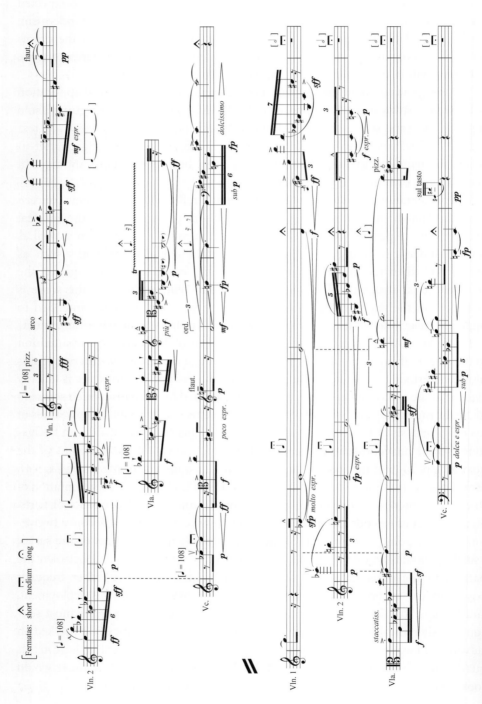

Example 5.3   George Rochberg, String Quartet No. 2, opening

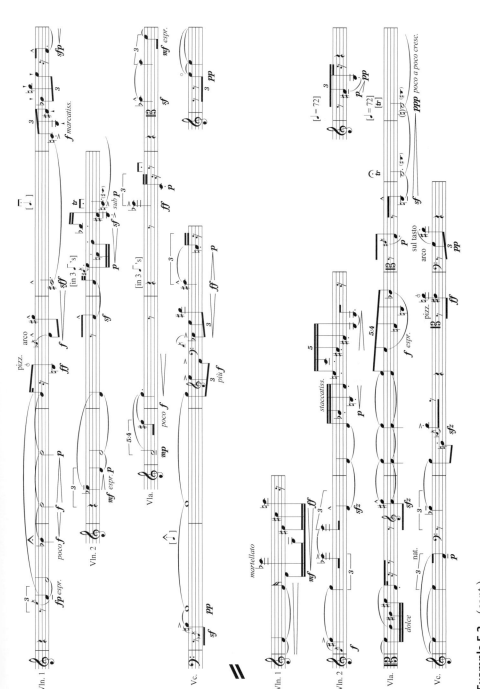

Example 5.3 (cont.)

Example 5.4 George Rochberg, String Quartet No. 2, pp. 24–5

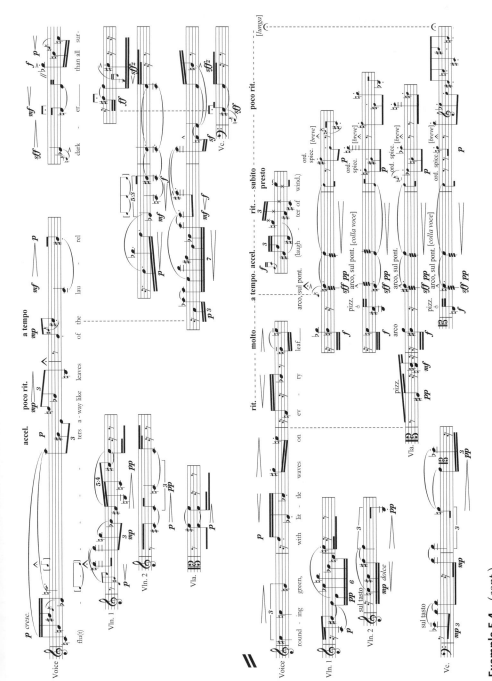

Example 5.4 (cont.)

Music for the Magic Theater

In 1964 Rochberg's son Paul died. This tragic event, as is routinely highlighted in most accounts of his career, led Rochberg to reflect critically upon his music and the methods that produced it. Now finding serialism 'over intense' he effectively renounced it, his last serial piece being the Piano Trio of 1963.[9] The music that comes in the aftermath of this personal tragedy is very different. During this period into the mid-1960s Rochberg began to experiment with musical collage, which, as was highlighted in the previous chapter, had a certain currency at this time. In a work titled *Contra mortem et tempus* (1965), scored for a chamber ensemble of violin, flute, clarinet and piano, and which predates Berio's *Sinfonia* by three years, Rochberg constructs a collage effect that, as described by Richard Taruskin, weaves 'a densely expressionistic contrapuntal fabric out of lines extracted from various atonal or twelve-tone works by Ives, Alban Berg, Edgard Varèse, Pierre Boulez, Luciano Berio and himself'. Taruskin goes on to highlight the fact that in keeping 'with so much modernist music, the collage was a "secret structure"' and that the 'works on which it drew were unlikely to be recognised by most listeners'.[10] However, in looking towards modernist music as a source for its collage effect in this work Rochberg was already constructing a distance to this music, framing it through a certain sense of detachment. The relationship to other music was to be further dramatized in another collage work, *Music for the Magic Theater*, also from 1965, which rather than appropriating modernism now looks to a broad, eclectic range of sources through the direct appropriation of different musics from different historical locations.

The composer, in his preface to *Music for the Magic Theater*, draws attention to what he considers to be the cinematic qualities of this work, with its 'discontinuous, non-narrative aural images combined in ways not unlike the handling of visual images in films by Fellini, Antonioni, Resnais and others. I am not commenting on similarities of context but rather on the relationships of compositional attitudes which tend toward the art of combination and the disruption of "normal" expectations of continuity and temporal relations.'[11] In this brief introduction Rochberg once again draws our attention to his interest in changing temporal and spatial relationships in music. The analogy with the work of the innovative film directors mentioned makes this quite explicit. The sense of disruption in much cinematic work of the period often broke the expectations of linear, narrative development. The cutting of image, and the moment of discontinuity, also enabled the sudden change from present to past tense. These are qualities that can readily be found in musical terms in *Music for the Magic Theater*, the title of which is a reference to the concluding stage of Hermann Hesse's novel *Steppenwolf* from 1927.

The work is scored for a chamber ensemble of fifteen players, including piano. It is presented in 'three acts', with each act in effect being a movement. The first act immediately introduces intertextual citation of other musical materials, making it clear that this is going to be a collage-based work within which, according to the composer, 'the present and past are all mixed up'.[12] Example 5.5 presents the opening of the work. The first music heard is Rochberg's 'own' but this very quickly leads to a quite direct reference to Mahler just before Fig. 2. The quotation is from the final Adagio of Mahler's ninth symphony (bar 13). This reference is not isolated; it becomes part of a web of such references to other music. Catherine Losada has published extended analyses of this work and comments on its status as collage:

> The [first] movement constitutes a prototypical model of a musical collage. It is composed of numerous successive short segments which are set off from the surrounding sections either by textural, stylistic or tonal juxtapositions, or by rests. These sections correspond to fragmentary quotations from a variety of pieces, with original material by the composer interspersed and superimposed in newly composed sections which relate to the quoted material in a myriad of ways.[13]

These short sections as Losada describes them accentuate the sense of disruption and juxtaposition in this work. In doing so they present a contrast to the layering effect of the Mahler material in the third movement of Berio's *Sinfonia* as discussed in the previous chapter.

If the first reference to Mahler's ninth symphony immediately suggests a collage effect made of intertextual citations to other music, the most notable, and memorable, aspect of the work is its appropriation of the music of Mozart in the form of the Divertimento in B♭ major K287. Rochberg's first act involves quotations from the allegro first movement of the Mozart Divertimento, but it is in the second act and its use of the Adagio of K287 that the appropriation of Mozart is most extensive and in which, as described by Rochberg, is the moment 'in which the past haunts us with its nostalgic beauty'.[14] Example 5.6 presents the opening of this movement in which we are given what the composer describes as a 'transcription' of the Mozart Adagio in the string parts to which the piano adds Mozartian decorations.[15] The first violin plays Mozart's melody, but it is played an octave higher than in the original, which gives a sense of otherness to the point of familiarity. As the act unfolds other elements will be added, but we always hear this as somehow Mozart; it is not a secret or passing reference. Rather, it places the old music firmly in the foreground and asks us to hear it again, both familiar and yet also different.

Throughout *Music for the Magic Theater* other references emerge in addition to the Mahler and Mozart examples discussed above. Losada outlines such references for the first act.[16] The composer also gives his own account of the wide-ranging sources used in this work, but goes on to provide an indication of how he saw and heard a point of

Example 5.5   George Rochberg, *Music for the Magic Theater*, Act I, opening

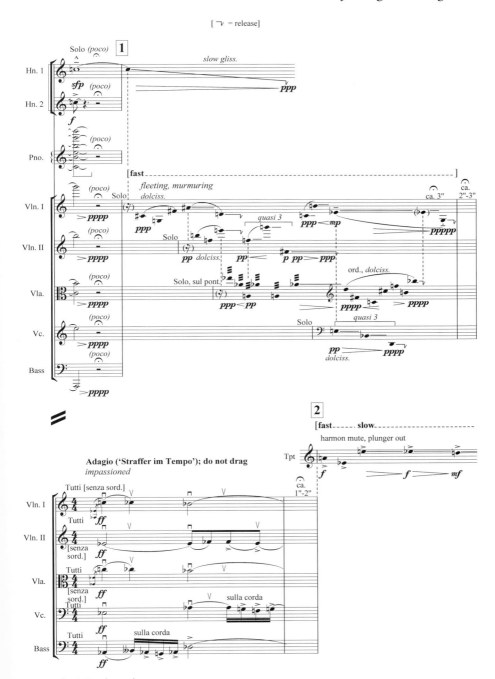

Example 5.5 (cont.)

Example 5.5 (cont.)

contact between them. This point is provided by what he described as 'the recognition of a three-note, downward chromatic half-step motif appearing prominently in each of the specific historical references I chose as major elements of the *Magic Theater* collage/assemblage'.[17] Rochberg provides a list of these references:

> Among the extensive sources which comprise the 'found forms' I used in writing *Magic Theater*, there are five in which the dominant chromatic motif appears prominently: Mahler, Symphony no. 9; Varèse, *Déserts*; Mozart, Divertimento, K287, Adagio; Beethoven, String Quartet, Op. 130, Cavatina; Rochberg, *Sonata-Fantasia* for piano.[18]

ACT II: in which the past haunts us with its nostalgic beauty ... and calls to us from the deeps
of inner spaces of heart and mind ... but the past is all shadow and dream – insubstantial ...
and we can't hold on to it because the present is too pressing ...

Example 5.6   George Rochberg, *Music for the Magic Theater*, Act II, opening

In addition to the 'found forms' identified in this quotation can be added Webern's Concerto Op. 24, Stockhausen's *Zeitmässe* and 'Stella by Starlight' in a transcription of a Miles Davis recording of this song.[19]

For the composer there is a point of connection between these 'found forms' in the shape of the descending motivic detail as suggested above, and clearly this generates part of the compositional logic of the work. But the different nature of

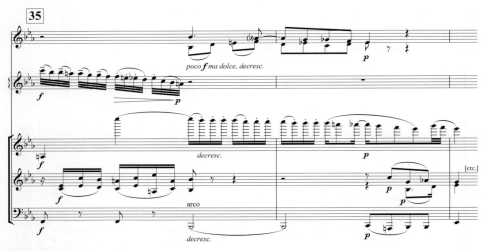

Example 5.6   (cont.)

each of the sources, including their different historical and stylistic locations, makes any process of unity, or at least coherence, very difficult to actually hear in this music, with the change of focus from one 'found form' to the next providing a meaningful representation of Rochberg's own description of the work's new cinematic qualities. In bringing so many different musics together in this work around the central position of the Mozart Divertimento, Rochberg is again articulating his engagement with new ways of hearing the temporality of music. For the composer 'the present and the past' may be 'all mixed up', but according to Taruskin: 'There is always a strict demarcation in *Music for the Magic Theater* between "then" and "now".'[20] I think this is a broadly accurate way of hearing this work. For example, the reference to the Mahler symphony is quite obvious to anyone familiar with that work, and, even if a listener had never heard this particular Mozart Divertimento before, this music would always signify Mozart and the classical style to any listener familiar with the broad tradition of classical music. We hear this point of familiarity as retaining something of its own identity. The process of collage may open up for Rochberg what David Metzer describes as 'vast fields of time', but in this work the past never becomes the present.[21]

In comparing Rochberg's *Music for the Magic Theater* to the examples of Nicholas Maw's *Music of Memory* and Robin Holloway's *Scenes from Schumann*, as discussed in the previous chapter, the differences are quite dramatic. Clearly the Maw example had something of a variation process around the source while Holloway attempted to recompose Schumann from the inside. In contrast, in *Music for the Magic Theater*, with particular reference to the Mahler and Mozart 'found forms', the citation is always transparent even if it is surrounded by so many other sounds that always render it as different. From this perspective it does share something in common with the third movement of Berio's *Sinfonia*, in which the Mahler 'core' text retained a strong identity in the new location.

Music for the Magic Theater is clearly a musical collage made up of many different intertextual sources. But does that automatically suggest that it is a telling example of postmodernism in music? Collage as a process and technique has its basis in the modernist visual art of the early twentieth century. We can see, for example, the cubism of both Picasso and Braque from that time as based upon a certain assemblage of objects and images. Of course Picasso, for example, was a definitive modernist and his appropriation of recognizable materials became part of a process of transforming such materials into his own, bringing them into the context of the painting, and often in a fairly general way. In contrast, what Rochberg is doing musically in *Music for the Magic Theater* is rather different. The reference to other music is highly specific and yet it also saturates the work. Such references pose questions about the identity and coherence of the work and in doing so subvert that particular set of modernist beliefs around questions of originality and unity. For Robert Fink, in *Music for the Magic Theater* Rochberg created 'a document as foundational for musical postmodernism as its more famous younger cousin, [Berio's] *Sinfonia*'.[22] While it is in the true nature of the debate about postmodernism that interpretation remains open I would find it difficult, and unnecessary, to disagree with Fink's conclusion.

String Quartet No. 3

The chapter of Rochberg's autobiography that covers both *Contra mortem et tempus* and *Music for the Magic Theater* is titled 'Unlocking the Past'.[23] This is an effective description of what Rochberg actually achieved through these two works. Once the past was unlocked for Rochberg a whole new set of possibilities became available to him and, in sharp contrast to his earlier modernist works, he would now explore further the possibilities of composing music that positively embraced the sounds of past musics. However, rather than continuing to explore the potential of an intertextual collage made of already existing music, it would be the pastiche reconstruction of the past with which Rochberg would become most identified. This important, and controversial, shift from collage to pastiche was enacted through the composition of the third string quartet (1972).

This five-movement quartet is based around newly composed music that intentionally sounds old. In the words of the composer, 'It was in its way a kind of collage – except that in this instance the "found" forms were all newly invented.'[24] Mark Berry, in his detailed discussion of this quartet, provides a useful summary:

> The allusions to past composers' work begins in the second movement and
> continues to the end of the quartet. At almost every point in the quartet, one
> can compare what is heard to other music in the western classical repertoire:
> non-tonal passages evoke the work of such composers as Bartók, Stravinsky, and
> Schoenberg, while other sections incorporating common practice tonality are
> written in styles characteristic of Beethoven and Mahler. These moments of
> music are constantly being introduced, abandoned, and revisited with no overt
> continuity between them; they operate together within one piece of music, but
> have only limited connections.[25]

In this summary Berry effectively highlights the evocation of the music of other,
past, composers; from modernism back to romanticism within often rapidly changing textures, which, once again, disrupt expectations of past and present within
music. Of the historical references suggested by Berry it is the central third movement that is most immediately noticeable as a pastiche exercise. This is a set of
variations in A major and suggests the soundworld of the late Beethoven string
quartets. For Berry it is Beethoven's Quartet in C♯ minor Op. 131 that is proposed,[26]
while Taruskin suggests that this movement 'in affect … alludes specifically to the
Cavatina from [Beethoven's] op. 130 and the "Heilige Dankgesang" ("Hymn of
Thanksgiving") from op. 132'.[27]

The general evocation of late Beethoven is evident from the opening of the third
movement (see Ex. 5.7). In this moment we hear the clear statement of tonality
through the key signature of A major and the outlining of the A major triad as the
initial harmonic event that is grounded by A as the bass of that harmony. The high
melodic line suggests something of the searching yet reflective quality of late
Beethoven while the variation process helps to provide a static dimension to the
slow-moving textures. The conclusion of this third movement (see Ex. 5.8) reaffirms
this as tonal music through the concluding cadential gesture in A major, a moment
which signifies the great distance between this and earlier works by Rochberg, such
as the second string quartet, among others.

This movement is framed by a march in the second movement that is continued
in the fourth movement. Berry accurately describes the second movement as 'an
atonal march that calls to mind the opening of Stravinsky's *L'Histoire du Soldat* [The
Soldier's Tale] or Schoenberg's *Serenade*, Op. 24'.[28] However, in keeping with the
pastiche nature of this music, in contrast to the specificity of intertextual relationships in the collage works, these are only suggestive, being at most allusions rather
than direct quotations. This process of generalized allusions to precursors is also
evident in the final movement, which is made up of several glances towards other
composers, including Bartók, Beethoven and, most recognizably, Mahler. As stated
above, this process of pastiche begins, for Berry, with the second movement. His

Example 5.7   George Rochberg, String Quartet No. 3, third movement, opening

Example 5.8   George Rochberg, String Quartet No. 3, third movement, ending

more detailed discussion of the first movement indicates that it stands outside the pastiche. According to Berry:

> The first movement has no obvious stylistic allusions – it is written in a non-tonal style – but is a gradually unfolding aural mosaic of musical fragments whose organization sets the pluralistic tone for the rest of the piece.[29]

Berry is correct to state that, unlike, for example, the second and third movements, there are 'no obvious stylistic allusions', but the interpretation of it as 'written in a non-tonal style' and its 'mosaic of musical fragments' suggests that it articulates some form of relationship to modernism. Its sharp, aggressive opening gesture (see Ex. 5.9) suggests a sense of energy and momentum that implies further processes of thematic

Example 5.9   George Rochberg, String Quartet No. 3, first movement, opening

development and progress. But, as Berry's analysis suggests, the role of interruption and juxtaposition in this movement prevents that potential from being realized. This fragmentary process, its 'mosaic of musical fragments' as Berry describes it, also suggests a possible retrospective look to Rochberg's own musical past as defined by his interest in new ideas of time and space in music as realized in the second quartet.

This material could at least suggest some earlier twentieth-century composers, with Bartók being one plausible suggestion that would connect with later moments in the quartet. However, when heard as part of the pastiche nature of much of what follows, this movement can best be interpreted as a kind of general pastiche modernism that can now be heard as sharing some common characteristics with the suggestions of Stravinsky and Schoenberg in the second and fourth movements. This interpretation now casts modernist music into a past tense along with the later allusions to Mahler and Beethoven. In constructing this pastiche version of modernism Rochberg is again pushing it into the past, and as he does so it becomes yet another historical reference.

This focus on pastiche as distinct from collage may render the modernist references in this quartet as historical, but in doing so it forms part of a process that is, when viewed within the context of postmodernism, of its time. Pastiche has emerged as an important element in much general literature on postmodernism. In previous chapters reference has been made to Fredric Jameson's highly influential book *Postmodernism, or, the Cultural Logic of Late Capitalism*. In this text Jameson features pastiche as a recurrent feature of a postmodern culture and presents this definition:

> Pastiche is, like parody, the imitation of a peculiar or unique, idiosyncratic style, the wearing of a linguistic mask, speech in a dead language.[30]

Imitation of a style, peculiar or unique, is clearly meaningful in terms of what Rochberg does in the third string quartet. The wearing of a 'mask', that of late Beethoven, can also be suggested as can the speaking of a 'dead language', with tonality perceived as a musical language that had died but which Rochberg now seeks to resuscitate. However, in this statement Jameson is comparing pastiche with parody; while pastiche is like parody, it becomes 'blank', a 'blank parody', through its 'neutral practice'. It lacks the motivations of parody: 'without any of parody's ulterior motives, amputated of the satiric impulse, devoid of laughter and of any conviction'.[31] On this account pastiche can free itself from expectations of parody – satire, laughter – but in achieving this neutrality, its blankness, it can become effectively uncritical, disengaged, detached. In constructing a pastiche version of late Beethoven, for example, Rochberg may be able to produce a music that sounds something like the precursor, but he cannot reconstruct the original critical identity of that music.

A postmodernism of reaction

The shift by Rochberg towards composing music that sounds intentionally old provoked distinct, at times hostile, critical reactions. In his autobiography the composer rather dramatically recalled the first performance of the third string quartet:

> The impact of the premiere of the Third [string quartet] at Alice Tully Hall in
> New York City … on May 15 1972, was stunning and electric. Shockwaves went
> through the audience, the critics, and eventually beyond. The critical furor it
> raised on all sides spread out from the performance itself into ever-widening
> concentric circles well past the release of the Nonesuch recording the following
> Year.[32]

The centre of the critical reaction was the slow movement and its evocation of late
Beethoven:

> The eye of the storm centred directly over the tonal third movement, the
> unabashedly romantic A-major theme and variations. I was excoriated by
> modernist supporters and loyalists for having betrayed serialism, for defecting
> from the ranks of the serialists.[33]

This sense of betrayal, of abandoning a core assumption about progress as indicated
by some of the criticisms levelled at this work, are summarized by the composer in
his collection of critical reactions:

> I read or heard that I was 'a traitor,' 'a reactionary'; worse still, 'a counterfeiter,' 'a
> forger.' My quartet represented an act of 'shameless regression,' 'a cop-out,' sheer
> indulgence in 'nostalgia,' a reversion to 'orthodox old-school romanticism in the
> Schubert-Schumann-Mahler tradition.' I was accused of making 'pastiche,'
> slavishly 'copying' earlier and better composers while simultaneously
> practicing 'tongue-in-cheek' and 'sly irony,' even producing 'travesty.' … One
> of the more inventive epithets that came my way declared me a 'ventriloquist.'[34]

The hostile reaction outlined by Rochberg in this extended quotation gives some
indication of the debate that this work provoked. The fact that such critical
responses were obviously couched in highly negative terms may simply suggest
that many of the individuals who responded did so through interpretive frameworks
conditioned by the experiences and assumptions of modernism. However, some of
these descriptions do seem valid. The work, at times, does seem to be a 'copy', there
may be a sense of irony and the suggestion of the 'ventriloquist' is intriguing.

It seems that, even in retrospect, this string quartet is an essentially conservative
gesture in that it only seeks to rearticulate old music. In doing so it could be viewed
as forming part of a 'postmodernism of reaction'. This is a terminology constructed
by art critic and theorist Hal Foster, who seeks to draw a distinction between 'a
postmodernism of resistance and a postmodernism of reaction'.[35] For Foster, a
'postmodernism of reaction' is 'singular in its repudiation of modernism'.[36] This
version of postmodernism for Foster may displace modernism but in doing so it
loses any real critical force or value. This conservative, reactionary interpretation of
this particular version of postmodernism has been linked to music as a way of

characterizing retrospective directions in music. Jann Pasler gives an extended overview of this direction:

> In music, we all know about the nostalgia that has gripped composers in recent years, resulting in neo-romantic works ... the sudden popularity of writing operas and symphonies again, of construing one's ideas in tonal terms ... many of those returning to romantic sentiment, narrative curve, or simple melody wish to entice audiences back to the concert hall. To the extent that these developments are a true 'about face' they represent a postmodernism of reaction, a return to pre-modernist musical thinking.[37]

In this statement Pasler is referring to events such as the Lincoln Center festival mentioned in the previous chapter, and it could be extended to include some of the music mentioned in that context as well as the music of Rochberg.

For some, postmodernism is most routinely described in such conservative terms. One such account is that of Jonathan Kramer, who states that 'when a composer or a piece is labelled postmodern, the postmodernism referred to is usually neocon-servative', and describes Rochberg as a 'quintessential postmodernist' whose 'compositions elide pre- and post-modernist elements'.[38] Other composers whose work can be seen to exemplify what Kramer describes as 'neoconservative post-modernism' include, according to Kramer, the then recent work of John Harbison, Steve Reich, Bernard Rands, Eric Stokes and Fred Lerdahl.[39]

Rochberg may have become a 'quintessential postmodernist' as Kramer suggests, and he did come to produce music that could be defined via a postmodernism of reaction in that it came to be preoccupied only with a relationship to the past, with the interesting tensions between past and present resolved into a nostalgic pastiche of old music. But this was a process that was also of its time, and the fact that it fits so neatly into Harvey's periodization of postmodernism, somewhere between 1968 and 1972, is not entirely coincidental. In situating it in this context we can hear Rochberg's third string quartet as one way of responding to Eco's proposal of postmodernism as the challenge of the past, of the already said. In making this response it also goes some way towards presenting one possible version of a musical equivalent to Hutcheon's historiographic metafiction, a possibility to which Hutcheon is clearly aware through her own passing reference to Rochberg's music.[40]

If the descriptions of the third string quartet as remembered by the composer have a certain validity, why do we need to assume that they can only be framed in such negative, critical terms? If the work is a copy then it only serves to pose interesting questions about processes of repetition and replication in postmodern-ism and the subversion of modernism's assumption of originality. Irony is a con-dition we have encountered in many different contexts in this book, and it can be presented as a positive indicator of postmodernism, while the image of the ventriloquist seems a playful analogy that poses meaningful questions about who is actually 'speaking' in this string quartet.

Rochberg's third string quartet may not be 'original' as such, but by provoking such debate it fulfilled important cultural and critical functions in its own time and afterwards. In restating the past in the way that it did, it became a music that, somewhat paradoxically, was timely. It continues to highlight the issues around a postmodern retrospection and in doing so makes a direct and radical critical commentary on the modernist preoccupation with progress in such a way that could be interpreted as highly resistant to such preoccupations. In doing so it also continues to pose further questions about the stability of the basic opposition between reactionary (conservative) and resistant (radical) forms of postmodernism as proposed by Foster.

Chapter 6

The music of John Zorn: 'a postmodernism of resistance'

Towards the conclusion of the discussion of the music of George Rochberg in the previous chapter reference was made to the distinction drawn by Hal Foster between what he interprets as two basic forms of postmodernism:

> a basic opposition exists between a postmodernism which seeks to deconstruct modernism and resist the status quo and a postmodernism which repudiates the former to celebrate the latter: a postmodernism of resistance and a postmodernism of reaction.[1]

According to Foster, in contrast to what is perceived by some to be the highly conservative nature of the engagement postmodernism makes with the past, as applied to the music of Rochberg, for example, and described as reactionary, a postmodernism of resistance is identified through a 'desire to change the object and its social context'.[2] This version of postmodernism takes on a critical dimension; not merely content to revisit and/or restate the past, it articulates a necessity for transformation. In doing so it could be argued that it reflects aspects of modernism's radical nature and extends the role of earlier avant-garde practices as critical responses to tradition and convention.

The claimed opposition between reactionary and resistant versions of postmodernism has been directly related to music. This was evident in Jann Pasler's comments on nostalgia as a 'postmodernism of reaction' as highlighted in the previous chapter, and it also features in the work of Jonathan Kramer. For Kramer, in contrast to those composers identified as representing a 'neoconservative postmodernism' at 'least some' of the music of John Zorn is seen as exemplifying a 'radical postmodernism'.[3] This is a highly qualified statement from Kramer which seems only to assign radicalism to a limited amount of music by Zorn and which in this context does not use Foster's 'resistance' but effectively replaces it with 'radical'. However, the music that Kramer does relate to a radical postmodernism is well suited to this positioning, even if it is by no means the only music that could be described as being both postmodern and radical.

John Zorn (b.1953) is an American musician who has been active in a number of different contexts, with this sense of difference already contributing to his association with postmodernism. The music produced in these often very different contexts and situations articulates many characteristics that are consistent with postmodernism: plural, fragmentary, different, diverse, other. Zorn is a composer, acknowledged as such regardless of the specific musical context, but, as a saxophonist, he is also involved in improvisational practices associated with jazz, producing music that acknowledges the importance of precursors and influences from jazz music, such as that of Ornette Coleman, among others. Zorn has composed music in collaboration with film, but also string quartets and a piano concerto, while also leading ensembles that reflect his interest in a radical Jewish culture. He has also looked towards rock music, at times generating music that, for example, has associations with the hard-core sound of bands such as Napalm Death. Zorn has also reflected the chance operations of John Cage and other experimental composers in the improvisational practices of his so-called 'game pieces' such as *Archery*, *Lacrosse* and *Cobra*, while, in one telling work, the piano concerto *Aporias*, he has taken a specific example of the late music of Stravinsky as a compositional model.

Zorn has also been identified with specific performance spaces in New York, such as the Knitting Factory, then Tonic, and, more recently, the Stone, all located in downtown New York, with this geographical designation also regularly used to describe radical, innovative musical practices and collaborations that originated from, or happened in, this location.[4] Zorn also exercises control over the production and dissemination of his music through his own record label, Tzadik, which issues a consistent flow of recordings of his music as well as that of many other musicians, including noted Zorn collaborators, but often with a particular emphasis on music that reflects a radical Jewish culture.[5] Zorn has also come to achieve a remarkably high profile, which is perhaps surprising given the difficult, consistently provocative sound of the music he produces. He is also often seen more generally as an important presence in contemporary music. John Rockwell, in the prominent role of music critic of the *New York Times*, defined Zorn as 'the single most interesting, important, and influential composer to arise from the Manhattan "downtown" avant-garde scene since Steve Reich and Philip Glass'.[6]

From the brief summary given above it is clear that John Zorn does many different things. There are several different versions of John Zorn. As indicated this already leads to the association that is often made between Zorn and post-modernism, even though he himself is not comfortable with this identification.[7] While the challenging nature of much of Zorn's music lends itself directly to Kramer's description of a 'radical postmodernism' it is also notable that this music is routinely described as avant-garde: a terminology that implies an essentially modernist belief in artistic progress and innovative transformation, possibilities to which postmodernism may be incredulous but with which Zorn is very comfortable.

Spillane

Given how effectively Zorn and his music reflect a wider postmodern condition it is not surprising that they are featured in several of the existing discussions of postmodernism in music, including Susan McClary's 'Reveling in the Rubble', in which Zorn is situated in relation to postmodernism along with other musicians that are seen as being 'concerned with performing some active negotiation with the cultural past for the sake of here and now'.[8] In Zorn's case this 'active negotiation' takes place through the wide range of sources, contemporary as well as (relatively) historical, that are filtered into his music. McClary's discussion of Zorn's music begins with reference to *Spillane* (1987). On the recording *Spillane* is described as being 'written and arranged by John Zorn' in collaboration with a number of musicians who have regularly contributed to Zorn projects as well as producing their own distinctive music, including Anthony Coleman (piano), Bill Frisell (guitar) and Bobby Previte (drums), among others. In his liner notes to the recording Zorn describes the creative process behind this music:

> Because I write in moments, in disparate sound blocks, I sometimes find it convenient to store these 'events' on filing cards so they can be sorted and ordered with minimum effort.[9]

This description draws attention immediately to the fragmentary nature of Zorn's creative process and compositional thought through the description of 'moments' and 'sound blocks', with the filing cards a convenient but highly individual way of organizing such material. However, the emphasis given to such moments and sound blocks in this description suggests certain parallels with earlier musics, such as the modernism of Ives, Varèse and Stravinsky, but also with Rochberg's interest in new concepts of spatial distribution of sound as discussed in the previous chapter, even if the result is very different.

The highly unique outcome of the filing card process in this instance is largely driven by the subject matter. *Spillane* is named after Mickey Spillane, the American author of crime novels many of which featured the detective character Mike Hammer. The sounds we hear in the approximately 25 minutes of the recording seem random. McClary effectively summarizes the first few minutes of *Spillane*:

> In the course of the first five minutes of *Spillane*, we hear a woman's scream, a jittery high-hat cymbal introducing a jazz combo, police sirens and dogs barking, another variety of jazz, a gong, a blur of synthesizers and vibes, a strip show complete with noisy patrons – and so it goes for twenty-five minutes.[10]

This is an accurate description of the sounds we hear at the outset. The effect is of a radical juxtaposition of unrelated fragments of sound. But, with knowledge of the title and its context it is possible, as McClary suggests, to find the trace of a coherent narrative through which 'the sequence of events in the piece makes sense – at least a kind of sense well established within late twentieth-century culture'.[11] We now hear the disjunct sounds within and through the context of film and the type of narrative scheme associated with the specific details of the detective story as defined by Spillane. This narrative and the limited but meaningful sense of coherence that comes with it are eventually defined by the spoken text, written by Arto Lindsay, a noted Zorn collaborator. The text is presented in a highly atmospheric way consistent with the voice-over effect of 1940s and '50s *film noir*, and articulated by the 'voice of Mike Hammer' and the 'voice of Mike Hammer's conscience'. The cinematic aspects of *Spillane* are also evident in other Zorn works, most notably *Godard*, named after the innovative film director Jean-Luc Godard, whose work was situated by Fredric Jameson as part of the 'empirical, chaotic and heterogeneous' nature of postmodernism.[12] Zorn's engagement with cinema is also reflected in his interest in composing music for film and collaborations with film directors, as evident from the works grouped within the series of recordings with the title of filmworks. Perhaps the most significant outcome of this interest is *The Big Gundown*, Zorn's tribute to the Italian film composer Ennio Morricone, a recording from 1985 that did much to bring Zorn's music to a wider audience.

The reference to both the literary and cinematic aspects of *Spillane* already begins to emphasize the breadth of context within which Zorn operates; most notably it defines the engagement with aspects of popular culture and the attempt to relate musical sound to visual imagery. The engagement with film and television as popular culture is acknowledged, for example, through Zorn's awareness of cartoon music, the musical accompaniment to the visual comedy, and in particular the music of Carl Stalling:

> Cartoon music is a very strong influence in the way I put together the disparate elements of my pieces … Stravinsky and Carl Stalling, who was the composer responsible for the soundtracks to many of the great Warner Bros. cartoons of the forties, were successful at that. Their mastery of block structure completely changed the way I see the world.[13]

It is clear that the cartoon genre that Zorn refers to would often contain moments of sudden change and a resulting discontinuity that can be defined in musical terms by seemingly disparate blocks of sound. The fact that Zorn can bring together the music of Stravinsky and Carl Stalling in one statement of influence provides yet another reflection of the wide range of his highly personal musical and cultural perspectives.

Forbidden Fruit

If we are in part dependent upon knowledge of the title of *Spillane* and its context to somehow make sense of its seemingly random disconnected sounds, then another Zorn work *Forbidden Fruit*, which appears on the same CD as *Spillane*, presents similar challenges but without necessarily suggesting a recognizable narrative scheme through which the music can be interpreted.[14]

Forbidden Fruit is scored for voice, string quartet and turntables. On the recording the string quartet is the Kronos Quartet, Christian Marclay operates the turntables 'using only records of string music', and the voice is that of Ohta Hiromi, which Zorn describes as 'one of my very favourite voices in the world'.[15] Zorn confirms the distinctive nature of *Forbidden Fruit* in comparison to the other works on the CD:

> To balance the dramatic, narrative style of *Spillane* and the hot, live band quality of *Two-Lane Highway*, I came upon the idea of writing something of a more 'pure music' …[16]

Zorn's suggestion of a 'more "pure music"' refers to the historical and stylistic context of the classical string quartet repertoire and the presence of this ensemble in *Forbidden Fruit*. This particular instrumental sonority had distinct historical associations with an 'absolute music', the eighteenth- and nineteenth-century discourse about music that elevated the independence of instrumental music into a condition of a self-contained purity that, by extension, became autonomous. Such music was, for some, contrasted with the dependency on word implicit in, for example, programme music and opera, and, because of its self-sufficiency, it was assigned a greater cultural value. In highlighting 'more "pure music"' through the sound of the string quartet Zorn is clearly looking in this particular historical direction. However, in *Forbidden Fruit* the pure sound of the string quartet is treated in a highly impure manner.[17] As in *Spillane* we get many different fragments of sound, although now the nature of these sounds is very different, with that sense of difference accentuated by the effect of the turntables, which is the maximum point of impurity in this context. The female voice and its text also accentuate the difference between this music and more traditional usages of the string quartet. Ellie M. Hisama provides the following concise summary of *Forbidden Fruit*:

> Like many postmodern artists, Zorn freely borrows from musics he admires, either sampling the works themselves or drawing from their aesthetic … As is characteristic of Zorn's compositions, 'Forbidden Fruit' is musical pastiche. Fragments of familiar musical themes fly by – Carmen's Habañera vamp; the opening of Mozart's Piano Sonata in B♭ major, K. 315; a phrase by the soloist in

Bruch's G minor violin concerto – only to have their cadences smudged or snatched away.[18]

Hisama is correct to identify the borrowing of various sources, and we are now familiar enough with intertextuality in other contexts to be able to agree with the assertion that this is a common procedure for 'many postmodern artists'. However, I think that the effect of *Forbidden Fruit* is better described as collage, and produced through intertextual processes, rather than pastiche. Zorn does not directly copy earlier composers as such. It would seem that, for example, the collage effect of Rochberg's *Music for the Magic Theater* might be a more plausible, if still somewhat distant, point of comparison for Zorn's *Forbidden Fruit* than the pastiche of the third string quartet. However, Zorn's references to other music are much more fragmentary and rapidly passing than Rochberg's even if some, such as that to Bizet's *Carmen*, are much more noticeable than others. The rapidly changing soundscape produced by these short fragments of sound leads Jonathan Kramer to the following description:

> Listening to *Forbidden Fruit* can be as dizzying as it is electrifying. You never know what is coming next, nor when. The stylistic juxtapositions are amazingly bold. If there were any discernible thread of continuity, the music would surely be more tame, more predictable, more ordinary. But there is not.[19]

Kramer's description may be, in some ways, an effective account of listening to *Forbidden Fruit*. The stylistic juxtapositions are bold, and the 'dizzying' feeling of not knowing quite where you are in terms of a structure or even direction is part of what makes it an 'electrifying' experience. However, while we may not know where we are in structural terms or as part of a narrative as such, the claim that 'you never know what is coming next, nor when' seems to exclude the impact of repeated hearings of this music. The most common, perhaps only, way of hearing *Forbidden Fruit* is through its availability on CD, an availability that invites more than one encounter. Through the impact of the repetition of the listening experience it is surely the case that we do come to know what is coming next, even if the rapid passing of sounds still makes this not as easy as listening to some music that is more obviously preoccupied with continuity and development. It may also be, when we become more familiar with Zorn's music in general, that, although the specific details may be surprising, we come to expect the unexpected and the unpredictable becomes predictable, with the constant changes of fragmentary ideas and sounds becoming defining, perhaps now expected, indicators of Zorn's consistently inconsistent style.

Clearly the female voice and the words that it articulates form important aspects of *Forbidden Fruit*. However, now voice and text do not suggest a possible narrative coherence; rather, they are further elements in the fragmented surfaces of this work. The voice and text have also generated an interesting and important debate about Zorn, his music and his wider ideas. Zorn has an ongoing interest in Japan and Japanese culture, and this is reflected in the text and voice of *Forbidden Fruit*, both of which are Japanese. Although the CD booklet offers an English translation of the text it still sounds as intentionally 'other' and, even without the specific meanings of the text, which is described by Hisama as intimating 'a sexual encounter between a Japanese female and some unnamed "he"',[20] the vocal performance, evocatively described by John Corbett as 'the whispery, exoticized voice', is clearly intended by Zorn to sound 'sexy'.[21] This suggestive sexual reference is extended through the photograph included in the CD booklet. This is a photograph of Japanese film star Ishihara Yujiro, whose death is claimed by Zorn as a motivation for *Forbidden Fruit*. However, it is Yujiro's wife, Kitahara Mie, who fills the foreground of the photograph, and whom Zorn describes in his liner notes as being 'unbelievably gorgeous in this photo'.[22] For Hisama this photograph forms a distinctive part of what is perceived as Zorn's problematic relationship to Japanese women, through which Zorn 'perceives the Asian woman's world as distinct from and opposite to his own. He eagerly wants to explore her world, and invariably ends up exoticizing it.'[23] In treating the woman as an exotic object there is clearly a play with the power of the male gaze that is intensified through the political structure of a Western perspective on what is now perceived as the oriental, exotic other constructed as an object of desire. The problematic nature of this construction is further extended through the awareness of Zorn's use of highly explicit sadomasochistic imagery as artwork for some of his other CD covers. Clearly Zorn's music often plays with images of transgression, and pain forms part of that image as articulated through, for example, painfully high volume levels, and specific moments, such as the violence of the woman's scream with which *Spillane* begins and which, for Hisama, is one of the elements in Zorn's work that is 'sexist'.[24]

While Zorn himself has provided certain justifications for this fascination, often linked to a notion of transgression as a positive quality, clearly this particular set of issues cannot easily be explained away as just another set of cultural references that Zorn seeks to employ as part of his seemingly random engagements with so many sounds and ideas. They may be the fragments of a postmodern culture but they are not divorced from the politicized meanings they carry. The extent to which this debate influences how we chose to listen to Zorn's music must remain a matter of individual interpretation, but while it might be wrong to dismiss Zorn and his music on the basis of these problems it is important that we recognize the validity of the points made by Hisama and others in relation to these issues.[25]

Naked City

Zorn formed Naked City in 1988 as a project that had the common identity and focus of a rock group, described by Zorn as 'my pop-band experiment'.[26] The group name of Naked City provides yet another statement of Zorn's New York location and his awareness of that particular environment; it also again reflects his interest in cinema, *The Naked City* being the title of a 1948 film in the *film noir* style directed by Jules Dassin and presented in an often quasi-documentary manner that is built around a story of murder and the search for the perpetrator. The film begins with a sweeping view of New York that then focuses in on specific situations and characters and uses precise locations to great effect, including a climactic scene set on the Williamsburg Bridge. The film inspired a television series, which ran from the late 1950s into the early 60s, and which repeated the quasi-documentary style of the film and again made great use of specific New York locations.

The members of Naked City were Joey Baron (drums), Bill Frisell (guitar), Wayne Horvitz (keyboards), Fred Frith (bass) and Zorn himself on alto saxophone. All of them had participated in many of Zorn's previous projects and all had been, and continue to be, responsible for their own highly individual and innovative musics. Although the group identity of Naked City is distinct from many of Zorn's other projects, this music does further extend already recognizable aspects of Zorn's work and his wider interests. The first Naked City recording, titled *Naked City* (1990), gives further indications of Zorn's interest in film and film music through versions of John Barry's 'James Bond Theme' as well as music by Ennio Morricone ('The Sicilian Clan'), Henry Mancini ('A Shot in the Dark') and Jerry Goldsmith ('Chinatown'). Zorn's background in jazz music is also acknowledged through the inclusion of a version of Ornette Coleman's 'Lonely Woman', which was originally featured on *The Shape of Jazz to Come*, Coleman's landmark recording from the end of the 1950s.[27] While this wide range of musical sources and references are now expected features of Zorn's music, the music Zorn composed specifically for Naked City continues, in fact intensifies, the rapid juxtapositions of fragmented sounds as evident in, for example, *Spillane* and *Forbidden Fruit*. Such juxtapositions led William Duckworth to evocatively describe Naked City as a 'super-tight bar band that can turn stylistic corners on a dime'.[28]

The rapid turning of 'stylistic corners' is most aurally evident in relation to 'Snagglepus', the seventh track on the CD. In its very brief time span it spins through a remarkable range of unrelated sounds. In his extended study of Zorn's music, Tom Service provides a detailed commentary on 'Snagglepus', and this stage of the discussion draws directly on Service's work.[29] The score for 'Snagglepus' consists of a series of written descriptions of discrete sections of musical activity defined and separated by double bar lines. However, although this description suggests a degree of structural cohesion it does not 'determine the arrangement of the sounds, their pitch, or any of the precise features preserved on the recording'.[30] Rather than giving a determined musical content, most of the sections are defined through an instruction, such as the first, which only indicates 'loud noise', which is certainly what we hear on the CD. It opens with a sudden blast of intense activity that cannot be described in conventional musical terms. Other sections indicate a texture and/or ensemble, such as, for example, 'fast thrash trio', 'piano solo', 'c boogie blues band' and 'jazz band trio'. When these sections come into focus the recognizable ensemble, such as jazz trio, and a rather stereotypical music associated with it, provides moments of familiarity. But this is a highly personalized musical notation in that it belongs to Zorn and Naked City; it is not conceived as a musical work, a 'score', that can be performed by any group of musicians. Clearly each realization of the instructions that constitute the score of 'Snagglepus' will be different, with the uncertain nature of the outcome providing a point of similarity to the play with indeterminacy evident in other experimental musics, but which John Cage initiated. It is also another point of contact with other Zorn projects, such as the game pieces and other improvisational projects.

Zorn recalls the unpremeditated, unpredictable nature of the outcome of the Naked City repertoire in general: 'And it was astonishing to see Joey [Baron], Bill [Frisell], Wayne [Horvitz], and Fred [Frith] come up with something different every night; every … night something different happened on the same tunes that we did, 20, 30, 50 times. Amazing!'[31] With reference to 'Snagglepus', Service describes the sequence of its various sections as remaining 'intact', within which 'the precise sounds in each section could vary wildly'.[32] The live performance of 'Snagglepus', recorded at the Knitting Factory in 1989, may be different in some details to the studio recording, for example, but it is still identifiable as basically the same music.[33]

Zorn decided to bring Naked City to what he considered to be its natural point of closure. As he later recalled: 'Toward the end of Naked City I realized I had taken that band about as far as I could, compositionally', and '[he had] started hearing classical music in my head again'.[34] Service suggests it is the way in which '"Snagglepus", and other tracks' became 'relatively fixed texts' that led Zorn to bring Naked City to an end in 1993.[35] The suggestion of the open-ended possibilities of such instruction-based 'scores' becoming 'relatively fixed texts' may originate from the basic fact that it was always the same group of musicians and instruments that were responsible for interpreting the score, and the group identity generated a sense of expectation and resulting consistency. Zorn recalled a point of exhaustion: 'I didn't want to travel around and regurgitate the same pieces over and over; I didn't want to become a repertoire band, presenting a music.'[36] Clearly the band had reached the point where 'something different' no longer happened every night.

However, whatever limitations may have been applied to Naked City or how exhausting it had become, the music generated by the group remains some of the most vital ever produced by Zorn. In their sharp cuts between different sounds, the moving between many different contexts, and their engagement with popular culture the Naked City recordings continue to provide a powerful projection of Zorn's predictably unpredictable musical world.

Masada

One of the most striking aspects of Zorn's many musical and cultural practices has been his rediscovery of a Jewish heritage and the positive assertion of a radical Jewish culture. The term radical Jewish culture was coined by Zorn to embrace the rediscovery and redefinition of Jewish culture within a new musical context. It was first announced as part of a festival held at the Knitting Factory, a key location in the New York downtown scene, in April 1993, which consisted of five days of new music under the collective title of 'Radical New Jewish Culture Festival'.[37] Since then Zorn and other musicians – such as Anthony Coleman, for example – have produced innovative work under the broad terminology of radical Jewish culture, and Tzadik, which in Hebrew means a 'righteous man',[38] has produced a constant stream of recordings that reflect this cultural orientation. The aim of Tzadik is to explore 'Jewish music beyond Klezmer' and to 'bring Jewish identity and culture into the 21st century'.[39]

In terms of Zorn's own music it is the group named Masada, and the music he composed for it, that most clearly demonstrates his own participation in a radical Jewish culture. The name Masada is loaded with symbolism, being the ancient, historical site of heroic resistance to Roman power. Masada consists of Dave Douglas (trumpet), Greg Cohen (bass), Joey Baron (drums) and Zorn himself on saxophone. The quartet led by saxophone and trumpet gives an obviously jazz-based direction to Masada, with the great Ornette Coleman recordings with Don Cherry (trumpet) from the late 1950s and early 1960s providing an obvious reference point. This reference is further extended by the absence of piano in both contexts, and consequent focus on linear rather than harmonic improvisation. However, if the sound of Masada looks towards jazz the material that Zorn has composed for this group has a very different origin. As Tamar Barzel describes it, Zorn's aim with Masada was to 'write innovative, Jewishly inflected music'. The basis of this music is the so-called 'Masada songbooks' of Zorn, which consist of several hundred pieces based on 'the pitch content of two synagogue modes'.[40] Ajay Heble describes the use of the musical material that emerges from this source as 'invoking and building on a traditional Jewish music, klezmer, which has remained popular despite the test of generations'.[41]

The emphasis on linear (melodic) improvisation based on recognizably Jewish musical material is the common characteristic of Masada. It is also a music that routinely has greater concern with continuity and development than many of Zorn's other projects and works. These defining qualities of Masada can be heard, for example, on the CD titled *Masada First Live 1993*, recorded live at the Knitting Factory in 1993 and which documents the first public performance by the group. The first track, titled 'Piram', is representative of Zorn's Masada music in general. The bass and drums establish a regular rhythmic pattern that is consistent with the expectations of a modern jazz. Zorn and Douglas present the linear melodic material over this basic pulse and its more intricate rhythmic details. This material may have its origins in Jewish culture but it basically signifies jazz music with the reference to Ornette Coleman aurally evident, and, from before Coleman, the classic modern jazz style of bebop is present in the interweaving of the lines and their increasing complexity.[42] The other tracks on *First Live* all have their own individual identity but they do tend to follow the pattern established on 'Piram'. The most obviously jazz orientated is 'Zebdi'. The long improvised lines on this piece, projected by Zorn and then Douglas, look back to both Ornette Coleman and Charlie Parker. The interplay between both Zorn and Douglas takes place over a consistent, rapid rhythmic pulse, while the drum breaks that occur towards the end intensify the signification of this music as jazz.

The focus on a radical Jewish culture so highly evident with Masada – and the articulation of that culture through the sounds and ideas of jazz – renders this music as highly distinctive. It also accentuates the potential of new hybrids formed between seemingly separate musical contexts and practices. The distinctive nature of Masada adds yet another facet to the difference and plurality of Zorn's musical persona. The consistency and continuity, through improvised thematic developments, in the Masada music now feels very different from, for example, the fragmented, juxtaposed sounds of *Forbidden Fruit* or *Spillane*. However, it does articulate once again that Zorn's music is always somehow also about other music.

Aporias

One recurrent aspect of the many versions of himself that Zorn constructs is that formed by the definition and identification of composer. Zorn is recognized as composer in all his projects, although many of them are shaped by the contribution made by other musicians and often involve improvisatory practices. However, in some works Zorn comes closer to the recognizable figure of the composer as defined within the broad parameters of the tradition of classical music. In this seemingly more conventional role of composer the music Zorn has produced has a more obvious concern with coherence and predetermined structure than is evident in the examples of his music that have already been highlighted in this chapter.

John Brackett has effectively discussed Zorn's role as composer, and the music that has been produced via that role, in his book on this music, one of the few extended studies and one that does much to enhance our understanding of Zorn. Brackett draws attention to the string quartet *Cat O' Nine Tails* (1988), a work that, like *Spillane*, *Godard* and *Forbidden Fruit*, consists of 'collage blocks' that are an 'integral part of the work's design' and includes 'quotations from Carter, Xenakis, Schoenberg, and Berg'.[43] This list of composers is notable for the identification with modernism, both in its early manifestations of the second Viennese school and the late extension of modernism in the work of both Carter and Xenakis. This citational gesture towards modernism is quite distinct from the encounter with popular culture in *Spillane*, for example, even if both works consist of highly fragmented surfaces.

This reference to modernism is also evident in Zorn's *Elegy* (1991), which, as Brackett indicates, 'draws much of its pitch material from Boulez's *Le Marteau sans maître*' and *Walpurgisnacht* (2004), which is based on Webern's String Trio Op. 20.[44] In contrast to the rapidly changing, fragmentary quotations in most of the music already discussed, Zorn also becomes much more interested in a developed, integrated relationship to the music of other composers. As Brackett explains:

> direct or even slightly disguised quotations give way to a method of composition where works by other composers are integrated into the overall fabric of Zorn's own compositions. With his more recent practices, the referential piece is subsumed and manipulated in the interest of the piece at hand. In other words, a variety of musical features – melodic lines, chords, rhythms, etc. – are used as source material whose compositional end is to serve and satisfy the individual logic, unity, and coherence of Zorn's *own* work. With these works, the listener may not even recognize any surface similarities between the 'original' work and Zorn's own composition, as the two are seamlessly blended together.[45]

On the basis of the above description we can see and hear a notable shift in Zorn's music from works such as *Spillane* and *Forbidden Fruit* into a concern with a much greater degree of integration than had previously been evident in his music. As suggested by Brackett there is a new level of depth to the still present source provided by other, already-existing music, but this source may not now be aurally evident and requires fairly detailed study in order to reveal these relationships. Brackett undertakes the required detail study in relation to a number of different examples of Zorn's music, including *Necronomicon* for string quartet (2003), *IAO* (2002), *In the Very Eye of Night* (dedicated to the film-maker Maya Deren; 2001) and *Untitled* for solo cello (2001). However, it is Brackett's account of Zorn's *Aporias* (1998) that does most to draw attention to the new levels of depth that emerged in Zorn's work around this time.

Aporias is subtitled *Requia for piano and orchestra* and is in effect a piano concerto, with the sound of the solo piano against the orchestral background making this generic reference clear even if the actual music is remote from the expectations of the concerto in its classical and romantic guises. The work consists of ten movements, each of which has a specific title: Prelude, Impetuoso, Con Mistero/ Misterioso, Languendo, Risentito, Freddamente, Religioso, Drammatico, Postlude, Coda. However, some movements are conceived as tributes, or memorials ('requia'), to individuals, often composers, whose work Zorn wishes to acknowledge as influences. For example, the sixth movement, Freddamente, is a tribute to John Cage, while the next movement, Religioso, acknowledges Olivier Messiaen. Other tributes reflect Zorn's other interests, including cinema – with the second movement, Impetuoso, a tribute to the actor and director John Cassavetes – and the visual arts, as reflected in the tribute to Francis Bacon in the third movement, Con Mistero/ Misterioso.

Within this network of tributes the musical materials are derived from a specific compositional source, Stravinsky's *Requiem Canticles* (1966). This was effectively Stravinsky's final work, through which his employment of serialism, a feature of his late music from the early 1950s onwards, reached its culmination while still providing meaningful reflections of a personal musical past. Zorn gives his own account of the relationship to this source and the compositional approach that is employed:

> One of the things that I do to give each classical piece structural integrity is use another composer's work from which to derive pitch information. With [*Aporias*], I used the *Requiem Canticles* by Stravinsky … Using someone else's work as source material gives a piece a kind of unity. Everything's coming from one place.[46]

It is interesting that Zorn describes *Aporias* as a 'classical piece', a description that he extends to other works. Zorn seems very comfortable with this designation and all that it implies in terms of specific musical traditions and cultural contexts. The situating of this music in relation to that context is extended through the assertion of a 'structural integrity' and the claim that the 'source material' provides 'a kind of unity'. The focus on these qualities distances this music from the effect made by other examples of Zorn's music, and in doing so draws attention again to the diversity of Zorn's musical practices, with the resulting plurality effectively legitimizing the definition of Zorn as a radical postmodernist. However, the specific nature of the claims made on the basis of 'structural integrity' and 'a kind of unity' would seem to distance this music from some definitions of postmodernism in music. At earlier stages of this book we considered aspects of Jonathan Kramer's list of characteristics of postmodern music, one of which claims that such music 'shows disdain for the often unquestioned value of structural unity'.[47] Much of the music considered thus far as examples of postmodernism in music has generally tended to suggest that unity does not have the value that it had in previous contexts; it may be that, if we translate Lyotard's 'incredulity toward metanarratives', which was central to the discussion of how we define postmodernism in general, into musical terms, then perhaps the assumed unity of music is one modern metanarrative that postmodernism refuses to believe in. In now looking towards Stravinsky's late work as a source, and building an integrated relationship to it, Zorn now actually seems to be running against one of the strongest aspects of postmodernism in music. However, Zorn may understand the compositional logic that underpins *Aporias* in this way but, without the benefits of Zorn's own comments, and, it could be argued, the insights of Brackett's detailed analysis of the relationship between the two works, it would be difficult to actually hear a sense of unity in *Aporias*. The textures still sound fragmentary, even if much less so than in *Forbidden Fruit*, for example, and, in identifying the precursor, Zorn is still producing music that can be described through an, albeit concealed, intertextual relationship to other music.

Each of the different examples of Zorn's music considered in this chapter presents its own distinctive qualities. When placed alongside each other they emphasize the wide range of different musics with which Zorn engages. While this comparison will accentuate the plurality and differences of Zorn's various musical projects, there are certain recurring factors, mostly concerned with the rapid, radical juxtapositions of fragments of sound that originate from many different places. The relationship to, and dependency upon, other music – Carl Stalling, Bizet, klezmer, Ornette Coleman, Stravinsky, among countless other examples – is one common characteristic of Zorn and much of the music he creates. There is so much emphasis on 'other' music that it is at times difficult to hear what the 'self' is, or how it might be constructed, in Zorn's music. The extent to which Zorn plays with such intertextual references suggests that Susan McClary's implied description of Zorn as 'reveling in the rubble' is highly apposite; he rummages through the fragmentary rubble of so many cultural contexts in such a way that this is perhaps one of the most obvious manifestations of postmodernism in music. The wide-ranging and seemingly never-ending nature of such processes for Zorn does much to substantiate Jonathan Kramer's description of it as a radical postmodernism, as does the rapidity with which the music changes between and within specific works. Zorn's music can also be placed again in relation to Foster's terms with which this chapter began; resisting easy accommodation with notional mainstreams and traditions, it knowingly transgresses cultural norms and radically transforms expectations of what constitutes the musical work.[48]

In looking to both classical and popular music for material Zorn provides a critical commentary on the often-arbitrary distinction between both broadly conceived contexts and offers a point of resistance to the division. The focus that Zorn places on both leads McClary to describe him as announcing 'his refusal to abide by what Andreas Huyssen has called the Great Divide between so-called high and popular culture, for he is heir to both'.[49] The claim that postmodern culture, as exemplified in this instance by Zorn, refuses to acknowledge the great divide between high (classical music) and popular culture, or at least blurs the boundaries, will form the starting point of the next chapter.

Chapter 7

Blurring the boundaries

The claim that postmodernism represents, or generates, a blurring of boundaries, a crossing over of the divide, between 'so-called high and popular culture',[1] is often argued for in much literature on postmodernism in general and also with specific reference to music. This proposal has already become evident in some of the texts that were featured in the first chapter of this book and which have been revisited at various points throughout. For example, Fredric Jameson identified the minimalism of Philip Glass and Terry Riley as a 'synthesis of classical and "popular" styles',[2] while Linda Hutcheon describes 'genre-boundary crossings' and highlights a specific recording by Philip Glass, *Songs from Liquid Days*, as a 'cross-over', being 'both a song cycle and a pop album',[3] and Susan McClary's positioning of John Zorn as a point of resistance to the division, as defined by his 'refusal to abide by' it, provided the conclusion to the previous chapter.[4]

The use of popular music by classical musicians and composers is clearly relevant to this discussion. Interesting examples include Glass's *Low Symphony* and *Heroes Symphony*, both based on the music of David Bowie, and the Kronos string quartet's recording of Jimi Hendrix's 'Purple Haze', among many possible examples,[5] while popular musicians have often looked to classical music, with the development of progressive rock in the late 1960s and early 1970s indicative of this. Emerson, Lake and Palmer's version of Mussorgsky's *Pictures at an Exhibition* is one transparent example of this direction, but there are others.[6] More significantly the newfound experimental direction of rock music in the 1960s presented parallels and inter-sections with a concept of a 'high'-art avant-garde.[7] From a later context, different from progressive rock, Elvis Costello's work with the Brodsky Quartet on his *The Juliet Letters* recording exemplifies the highly conscious attempt to blur any recognizable boundary between classical and popular musics.

For Steven Connor, in postmodernism, 'the gap between classical and popular music has been narrowed'.[8] He does not cite specific examples in support of his claim, but the music listed above could be used to reinforce it. It can also be argued that much of the commercialization of classical music in recent times – aggressive marketing, use of sexual image, classical crossover as genre – are other, further manifestations of the blurring of the distinction between classical and popular musics.

The great divide

In more general terms the great, historical divide between the two cultural spheres is defined and debated, as McClary suggests, in the highly influential work of Andreas Huyssen.[9] In the introduction to the collection of essays grouped under the title of *After the Great Divide*, Huyssen begins with a characterization of modernism based upon its 'insistence on the autonomy of the art work, its obsessive hostility to mass culture, its radical separation from the culture of everyday life'.[10] The claim of autonomy made by modernism in its high form became part of its distance to 'the culture of everyday life', with the presence of mass (popular) culture acting as a threat to the aesthetic purity of a certain version of culture that denies the presence of a social reality.[11] The identification of mass culture as threat to modernism is most dramatically evident in the critical theory of Adorno, within which it is dismissed as false.[12] For Huyssen the point of division between both spheres was 'always challenged as soon as it arose'.[13] There have been 'a plethora of strategic moves tending to destabilize the high/low opposition from within'; however, such moves made no lasting impact.[14] It is only through postmodernism that this changes, with the divide no longer seeming 'relevant to postmodern artistic or critical sensibilities'.[15] The claim that this division is no longer 'relevant' could be read as another statement of Lyotard's 'incredulity toward metanarratives',[16] in that we can now no longer invest belief in the distance, or difference, between the two cultural spheres as ideologically constructed by modernism. In making this move postmodernism is now seen as once again rejecting a core assumption of modernism: the privileged status of 'high' over mass, popular culture.

In contrast to the resistance of modernism postmodernism comes to positively embrace the potentially interesting possibilities and opportunities that emerge through the blurring of the all too neat binary opposition:

> The boundaries between high art and mass culture have become increasingly blurred, and we should begin to see that process as one of opportunity rather than lamenting loss of quality and failure of nerve.[17]

The examples of specific musical works and practices mentioned above, and the case studies that follow, can now be heard as the realization of some of the potential that is released through this rejection of the rigid certainties that were enshrined in the great divide.

In the remainder of this chapter some specific musical contexts and practices will be highlighted and discussed further in relation to the issues outlined above. As suggested by both Jameson and Hutcheon, minimalism, more specifically the music of Philip Glass, will be significant, but in the first instance the focus will move back to the music of Michael Daugherty that was discussed in chapter 2.

Dead Elvis revisited

Michael Daugherty's *Dead Elvis* was described in chapter 2 as an interesting example of a postmodern intertextuality, based on the use of the *Dies Irae* and the associations that this invoked. It also made reference to the music of Stravinsky and cited the song 'It's Now or Never' along with a more general evocation of 1950s rock 'n' roll.

It has been claimed that 'Daugherty may just provide the link to pop culture that classical music so desperately needs'.[18] In *Dead Elvis*, and many other works, Daugherty can indeed be heard as making a link to popular culture from contemporary classical music. Through playing with the sounds and images of a historical popular music he is blurring the boundaries between classical and popular musics and in doing so presents another reflection of a wider postmodern culture. However, there are some problems with this interpretation. Daugherty's music in general, and *Dead Elvis* in particular, may engage with popular music but does it actually cross or blur any boundary? In responding to this question it is important to underline the basic fact that Daugherty is a *composer*, whose music is promoted by specialist publishers of classical music and performed by ensembles that are almost exclusively identified with the world of 'high' culture as defined by classical music.[19] In other words, we are more likely to hear this music in a traditional concert hall than on the street or in a club.

Daugherty views popular music from the vantage point of classical music and from that position he does not merely provide a 'link', or blur the boundaries, between popular and classical, but could actually be interpreted as appropriating popular music and in doing so drawing it into the world of classical music, a process that strips popular music of its identity. It is also notable that on the recording of *Dead Elvis* the work is performed by the London Sinfonietta, a specialized contemporary music ensemble who, while engaging in some fairly broad projects and performing music by composers who might routinely be described as postmodernist, also perform, and are perhaps best known for performances, of modernist, at times canonical modernist, music. Also notable is the fact that all such performance activities routinely take place in traditional concert venues.

This focus on the identity of Daugherty as composer as opposed to, for example, a pop star, and the performance situation of the music, does not necessarily negate the identification of *Dead Elvis* as a vivid example of postmodernism in music. Nor does it automatically displace the more general claims outlined above. But this specific example does begin to suggest that the proposed shift from a binary opposition between 'high' (classical) and popular cultures as constructed by modernism to a crossing or blurring of the boundaries within postmodernism is not as clear cut as is often suggested.

This brief return to Daugherty's *Dead Elvis* can also act as a reminder of the historical context to which this music referred, the 1950s, but it also reconnects with questions of interpretation. Through reference to the concept and practice of intertextuality I have suggested that, as well as hearing the various musical sources with which Daugherty plays, the iconic image of Elvis Presley that is treated ironically in this work somehow leads me to think about the art of Andy Warhol, within which the iconic status of Elvis played a significant part in the transference of images from popular culture into art through Warhol's work of the 1960s.

The work of Warhol, and other artists associated with the label of pop art, including Roy Lichtenstein's play with cartoon images, was one of the first, and most demonstrable, examples of how postmodernism might blur the boundaries between 'high' and popular cultures. As well as using icons of popular culture, such as Elvis, Warhol repositioned everyday objects, most symbolically the Brillo box, into the context of art. Art historian and critic Arthur C. Danto has made great claims for Warhol and pop art, highlighting the convergence between art and everyday life, and retrospectively stating that 'there was no special way works of art had to look in contrast to what I have designated "mere real things"'.[20] In other words, there was no inherent need for art to be different, or distant, from the objects that surround us, and which we make use of, in our everyday life. In the case of Warhol, 'nothing need mark the difference, outwardly, between Andy Warhol's *Brillo Box* and the Brillo Boxes in the supermarket'.[21] But of course there is a big, and rather obvious, difference; the conscious act of viewing Warhol's *Brillo Box* in an art museum, hardly a space that is normally reflective of everyday life, and how the original objects were used, or even looked at, need not be seen as necessarily similar. When we cross the line to go into an art museum or gallery the work within it may be reflective of what exists outside in the real world, but it still retains a strong sense of difference, and this difference still marks objects that are transferred from outside to inside the museum.

However, Warhol did make this play with familiar everyday images and objects, and therefore did pose interesting questions about the nature of art, particularly in contrast to the previous dominance of abstract expressionism and its highly self-reflexive quality. This play, and the issues which flow from it, leads to Warhol's work assuming an important position in the emergence of postmodern practices of the early 1960s as indicated by Jameson's positioning of it in his list of names and styles which exemplify the new context.[22] It is also notable that the reflections of objects and images of popular culture and everyday life in the work of Warhol, and other artists associated with pop art, such as Roy Lichtenstein, continue in the work of more recent artists. This can be seen, for example, in the transference of 'ordinary' objects into art in the often-autobiographical work of Tracey Emin, while the work of Douglas Gordon makes extensive use of popular culture, primarily cinema, as an artistic reference. Notable examples of Gordon's work include *24 Hour Psycho* (1993), in which we are presented with a slow-moving screening of Hitchcock's *Psycho* (1960) that lasts in full for twenty-four hours, and *Zidane* (2006), a film made by Gordon in collaboration with Philippe Parreno. This film is based on footballer Zinedine Zidane and follows him through the course of a game, using his body as a moving form that is viewed from different perspectives. The soundtrack to the film features music by the group Mogwai, whose work is often described as 'post-rock', a very loose stylistic label that suggests a rejection of some of the basic premises of rock music and the projection of new, often instrumental textures. It also has a loose but suggestive resonance with postmodernism.[23] The music Mogwai produce for the film largely consists of slow-moving but intense instrumental textures that create an imaginative aural background to the visual image. This collaborative project, rather than merely crossing the great divide, actually blurs many potential boundaries – art, cinema, rock music, dance, sport as popular culture – resulting in something quite new that defines its own context and interpretive response.[24] It may also be the type of collaborative project that Connor is thinking of in his claim that it 'would be possible to characterize the postmodernism of music not in terms of the stylistic changes and changes to musical language that take place in scores and in concert halls, but in terms of the explosion of collaborations and fusions'.[25]

Minimalism

If the reference to Warhol and pop art gives some indication of a blurring of boundaries from within a historical time frame of the early 1960s then minimalism, which also emerged as an art movement at that time, gives another such reference and one that, as has already become evident, often features in discussions of postmodernism.

Minimalist art, and its emergence in the 1960s, occurred specifically in New York. The term was, and in some way remains, identified with the work of artists such as Frank Stella, Donald Judd, Richard Serra, Carl André and Robert Morris. As the term implies, the reduction to a minimal essence, or material, is a common factor. It is significant that many early examples of minimalist art are simply titled *Untitled* or only suggest a material or object in a quite general way. For example, the sculpted works of Donald Judd often consist of coloured box-like objects that have no representational connotations, nor do they suggest any kind of social function or context. One defining example of such minimalist art is provided by Judd's work *Untitled (Stack)* from 1967, which forms part of the collection of the Museum of Modern Art in New York. This work consists of a series of twelve identical boxes fixed to the wall in a straight, vertical line with exact spacing between each box. The boxes do not have any purpose or imply a 'meaning' as such. In other words, this process of reduction becomes essentially abstract, resulting in formed objects that can be conceived in broadly formalist terms and understood as socially autonomous. From this perspective, such art can be equated with a high modernism and its preoccupation with a pure form, and positioned as a maximum point of difference to the engagement made by Warhol with popular culture and everyday life.

However, minimalist art is also concerned with repetition. There are many works by Judd in which there is an arrangement of objects into a pattern or series as evident in the serial arrangement of *Untitled (Stack)*. The focus on repetition is also highly evident in the work of Carl André, whose best-known, and somewhat notorious, work has involved the placement of bricks in an arranged series on the floor. A good example of André's approach is evident from his *144 Lead Square* (1969), also owned by the Museum of Modern Art in New York. This work consists of the specified number of identical lead squares that are arranged in a larger square on the floor. It is repetitive and reductive in that all the squares are exactly the same shape, size and material.

There is also a process of repetition across works. Once one has a general familiarity with Judd's work it becomes instantly recognizable, as does André's, and it is often difficult to determine the difference between one work and the next. This focus on repetition and the displacement of the individual identity of the art work would now seem to pull minimalism away from a high modernist aesthetic of art. It will also become possible to see, and hear, the processes of repetition in minimalism as a meaningful reflection of the role played by repetition in wider cultural and social contexts, possibilities that are pursued in a highly imaginative way in Robert Fink's work on musical minimalism as cultural practice.[26]

The two defining processes of minimalism in art, reduction and repetition, translate directly into what we understand of as a minimalist music, the origins and development of which also begin in the early 1960s and come to a point of realization during the late 1960s and into the early 1970s. Composers such as Terry Riley (b.1935) and La Monte Young (b.1935) feature extensively in the history of minimalism, while Steve Reich (b.1936) and Philip Glass (b.1937) are central both to minimalism and the conscious rejection of modernism. For Reich, from the perspective of the mid-1980s, modernism held no meaningful place or value in an implicitly postmodern world. In response to Tim Page, Reich states:

> Don't get me wrong. Berg, Schoenberg and Webern were very great composers. They gave expression to the emotional climate of their time. But for composers of today to recreate the 'angst' of [Schoenberg's] 'Pierrot Lunaire' in Ohio, or in the back of a Burger King, is simply a joke.[27]

Glass, also reflecting back on the 1960s, retained a sense of horror of serialism as practised by Boulez and other composers. He recalled a 'wasteland, dominated by these maniacs, these creeps, who were trying to make everyone write this crazy creepy music'.[28] This is an extreme reaction, one that is difficult to rationalize, but it does in its own highly individual way articulate the rejection of modernism by someone who found a distinctive compositional voice in the 1960s. Through this rejection of modernism what emerges is a music that has a clear correspondence with minimalist art and which can be described using similar terms. This is now a music of reductive materials treated in a repetitive way that invites comparison with aspects of rock music and also reflects the influence of other non-Western cultures.

Philip Glass

The early music of Philip Glass is already definitive of minimalist music as evident from works such as *Music in Fifths*, *Music in Contrary Motion*, *Music in Similar Motion* and *Music in Eight Parts*, all from 1969 and therefore situated within the historical outline of postmodernism that was presented in chapter 1.[29] These titles are already significant. They reflect only a material, or process, without reference to any descriptive, illustrative qualities, and suggest a parallel with the abstract nature of much minimalist art. There is a clear indication of the highly reduced sense of what the musical material might be: a single interval, a motion, and the number of parts. *Music in Contrary Motion* is a representative example of Glass's music from the late 1960s, with its title only defining the process of the music. The first page of the score is given as Ex. 7.1.

The minimal nature of the musical material is immediately evident. It consists of two parts, lines, in contrary motion. The upper line begins with a five-note segment of A–B–C–D–E. This limited range of pitches is highly economical as is the lower line, which begins on E and simply mirrors the upper line. The almost mechanical working through of this minimal pitch material is intentionally inexpressive and highly repetitive, and subverts any expectations of contrast. The somewhat austere nature of this music is reinforced by Glass's performance of it on electric organ on the recording, with the electronic sound further enhancing its mechanistic, inex-pressive aura.[30]

On the basis of the above description this music clearly articulates a relationship to minimalist art, and minimalism is perhaps the only way in which this music could be described. But, given that this music seems only to be about its own formal processes, how does it relate to postmodernism? For Keith Potter, 'the early phases of American musical minimalism', which would include this specific example, can be 'interpreted as essentially modernist'.[31] This essential modernism could be based upon that austere formal quality outlined above, it seems a music that is only about

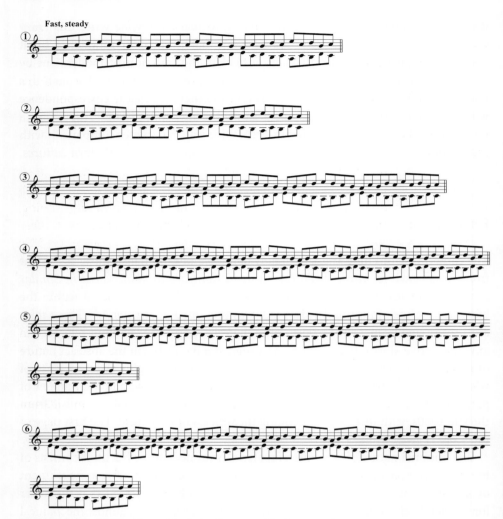

Example 7.1 Philip Glass, *Music in Contrary Motion*, opening

its own processes, and Potter does make an interesting reference to formalist thought in relation to modernist interpretations of early minimalism.[32]

However, it can be interpreted through and within postmodernism. This example, like all of Glass's music, has no real concern with the ongoing development and transformation of musical ideas, processes that were central to musical modernism. It also avoids the tensions and resolutions of earlier, traditional conceptions of musical form. Through its additive processes it expands the duration of the music but in a way that avoids such expectations of inevitable goal and conclusion through what Glass describes as an 'open form', which does not end or resolve, 'it just stops'.[33] This open form, potentially endless, suggests that this music could be included in David Harvey's characterization of postmodernism as 'new dominant ways in which we experience space and time', with the changing nature of that experience reflected in new representations of music's temporality.[34] The actual 'electric' sound of this music also adds something different. As well as suggesting a certain austere formalism, this sonority in combination with the basic pulse and rhythmic repetitions leads to certain similarities with rock music of the period, in which expanding durations and changing sounds were part of something new and challenging.

While these points of similarity with aspects of rock music may lead to a post-modern blurring of boundaries, it is also possible to see and hear this music through Lyotard's micronarratives of postmodernism.[35] This music is its own self-defining, self-legitimizing fragment that may be shaped through the comparison with other contexts, such as visual art and rock music, but it is part of its own story. This interpretation gives meaning to the 'abstract' qualities of this music while at the same time placing it in a wide context.

Other, later projects by Glass make a more direct reference to popular music. The aforementioned *Songs from Liquid Days* and the *Low Symphony* are two of the most obvious examples. Linda Hutcheon has described *Songs from Liquid Days* (1986) as 'both a song cycle and a pop album'.[36] This is in many ways an effective description of this recording. It contains a sequence of six songs, with the words for each song provided by an important figure from, or who relates to, popular music: Paul Simon, Suzanne Vega, David Byrne and Laurie Anderson. While this sequence does suggest the song cycle as a historical reference it is notable that it does not have the sense of a poetic unity (single author) of some of the defining examples of the song cycle genre. It also has a strong similarity with the 'pop album'. However, although Simon, Vega and the other songwriters provide the words they do not actually perform them, which tends to shift the focus away from the strong, often singular, relationship between composer and performer within popular music.

The first song, 'Changing Opinion', has words by Paul Simon and is sung on the recording by Bernard Fowler. Example 7.2 presents the instrumental introduction. Perhaps the first obviously notable feature is the key signature of C minor. This already defines this music as tonal, as does the basic triadic harmony as presented in the reduction, with the reusing of tonal materials evident in other examples of Glass's work.[37] This very simple tonal harmony may be part of Glass's attempt to produce a pop-music song, but it can also be heard as another reduction to a basic musical material that is subject to a process of repetition.

When the voice enters, the reduced nature of the musical materials is made clear (see Ex. 7.3). The word setting follows a very basic pattern and the melodic line outlines the basic tonal shape of the harmonic context of the C minor tonality, beginning on C to which it returns (bar 41) before rising to the sustained G from

Example 7.2   Philip Glass, *Songs from Liquid Days*, 'Changing Opinion', introduction

bar 45. Other songs in the collection move through similar strategies, while each song projects an individual mood. There is a degree of consistency across the songs in terms of sonority, texture and harmonic language, but there is less sense of how the songs actually come together into a cycle or unified concept.

If *Songs from Liquid Days* looks to both song cycle and pop album, Glass's *Low Symphony* (1992) engages with, as the title indicates, the historical genre of the symphony, one of the cornerstones of the classical tradition. But it takes as its starting point the music of David Bowie, specifically his *Low* album (1977), conceived in collaboration with Brian Eno and which articulated Bowie's own aspirations towards art, including reflections of minimalist musical practices with which Eno was very familiar.

The *Low Symphony* is effectively a commentary on Bowie's music, which is used as a starting point of a symphonic process that makes this material its own. As Glass explains: 'My approach was to treat the themes very much as if they were my own and allow their transformations to follow my own compositional bent when possible.'[38] However, Glass also concludes that in 'the end I think I have arrived at something of a real collaboration between my music and theirs'.[39] Each of the three movements of the symphony takes its starting point from one of the instrumental tracks on Bowie's *Low*. The first movement is based on 'Subterraneans', the second movement comes from 'Some Are' and the final movement is based on 'Warszawa'. Once we know the Bowie material is being used as the source it does become recognizable. However, this is enveloped in an orchestral texture that still sounds far removed from either an identifiable popular-music framework or the specifically electronic sound of the Bowie album.

As Glass has come to make more overt gestures towards popular music his work has perhaps lost some of the energy and critical edge that was central to his music

Example 7.3 Philip Glass, *Songs from Liquid Days*, 'Changing Opinion', bars 37–48

from the late 1960s and early 1970s. This earlier music was, somewhat paradoxically, the moment that Glass in not trying so hard to self-consciously engage with popular music projected meaningful parallels with the counter-culture, experimental aura of rock music of the time.

The references made to popular music in both *Songs from Liquid Days* and the *Low Symphony* coexist with the increased popularity of Glass's music, a factor that has also been enhanced by both his role as a composer of film music and the performances of his own ensemble. The popularity, and availability, of this music is far removed from its original starting points in 1960s downtown New York. In the directions it has taken from that time and place, Glass's music has moved towards the kind of blurring and crossing of boundaries that are widely discussed in relation to postmodernism and of which Glass can be seen as definitive, but the musical contexts and materials that are utilized are always viewed from the perspective of Glass as composer.

Laurie Anderson

Laurie Anderson (b.1947) comes from a deep background in performance art, and has produced multimedia work that has involved visual art, physical movement and film as well as music. In the early stages of her career Anderson interacted with many other artists, dancers and musicians, including Philip Glass, as part of a downtown New York alternative art scene. As she later recalled: 'New York in the early '70s was Paris in the '20s … We were very aware that we were creating an entirely new scene (later known as "Downtown").'[40]

In a number of her early performance-based works Anderson sought to incorporate music and other types of sound as part of a real, physical environment. For example, in *Duet for Door Jamb and Violin* (1976) the physical space provided by a doorway creates sound. Anderson gives her own description:

> This duet is performed on the threshold. The length of the bow stroke [of the violin] is determined by the width of the door. Contact microphones are attached to the jambs at the impact points, amplifying the staccato, knocking sound as the bow bangs back and forth. When the violin is electric, the violin speakers are located in one room and the door jamb speakers in the adjoining room. During the performance, tonal and percussive are alternatively separated and mixed by kicking the door open and shut.[41]

This description, which can only give an indication of what it might feel like to witness a performance, does reflect the importance of the performance environment as physical space and the interaction between what might be conceived as both musical and non-musical sound, factors that Anderson would be much preoccupied with in other projects of this time. However, this duet also reflects a general experimental direction and can be seen in relation to the establishing of such experimental practices in the work and presence of John Cage. Other interesting examples of Anderson's early experimental performance-based works of the period include the series titled *Institutional Dream* (1972–3) and *Duets on Ice* (1974). *Institutional Dream* actually involved Anderson sleeping in public spaces, including Coney Island beach, New York, which is captured in a photograph,[42] and *Duets* featured Anderson playing violin live while being accompanied by a recording of a violin that was hidden in her instrument. These violin sounds were heard against the background of street noise in various New York locations. She performed wearing ice skates the blades of which 'were encased in blocks of ice. When the ice melted, the concert was over.'[43] These performance events again reflect Anderson's preoccupation with place and environment, but, as well as providing a site for performance, this is also the space within which Anderson herself as a physical presence is situated. This interaction of space and body would be extended in Anderson's later works, but often in a more subtle and accessible form.

The musical content in these experimental performance art events might be only one element, but Anderson did move towards more musically specific projects without losing sight of the background in performance art or the potential of multimedia concepts. In the many different music-based projects of Anderson's career, *United States I–IV* (1983) stands as a definitive moment, a work of extended duration that incorporates a vast range of materials, ideas and sources. Susan McClary describes this work as being hailed 'as a landmark by postmodernist theorists' and seen as 'thematizing the contradictions and tensions of late-capitalist society'.[44]

'O Superman', a surprising hit single in the British charts in 1981, emerged from *United States*. However, when heard as a single track it can contrast the epic scale of that work as well as forming part of a suggested change of direction from the earlier stages of Anderson's career. The album *Big Science* (1982), which also contains 'O Superman', further extends the move into a more accessible style and format.[45] 'O Superman' and the projects that followed can be heard as another postmodern blurring of boundaries, moving from an already blurred performance art into a more explicitly popular context. However, although 'O Superman' reached a wide audience it is still a rather individual piece of music, especially in terms of its commercial success. It sounds minimal, in that it is based on the repetition of very limited musical materials, with a simple tonal background. As McClary describes it: 'The musical constant in "O Superman" is a pedal on middle c on a single syllable: "ha ha ha"' while 'two alternating chords inflect the pedal harmonically: an A♭ major triad in first inversion and a root-position C minor triad.'[46] These few, closely related, harmonic materials are effectively a process of reduction to a clear, essential tonality. However, this is not a goal-orientated tonal process; there is no real reflection of the tensions that require resolution within the shared vocabulary of common-practice tonality. In describing it as 'basic', or 'simple', which are also words that have been used to describe aspects of minimalism, we are not making a critical judgement on this music. Rather, it is possible to hear this music as in itself a critical gesture towards the assumptions of complexity as generated by modernism. It is also possible to hear the electronic sound of the voice as part of a critical commentary on technology and its impact on the body.

Anderson makes these critical gestures from the perspective of a woman composer. In the words of McClary, Anderson is 'one of the most influential women composers of her time',[47] and McClary's discussion of Anderson and her music in *Feminine Endings* gives substance to that claim. It is also clear that Anderson assumes an important position in the debate about the blurring of boundaries within, and through, postmodernism. The shift she made from essentially avant-garde performance artist to something closer to, but not quite being, a popular musician is significant in this context. For Anderson herself, this distance is unproblematic. In response to a question from William Duckworth asking whether friends had thought she had 'sold out' by signing a record deal with Warner Brothers, she responded:

> My friends were happy. People I didn't know, I'm sure, thought I had sold out. But I had a choice at that point, which was to keep doing concerts for fifty people, or to make records.[48]

This is a rather stark juxtaposition of possibilities between obscurity and access. But in retrospect the recordings made by Anderson that are available to a wider audience than would otherwise have been possible do not necessarily sound compromised and, as has already been stated, even the commercially successful 'O Superman' has both a critical dimension and a distinct difference from any notional mainstream of popular music.

Although the direction Anderson's career has taken can be seen as part of a postmodern blurring of boundaries, this proposal does not necessarily position her work as the point of convergence between 'high' (classical) and popular cultures. Anderson's starting point, unlike the status of composer in the examples of both Glass and Daugherty, was that of an already blurred performance art. Even if some of her work can be described in more popular terms it still projects a critical distance from many of the assumptions about popular culture and continues to resonate with multimedia, performance-based sounds and images.

Carla Bley

In contrast to Laurie Anderson's beginnings in experimental performance art Carla Bley (b.1938) comes from a clearly defined background in jazz music. Bley's career began in New York and involved working with jazz musicians such as composer George Russell and pianist Paul Bley, her first husband. Carla Bley became known primarily as a jazz composer and Paul Bley has recorded and made known some of her most distinctive compositions, which reflect a background influence of jazz composers such as Thelonious Monk and Charles Mingus.[49] With her second husband, Michael Mantler, also a composer, Carla Bley became deeply involved in the formation of a self-reliant organization of jazz musicians, which became the Jazz Composer's Orchestra Association. Other important contributions include her work with Charlie Haden's *Liberation Music Orchestra* (1969), a project that reflected the political engagement of many jazz musicians in the late 1960s into the early 1970s.[50]

However, in one massive project from the early 1970s, *Escalator over the Hill* (1971), described by Stuart Nicholson as an 'eclectic "jazz" opera',[51] Bley produced a work that she is perhaps still best known for and which is of most direct relevance in this context. In *Escalator over the Hill* Bley constructed a music that blurs many boundaries, incorporating musical ideas which have their origins in classical, jazz and popular musics, while also involving musicians from many different backgrounds.

Escalator over the Hill was initiated in 1968, and the recording was completed in 1971 and captures the energy and imagination of the period.[52] It is a setting of words by Paul Haines and, although often described in relation to opera, there is little sense of a coherent narrative structure or how it might have looked had it actually been staged. The music moves across many different styles, often suggesting Kurt Weill's theatre music but also looking to Indian music and rock music. As well as utilizing this wide range of musical references, the album featured a vast number of musicians from many different backgrounds, although many did start from within jazz. Notable contributors include Jack Bruce, who had been until quite recently singer and bass player with the seminal rock group Cream, whose music reflected the transformation of blues into rock but also the spontaneity of improvisational practices associated with jazz music. Linda Ronstadt, with a background in country rock music, also makes a distinctive vocal contribution. Other musicians such as Dewey Redman (saxophone), Enrico Rava (trumpet), Leroy Jenkins (violin), Charlie Haden (bass) and Paul Motian (drums), among others, had already made notable contributions to jazz music, while guitarist John McLaughlin had already become a significant figure in the developing fusion of jazz and rock music.

The music not only brings different musicians together but also moves through and between different musics within a highly sectionalized framework that has at most only a very limited sense of unity and coherence. The opening 'hotel overture' is a highly structured, composed musical background over which the soloists, most notably Gato Barbieri's tenor saxophone, project strong, highly charged lines. This is music that obviously comes from, and relates to, jazz. But the following section, 'this is here', would be much more difficult to define in terms of specific musical context or stylistic reference. As the work unfolds other sounds and textures come to the surface, from free jazz to psychedelic rock. These are already highly diffuse musical contexts and their close proximity to each other within this work adds to its already eclectic, non-unified nature. The wide-ranging nature of these musical sources already suggests that the description of this work as 'eclectic' is highly apposite; in fact, it may be a slight understatement. This eclecticism comes from many different directions and blurs many different boundaries, and this already suggests that postmodernism is an appropriate location for this remarkable work.

It is difficult to say what *Escalator over the Hill* is really about in terms of the words and situations, but the work begins with an overture, the 'hotel overture' performed by the large ensemble. This establishes an idea of a hotel that will be developed through the suggestions of rooms as spaces that contain presences, voices. The hotel comes to be defined as 'Cecil Clarke's Old Hotel'. Other sections refer to parts of the hotel: 'in the courtyard', 'in the lobby', 'in the room'. There is also reference to the hotel as space in the naming of specific ensembles, such as 'hotel lobby band' and 'Jack's traveling band'.

Escalator over the Hill happened within the time scale of an emergent postmodernism in the late 1960s and early 1970s as defined by Harvey's 'new dominant ways in which we experience space and time'.[53] One of the things that *Escalator over the Hill* is about is the passing of time – time waiting in hotel rooms, the journey, the past – and the poetic image of the escalator moving but also disappearing out of sight, 'over the hill'. The conclusion of the recording defines this meditation on time through the ending of the original LP on a locked groove, which made the sound in effect endless, while the CD reissue ends on a hum that runs for approximately 20 minutes before finally fading.

Each of the examples discussed above – Daugherty, Glass, Anderson, Bley – has produced music that can be heard as blurring many boundaries within postmodernism and as such they celebrate the potential that is unleashed in the new context. However, this claim may need to be distinguished from any assertion that they actually cross, blur or merge the great divide between 'high' culture and the popular. Daugherty and Glass may, in different ways, look to aspects of popular music but are they ever really fully positioned in a new space in between? Anderson starts from an already somewhat blurred position between music and other art forms, and Bley in

Escalator over the Hill is always looking in many different directions, never just between classical and popular, while jazz is a music that was always a musical and cultural hybrid. But all these examples pose interesting questions about the mobility between what was perceived to be distinct musical categories before postmodernism, and they all in different ways produce music that articulates various points of connection with aspects of a wider debate about the historical moments and stylistic identities of postmodernism in music.

Chapter 8

The music of Sofia Gubaidulina (and others): 'as if the history of music were at an end'

Sofia Gubaidulina (b.1931), as a citizen of the Soviet Union, who studied in Moscow during the 1950s and 60s, was shaped by the political realities of the Cold War. After a period of slow development and relative obscurity her music began to reach a wider audience in the mid-1980s, the point at which she was allowed to travel outside the Soviet Union, and which coincided with the shifting political landscape towards the new conditions that would be formed in the post-Cold War world after 1989. Gubaidulina's positioning in, and relationship to, this changing political context can be seen as part of a shared and comparative experience with other composers of a similar generation and background. Alastair Williams suggests an obvious association between Gubaidulina and Alfred Schnittke (1934–98): 'two strong individualists whose lives nevertheless share core experiences'.[1] These common experiences included the enduring of the 'intolerable Soviet regime'. Both composers worked in film music in order to support themselves, and both were influenced by the music of Shostakovich. Although oppressed by the Soviet system they would later share a 'deep apprehension at what the collapse of the same system left behind'.[2] Gubaidulina believes that we are all 'existentially shaken by what has happened to our country'.[3] Against this background Schnittke and Gubaidulina would, in different ways, compose music that reflects what Williams describes as an 'ambivalence towards modernist systems'.[4]

Schnittke – Concerto Grosso

In the music of Schnittke this 'ambivalence towards modernist systems' is articulated through a self-defined polystylism. This terminology reflects a highly plural notion of what constitutes musical style as defined by the play with elements drawn from different musical styles, including primarily the juxtaposition of new and old music. In much of Schnittke's music we encounter sudden changes, or a dissolve effect, between different musics that reflect distinct historical and stylistic origins. This description suggests a point of convergence with some of the music discussed in chapter 4, even if the reference is not towards musical romanticism as such, and the effect is very individual. It suggests an intertextual relationship to already-existing

132

music, but this relationship is not directed only to specific details, such as an identifiable moment in, or material from, earlier works; it is also often located at the level of more general characteristics of style and genre. This emphasis on a coexisting plurality of style as asserted by the term polystylism brings Schnittke's music into the wider perspectives of postmodernism in music.

Schnittke's relationship to old music is already evident in many of the titles of works that refer to historical genres – symphony, concerto, string quartet – while some works do relate to specific precursors, including Mozart and Haydn. In the series of works titled Concerto Grosso, Schnittke's engagement with old music, and his polystylism, comes most clearly to the surface. The title of Concerto Grosso already indicates the music of the baroque, specifically J. S. Bach and Handel, as a point of reference. Schnittke's Concerto Grosso No. 1 (1977) has been described as using a polystylism that is 'torn between a clashing pluralism and a yearning for the certainties of tradition'.[5] This description captures an essential tension between a recognizable playfulness with past musical materials and a sense of loss for the value that such material once held. This critical tension pervades much of Schnittke's music. Such factors are aurally present in the Concerto Grosso No. 3 (1985) for two solo violins and string orchestra, which also utilizes harpsichord, piano, celesta and bells. The first movement, of five, begins with a remarkable pastiche realization of a baroque-sounding music that is clearly intentionally retrospective (see Ex. 8.1).

The initial harmonic event, the chord that initiates the first movement, indicates a G minor tonality. This tonal reference immediately signifies old music. We hear the ensemble play through a rapidly moving sequence-based contrapuntal texture that immediately recalls the Brandenburg Concertos of J. S. Bach as well as other examples of the genre. This generic reference is reinforced by the presence of the harpsichord, which suggests the continuo role within the baroque ensemble. This beginning also seems to recall the engagement with baroque music in the neoclassicism of earlier twentieth-century composers, including Hindemith, whose *Kammermusik* series also often made a quite explicit gesture towards the concerto grosso. However, having established the rhythmic, textural and thematic consistency that is typical of the baroque period and concerto genre there is a sharp, dramatic intrusion. The music suddenly changes; it comes apart, breaking down into fragmentary textures that seem to have little relationship to the opening gesture (see Ex. 8.2).

This moment of rupture at Fig. 4 is defined by a strong vertical harmony marked *ff* and the sounding of the bell, which heralds the change. There is no real sense of preparation for this moment; the contrapuntal lines do not move inevitably towards this point. Also, although D is featured as the bass of this harmony, there is no recognizable harmonic relationship to the suggested G minor tonality of the opening material. Any possible indication of a harmonic connection between D and G is

Example 8.1 Alfred Schnittke, Concerto Grosso No. 3, first movement, opening

immediately undermined by the highly chromatic nature of the other pitches of this chord.

   After this interruption we still hear aspects of a baroque-sounding music, but they are fragments that lack any sense of coherence or direction. The two solo violin parts now seem out of step with each other, while the upper lines of the ensemble articulate a glissando effect that has a maximum distance from what has come before. This distance is also reflected in the bass line, which, following the D at Fig. 4, now moves ceaselessly around neighbouring pitches. This process of fragmenting, breaking down textures and disrupting any notional consistency or unity, is defined at the conclusion of this first movement. At this point the texture reduces to eventually leave only a descending bass line that moves downwards through a chromatic motion to arrive on a sustained C♯ (see Ex. 8.3). This ending is now very different from the G-minor-based baroque texture with which the movement began.

   The composer himself provides a highly evocative description of this movement:

> It begins 'beautifully', neo-classically – but after some minutes the museum explodes and we stand with the fragments of the past (quotations) before the dangerous and uncertain present.[6]

Example 8.2 Alfred Schnittke, Concerto Grosso No. 3, first movement, from Fig. 4 to Fig. 5

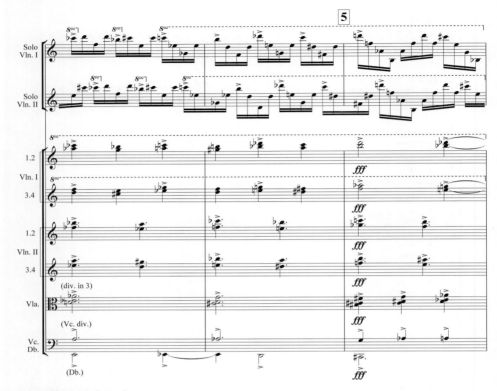

Example 8.2   (cont.)

The image that the composer evokes of the beautiful beginning (Ex. 8.1) that then explodes (Ex. 8.2) captures the essence of this movement, but it also provides an insight into Schnittke's music in general, of which this is a good example, and its association with postmodernism. It is notable that in this description it is the 'museum' – the repository of the past – that explodes. It is taken apart, deconstructed into fragments that can never return to their original unified state. We are familiar now with fragments of past music being quoted and redefined, but also with how a postmodern culture becomes a series of fragments. This music is a meaningful musical illustration of such processes. In this instance Schnittke does not directly invoke postmodernism to describe his own music but he is using language, and composing music, that already relates to what we now understand as postmodernism.

Gubaidulina

If Schnittke and Gubaidulina share a common background and starting point, the music they have composed has looked in different directions, with the coexistence of

1) Vierteltonerhöhung / un quarto di tono più alto [quarter-tone higher]

2) Vierteltonerniedrigung / un quarto di tono più basso [quarter-tone lower]

Example 8.3   Alfred Schnittke, Concerto Grosso No. 3, first movement, ending

Example 8.3   (cont.)

these different directions also defining their own spaces, telling their own story, within the broad pluralities of postmodernism. Gubaidulina's music and its changing reception have been marked by large-scale political realities, but what makes her music so distinctive in the context of the debate about postmodernism in music is the sense of retreat from that reality and the withdrawing into a profound sense of selfhood. Such qualities may suggest that Gubaidulina's music might have some point of connection with that of other composers who emerged from an East-European background – Arvo Pärt and Henryk Górecki – and whose work has been described through the rather misleading and unhelpful term of a 'holy minimalism'.[7]

Pärt and Górecki

In the case of Estonian-born Arvo Pärt (b.1935), his early career included an engagement with serialism that was strongly discouraged at the time. This was followed by a developing interest in the music of J. S. Bach that culminated in a work titled *Credo* (1968), a setting of a religious text for choir that is supported by orchestra and solo piano. The musical starting point for this work is the C major Prelude from Book 1 of J. S. Bach's 48 Preludes and Fugues, which we hear played on the piano in a highly literal way, after the intentionally Bach-like initial choral statement, and which is then accelerated into a process of minimal repetition that becomes distorted and fragmented. The subsequent events of the work are defined through juxtapositions of intense and reflective orchestral sound, bold choral statements and the intrusions of the piano part. The return of the piano to the Bach prelude leads towards the concluding climax and a reminder of the opening choral statement.

The essentially tonal nature of the initial musical material, and its explicit Christian symbolism, already marked it as highly individual. While that symbolism 'provoked an official scandal',[8] it would also become a defining factor in drawing a wider audience towards this music. By the mid- to late 1970s the composer established an international reputation based upon a sequence of works – including *Cantus in memoriam Benjamin Britten*, *Fratres* and *Tabula rasa* – which now involved a clarification of musical form and content in conjunction with an essentially contemplative aura. Following Pärt's move to the West in 1980 these works, and others, would come to find an audience through the increasing availability of recordings. For David Clarke, Pärt's 'very rise is symptomatic of the post-modern era we have now entered, under which modernism's one-time central position in 20th century art has itself been dislodged'.[9] The positioning of Pärt's music as symptomatic of postmodernism is based not only in the distance between this music and the assumptions of modernism, but also in changing values and modes of reception. According to Clarke:

> The wave of enthusiasm for Pärt's music – or at least for those works written since the late 70s – belongs to the same syndrome that has driven Górecki's Third Symphony and Tavener's *The Protecting Veil* to the top of the CD charts.[10]

This syndrome, which was highly prevalent in the early 1990s, when Clarke was writing, may have been driven, as he suggests, by a critical reaction against an 'alienating atonality' and 'complex structural abstraction' in 'modern music'.[11] In contrast, the 'religious aura' of the music listed by Clarke 'has a strong allure for a secularised culture that no longer has any collective way of articulating the spiritual'.[12] Of course, Clarke will proceed to complicate this scenario, but it is difficult to avoid the convergence between a notable simplification of form and the aura of spirituality that accrues to this music. Clarke also mentions the third symphony of the Polish-born Henryk Górecki (1933–2010), and the popularity of this work in the early 1990s was truly remarkable, not only the commercial success of the CD, but also, as Luke Howard documents in admirable detail, the sampling of, and references to, this music in many different popular music contexts.[13]

Gubaidulina – *Offertorium*

Although Gubaidulina's music has reached a wider audience than many contemporary composers and there is a shared concern for a sense of spiritual transcendence in music that could reflect, after Communism, what Mikhail Epstein defines as a 'post-atheism',[14] the actual sound of her music is very different from that of Pärt and Górecki.

One of Gubaidulina's most significant works is *Offertorium* (1980), in effect a concerto for violin and orchestra that is dedicated to violinist Gidon Kremer, who did a great deal to bring Gubaidulina's music to a wider audience and who is responsible for the recording through which the work is best known. *Offertorium* begins with another retrospective gesture, the sounding of the 'royal theme' from J. S. Bach's *Musical Offering* (see Exx. 8.4a and b), but the notes are distributed throughout the orchestra in what Alex Ross describes as 'Second Viennese School style'.[15] This reference to the second Viennese school suggests that it is reflective of the conception of the *Klangfarbenmelodie*, the sound-colour of melody, as related specifically to Webern, whose highly transparent textures and sparse lines were highly influential on later, modernist composers. For Gubaidulina this moment, through the use of the Bach theme and its Webernesque articulation, serves to 'unite the two personalities in the history of music who have produced the greatest impression on [her]'.[16] In retaining the actual pitches of Bach's theme Gubaidulina brings both

Example 8.4a   J. S. Bach, *Musical Offering*, 'royal theme'

Example 8.4b Sofia Gubaidulina, *Offertorium*, opening

baroque counterpoint and twentieth-century modernism into close proximity and in doing so treats both as historical subjects.

This opening statement is given as Ex. 8.4b and summarized in outline as Ex. 8.4a.[17] The accuracy with which Bach's theme is preserved, as is its modernist distribution, is immediately evident. The initial phrase of the theme – D–F–A–B♭–C♯ – now begins on the trombone, then moves to bassoon, trumpet and then the horn, but it is notable that this opening statement withholds the final D of Bach's theme, leaving the work open rather than closed at this stage.

In her study of this work, which forms part of a consideration of music from a feminist perspective that is informed by the philosophy of Deleuze, Sally Macarthur highlights a certain deconstructive violence in Gubaidulina's music:

> Unlike that of her former Soviet compatriot Kancheli, Gubaidulina's music does not concern itself with the struggle between violence and silence, yet the struggle between these two determinants is perceptible in her music. Rather, and this is the case in *Offertorium*, some of her music will set up a theme or an idea or a musical argument and then set about demolishing it. Gubaidulina will often employ her musical equipment like a weapon, wielding it upon the themes or remnants or fragments of themes she composes until they are metaphorically pulverised into musical mulch before reconstituting them in entirely new ways. She adopts a cyclical process of composing, decomposing and recomposing the music: to recall Jankélévich, 'violence [in Gubaidulina's music] … massacres determinants that are nonetheless constantly being reborn'.[18]

While the possible comparison of the music of Gubaidulina and Kancheli would be interesting, it is Macarthur's suggestion of the setting up of a thematic idea only for it to be demolished that is of most immediate relevance. In *Offertorium* this process, as Macarthur indicates, appears to be realized. The opening projection of the Bach theme is revisited but only for it to be deconstructed and finally, as a moment of resolution, returned to in something like its original form even if its projection will sound rather different from its initial appearance. The composer herself describes the theme as offering 'itself up as a sacrifice',[19] and there is an underlying relationship to the original thematic material that can be defined as deconstructive.

This engagement is already evident at the outset of the work. Following the Webernesque unfolding of the Bach theme, the solo violin enters with the repetition of the pitches F and E (see Ex. 8.4b), resisting the downward pull towards D as in the original source. The composer extracts this semitone from the Bach theme and interrogates its thematic potential. As the work progresses through its single-movement, three-section formal shape, the semitone gesture is subjected to further interrogation through changing articulations and transformations.

There are moments of real intensity, and increasing textural and harmonic complexity which validate the identification of violence as a force of meaning in this work before we reach the conclusion, which consists of an expansive, contemplative transformation of the thematic material. The sustained high D in the solo violin part finally defines this ending while the bass line gravitates downwards towards its sustained D (see Ex. 8. 5).

This ending in effect completes the theme with the resolution of the move from F through E to D having been suppressed until this moment. Alex Ross provides a highly evocative description of this concluding moment:

> By the end, Bach's theme has somehow mutated into an ancient-sounding liturgical melody, passing through a murmuring orchestra like an icon in a procession.[20]

The proposed image of the icon in a procession translates Gubaidulina's music into visual terms, but it is a meaningful translation that reflects well the spiritual journey that this music takes. In purely musical terms it can be described as one of three octaves, from the missing D of Bach's theme in its original register to its final placement three octaves higher. But this process, and the moment of arrival, also acts as a musical representation of a transcendent purity. Between these two points – the initial withholding of D and its concluding realization – many, often violent, things occur, but the 'icon' remains intact to secure its elevated place in the concluding procession. Ross's description of this process as part of 'an ancient-sounding liturgical melody' again suggests a sense of history to this music. This is not a musical past as conjured up through the specifics of intertextual quotation, although the initial use of the Bach theme could be positioned in this way, but it is a more generalized evocation of a mythologized past, perhaps a utopian one, that is seen as a spiritual retreat from the harsh reality of the real world. But, if this signifies a removal from the contexts of that reality, this is not a return to a vision of music as autonomous. This is a music that is loaded with an abundance of meanings.

However, if this is an effective description, the definition of this music as postmodern now seems more difficult. The reference to Webern, and the increasing complexity of the music as it unfolds, could suggest that it retains a definition of a musical modernism. The final arrival on D could also be heard as a resolution, a goal, perhaps even as a source of unity. These possibilities now look towards the question asked in many different ways and in different contexts in this book thus far: why should we describe this music as postmodern? Judy Lochead provides a highly effective description of Gubaidulina's music in general, which already begins to provide a meaningful answer to this question:

Example 8.5   Sofia Gubaidulina, *Offertorium*, ending, from Fig. 134

Example 8.5   (cont.)

Example 8.5   (cont.)

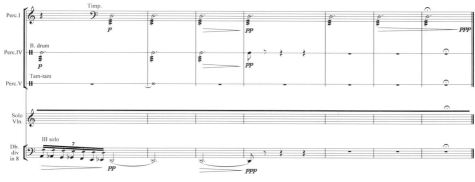

Example 8.5   (cont.)

> Gubaidulina's music speaks to the postmodern desire for a pre-modern world using
> figures and sounds which allude to a medieval world of a muted expressivity that
> claims access to essential being. Yet this pre-modern expressive mode is won by
> utilizing avant-garde musical techniques, and hence the discourse about
> Gubaidulina's music is bound up with the modern as well as the pre-modern.
> While seldom named as such the postmodern is everywhere evident in
> Gubaidulina's music and in the critical discourse that accompanies it.[21]

I think that the description of a 'postmodern desire for a pre-modern world' is a very
good way of describing this music. It makes sense of the starting point of the Bach
theme in *Offertorium* but more generally it brings into focus the importance of
expressive qualities that were seen, perhaps unfairly in some instances, to have been
suppressed in later versions of modernism. But if this is postmodern music there is
still a meaningful trace of the modern in Gubaidulina's version of the postmodern.

The music of Gubaidulina does not always sit too easily within a description of a
'holy' or 'mystical minimalism', but it is always concerned with the spiritual in
music. It gives sound to a mythologized 'pre-modern' world that denies the assertion
of an inevitable historical progress, rejects the consequences of modernity by now
treating modernism as just another historical subject, and returns into its own
fictionalized postmodern construction of the past.

The suggestion of a 'pre-modern world' and the allusion to a 'medieval world of
muted expressivity' are readily evident in other works by Gubaidulina and could be
seen to form part of what Alexander Genis considers from a purely Russian
perspective to be an 'archaic postmodernism', even though his discussion does not
actually extend to music and his context is quite distinct.[22] For example, in
Gubaidulina's large-scale orchestral work *Pro et contra* (1989) we hear hints, rather
than literal statements, of Russian orthodox chant that have a deep if distant sense of

history. This suggestion of a distant history is also evident in works such as *In croce* (1979) for bayan, a Russian accordion, and cello, and *Silenzo* (1991) for bayan, violin and cello. The titles of these works already begin to suggest a concern with an apparently lost spiritual expressivity in music, with the use of the bayan adding a feeling of a distant folk-like origin to the music. These factors are most clearly defined in *Seven Words* (1982), for cello, bayan and strings, another extended purely instrumental work that is intended to convey a recognizable symbolism while also carrying historical traces that somehow remind us of earlier attempts, by Schütz and Haydn, to tell this particular story through music.

In a brief overview of what he describes as 'mystical minimalism' – which involves reference to Górecki, Pärt and Kancheli and which at least in terms of the 'mystical' may be extended to Gubaidulina – Alex Ross claims that they are 'writing as if the history of music were at an end'.[23] This statement captures a certain timelessness of some of this music, both in terms of at times almost static forms and textures, but also through a wider positioning of a disruption of the assumed directions between past, present and future.

Ross does not really justify his conclusion, which comes very early in his essay, and such justification would not perhaps be fully required in the largely journalistic context in which he is writing. But, while it might be desirable to avoid over-interpreting this brief comment by Ross, it is very intriguing and does invite further speculation. The claim of an 'end of history' has been made in many different contexts, but in terms of philosophy it has its origins in the early nineteenth-century Idealist thought of Hegel, in which the end of history comes as a consequence of a dynamic, goal-orientated view of historical change, a metanarrative which postmodernism refuses to invest belief in.[24] The 'end of history' has been restated in a different way in more recent times by Francis Fukuyama, who sees the post-Cold War world as constituted in highly conservative political ('democracy') and economic ('market economy') terms as if not perfect then at least seemingly beyond change and therefore beyond history.[25] Of course, Ross is not making a direct reference to either Hegel or Fukuyama, but there is a sense in which modernism was seen, or saw itself, as a consequence of an inevitable historical progress while the emergence of postmodernism, in contrast, involves a new historical awareness. This awareness does not extend to projecting a future but rather becoming more, after modernism, preoccupied with the past. The music discussed in this chapter, along with examples discussed earlier in this book, can be heard as part of that historical awareness. It does not reach the moment at which it seems 'as if the history of music were at an end' as a state of perfection, but it does form part of a realization that, at the very least, any possibility of consistent, coherent stylistic renewal and progress is now deeply problematic.

Chapter 9

Repetitions and revisions: from bebop to hip hop

In his epic history of jazz music Alyn Shipton begins his discussion of what he considers to be 'postmodern jazz', the focal point of this chapter, with the following statement:

> Up until the 1970s, the story of jazz is a straightforward narrative. It is one in which there may be changes of emphasis … but there is a clear sense of development, of the music moving forward.[1]

It is possible to outline the main developments in jazz music in a recognizable chronological framework and to trace the impact of major contributors to the music. However, on the basis of Shipton's account this comes to an end through what he terms the 'information age'. This is the point at which the abundance of information, through the impact of technology, disrupts that 'straightforward narrative', a disruption that coincides with, and can be defined by, postmodernism.

It is significant that Shipton situates this moment of ending in the 1970s, which coincides with much of the historical territory already covered in this book as defined by David Harvey's noted emergence of postmodernism somewhere between 1968 and 1972, the third stage of the historical outline sketched in chapter 1. From this point, as Shipton argues, it becomes more difficult to follow lines of stylistic evolution. Rather than moving forwards, jazz moves sideways into fusions with rock music, backwards in terms of revivals and recycling, fuelled in part by the increasing availability of recordings as historical documents, and away from any wider audience through the continuation of the avant-garde aspirations of free jazz.

However, jazz music may have appeared to move forward in a relatively straight line up to this point, but, as the details of Shipton's history often reveal, this is a rather misleading image. Many jazz styles overlap and intersect rather than merely following one after another. The close proximity between, for example, swing and bebop, the reception of which is imaginatively contextualized by Bernard Gendron, posed questions of what constituted the new and the modern in jazz in the 1940s.[2] Jazz is also a music that may have become even more diverse after a certain point, but it was always already plural, always a cultural and musical hybrid. According to Krin Gabbard:

> Jazz is a construct. Nothing can be called jazz simply because of its 'nature'. Musical genres such as the military march, opera and reggae are relatively homogenous and easy to identify. By contrast, the term jazz is routinely applied to musics that have as little in common as an improvisation by Marilyn Crispell and a 1923 recording by King Oliver and his Creole Jazz Band.[3]

This statement accurately reflects the constructed nature of what we might understand by jazz. There are clearly certain musical qualities (rhythmic, improvised) and sounds (drums, saxophones, trumpets) that may routinely signify jazz music, but there is also, in comparison to the 'relatively homogenous' musical styles Gabbard cites, a powerful sense of plurality to the many different musics to which the label jazz is applied. The examples given by Gabbard to underline this pluralism are well, if carefully, chosen. They occupy different points of the historical spectrum, Oliver as part of the origins of the music, and Crispell as a more recent reminder of one of the places at which the music has arrived. They also suggest polarities of race and gender (Oliver as black man, Crispell as white woman), which accentuate the increasing diversity of what the music has become.

Oliver recorded in the early 1920s with his Creole Jazz Band, which featured the young Louis Armstrong. Oliver's personal history, as part of the migration from New Orleans to Chicago, and the music he made, situates him at a crucial juncture in the history of jazz. It is also a moment at which the impact of technology occurs through the recording of what had been a spontaneous, oral tradition. For example, a classic early jazz recording such as Oliver's 'Canal Street Blues', a standard twelve-bar blues form recorded in 1923, is now preserved, transformed into digital format and consumed as CD. It exists as a source of information, available for interpretation by historians, audiences and musicians. It, and other recordings of the period, allows us to have at least some indication of the sound of the music in the early 1920s and, given the absence of notated scores, this information is invaluable. But such recordings also become canonical, forming a tradition to which later music is compared or from which it is seen to depart.

In contrast, Crispell's music also comes to us in the recorded format of CD, but, unlike the transferring of an old recording in the case of the Oliver example, this is a music already conceived in the digital era. Crispell's CD titled *Amaryllis*, recorded in 2001 on ECM records, stands as a good example of her music. The first track of the CD, evocatively titled 'Voice from the Past', opens with a ruminative bass line from Gary Peacock. While Paul Motian's drums give some sense of pulse there is no real feeling of energy and direction to the music. When Crispell's piano enters it is soft, reflective, contemplative. Although there are some structural signposts, both harmonic and melodic, there is little indication of a predetermined formal scheme to this music and it seems to float free. This is music that is some distance from the cyclical form and rhythmic consistency of jazz as defined by Oliver.

Emerging from Gabbard's comments on jazz as a construction, the brief comparison of Oliver and Crispell highlights the sense of plurality and diversity of music still defined as jazz even when there seems little point of contact between the different musics. Such diversities and differences further complicate any notion of jazz as a tradition, and yet what constitutes the jazz tradition, how it might have been constructed, and the values that are ascribed to it have always been questions that provoke debate, at times of a highly conflicted nature. As postmodernism interestingly complicates the relationship between past and present it follows that it must do something critical to any conception of tradition.

Wynton Marsalis

There have been many attempts to effectively sustain or preserve a notional tradition of jazz music. One of the most sustained efforts has been that of Wynton Marsalis (b.1961), a prodigiously talented trumpeter from New Orleans who emerged in the early 1980s and has continued to exert a strong influence on perceptions of what constitutes jazz music and its tradition.[4] Marsalis's look towards the past has been seen as part of a 'neoclassical agenda',[5] while Shipton situates the retrospective turn that is personified by Marsalis within his discussion of postmodern jazz. According to Richard Cook:

> If his [Wynton Marsalis] first bands sounded like oblique descendents of the already-oblique Miles Davis groups of the early 60s, that shell was soon shucked in favour of Mingusian ensembles, Ellingtonian voicings, New Orleans survivals that could embrace Jelly Roll Morton and Joe Oliver. It looked able to spread in any direction but always *within jazz*.[6]

This summary by Cook suggests that there is a wide range of different musics to which Marsalis relates – the structured ensemble sound of both Ellington and Mingus, the New Orleans origins of the music through both Morton and Oliver. However, if this suggests a sense of diversity this does not extend beyond the recognizable parameters of jazz music to embrace 'other' music.[7] This version of the jazz tradition may be broad but it is also reductive in terms of a preoccupation with essentializing specific characteristics of the music.

Miles Davis

The most significant name mentioned by Cook in the above list is that of Miles Davis (1926–91), which is highlighted specifically in relation to his quintet recordings of the early to mid-1960s.[8] In other words, if Marsalis looked towards Davis it is the music Davis produced immediately before his move into experiments with jazz and rock music in the late 1960s and early 1970s that is seen as relevant.

Davis had been a central line of an evolving jazz tradition that begins with bebop and the young Davis's contribution to alto saxophonist Charlie Parker's radical, small group (usually quintet) sound in the mid- to later 1940s. The frenetic, high intensity of what become known as bebop was contrasted by Davis's naturally restrained trumpet sound. Davis developed his own musical directions after Parker, often in many different directions, but always within a jazz-based context, and often continued the practice of playing a standard repertoire. However, following the series of classic quintet recordings in the mid-1960s Davis began to move towards an attempted fusion of jazz and rock music in the late 1960s through a series of recordings that begins with *Miles in the Sky* (1968) and *In A Silent Way* (1969), and which is then developed further on *Bitches Brew* (1970) and *On the Corner* (1972). On these recordings Davis increasingly used electric instruments – guitar, keyboards – to create a dense background of sound over which often-sparse lines are projected. Many of the then younger musicians who contributed to some of these recordings – Herbie Hancock, Chick Corea, Wayne Shorter, John McLaughlin, among others – would go on to pursue their own fusions and collaborations.

This blurring of the boundaries between jazz and rock music was timely, coinciding with the increasing expectations and ambitions of rock music and finding a new audience after what was seen by some as the demise of jazz. However, it was also perceived as a threat to the jazz tradition from one of its central protagonists. For critic Stanley Crouch this was 'the fall'. He dismissed *In A Silent Way* as 'no more than droning wallpaper music' and claimed that with *Bitches Brew* 'Davis was firmly on the path of the sellout'.[9] It is this 'version' of Davis that Marsalis, and others, want to exclude, while preserving what Crouch identifies as Miles Davis before what he mistakenly describes as 'rock and roll'.[10]

Standard Time

The Marsalis recordings on which a highly selective view of jazz music is clearly presented are those titled *Standard Time* and which feature a selection of well-known jazz standards played in the small-group format with which we are familiar from bebop on to Davis's own quintet recordings of the 1960s, among many other possible examples. On *Standard Time Vol. 2: Intimacy Calling* (1991) Marsalis begins with 'When it's Sleepytime Down South'. In his discussion of Marsalis, the performance of standards, and concepts of tradition, David Ake provides a highly stimulating critical account of the issues and highlights the intentionally retrospective aspects of this specific recording:

The opening track of *Standard Time*, 'When it's Sleepytime Down South,' shapes much of the stylistic palette to follow. Marsalis's bucket-muted trumpet and concise melodic ideas lend 'Sleepytime' a gentle quality that harkens back to the sounds of the 1930s and early 1940s.[11]

On the basis of Ake's description we can hear this as a performance of a song from the early 1930s realized in a manner that is consistent with that earlier moment. This now begins to suggest some factors that are familiar from earlier stages of this book. Perhaps this now begins to sound like a jazz version of the challenge of the past that was explored in different musical contexts in chapter 4. It may also suggest a performance-based parallel with Rochberg's pastiche version of late Beethoven as featured in chapter 5.

Processes of revisiting and reinventing already known material are inherent within jazz music, and they form a kind of intertextuality within which we may hear traces and reflections of past material in a new light. Ingrid Monson character-izes this as 'intermusicality', which is defined as 'something like intertextuality in sound'.[12] The examples that Monson gives of this 'intermusicality' include John Coltrane's radical reinvention of 'My Favourite Things', which is transferred from Broadway musical into a jazz music that ultimately transcends the forms and contexts of the original song. However, the interaction implicit in both intertextual-ity and intermusicality is arguably absent from Marsalis's rendition of 'When it's Sleepytime Down South'. On this recording, and many others, Marsalis looks to rupture the close relationship between repetition and revision that is inherent within jazz music, focusing on repetition without subjecting what is repeated to significant revision.[13]

Such issues are also highly prevalent on Marsalis's *Standard Time Vol. 1* (1987), on which the rhythm section of piano, bass and drums supports Marsalis's trumpet. This recording begins with a version of Duke Ellington's 'Caravan' and also includes standards such as 'April in Paris', 'Memories of You' and 'Autumn Leaves', among others, all of which are familiar to a jazz audience and played within the consistent framework of a small-group modern jazz. It also includes two different versions of 'Cherokee'. 'Cherokee' was composed by Ray Noble in 1938 and was effectively reinvented by Charlie Parker and Dizzy Gillespie with a new title of 'Koko' in 1945.[14] The Parker version has become a classic example of a mid-1940s bebop style as defined by a remarkably rapid tempo, swift, passing chord changes and an intense level of instrumental virtuosity.

Although on *Standard Time Vol. 1* Marsalis adheres to the Noble original rather than the Parker revision, the performances of it are clearly within the traditions and conventions of jazz that emerge from bebop as defined by its recurring intensity and virtuosity. However, although Marsalis's remarkable ability to reconstruct the performance conventions of an earlier jazz music on both versions of 'Cherokee', and in different ways on the recording as a whole, may pay homage to the jazz tradition, in this process of rather literal reconstructions there is a denial of the experimental essence of that earlier moment. Bebop was, in the words of Bernard Gendron, the music that 'gets credit in the jazz canon for being the first modernist jazz, the first jazz avant-garde, the first jazz form in which art transcends entertainment'.[15] This is an accurate description. Bebop, as initially defined by Parker, projected many images and practices associated with an avant-garde. In becoming an art form that transcends the contexts of entertainment that had enveloped jazz music bebop becomes another blurring of boundaries:

> The historical transition of jazz from an entertainment music to an art music, initiated by the bebop revolution in the mid-1940s, set in motion a fundamental transformation in the way in which the barriers between high and mass culture would henceforth be negotiated.[16]

In terms of the 'fundamental transformation' that Gendron traces it is possible to see this moment of jazz history as at least an anticipation of the blurring, and crossing, of boundaries between 'high' and 'low' that would later become more evident in postmodernism even if the music still carries strong associations with aspects of modernism.[17] On the basis of Gendron's interpretation we can see that this canonical moment in the jazz tradition is one that is still marked by mobility and plurality, moving between the broad contexts of art and entertainment, and, through its dynamic strategies of revision, is resistant to easy containment within a solidified tradition.

In looking nostalgically to the jazz tradition, including bebop, Marsalis indicates a deep knowledge of the music and he is clearly extremely capable as both soloist and leader within the contexts and conventions of that tradition. However, in the attempt to repeat that tradition Marsalis, paradoxically, does not preserve the 'modern' sound of early jazz, bebop or Miles Davis before his fusion with rock music, but rather views that past through a nostalgia that can be positioned within the broad context of postmodernism. In looking to the past Marsalis, like so much of the music discussed in this book, has produced a music that is of its own postmodern time.

Have a Little Faith

Marsalis is not the only jazz musician whose music can be heard in this way, and nostalgic repetition is not the only way in which postmodernism in jazz music may be manifest. While some of the examples given by Shipton tend to look back to the tradition – including Scott Hamilton – there are others that look in different directions. We have already encountered the music of John Zorn and his relationship to jazz, and many of the musicians Zorn has worked with come from a background in jazz music. One notable example is that of guitarist Bill Frisell, who made an important contribution to Zorn's Naked City group. Frisell's own recordings include music from a wide range of sources, not always easily identifiable as jazz. His *Have a Little Faith* (1992) features an eclectic range of American music, including Foster, Sousa, Charles Ives, Copland, Muddy Waters, Bob Dylan, Madonna and John Hiatt.

As Ake's comparison of Frisell's *Have a Little Faith* and Marsalis's *Standard Time* indicates there are some obvious differences, which not only relate to repertoire but also include instrumentation.[18] However, while Frisell's appropriation of Copland and Ives seems beyond jazz, there are some precedents in the form of various jazz/ classical crossovers as defined by the so-called 'third stream'. More recently, pianist Uri Caine's radical reinvention of both Mahler and Mozart provides highly stimulating postmodern realizations of this particular blurring of boundaries. This is most evident in Caine's recording titled *Urlicht/Primal Light* (1997), which is presented as a collaboration between Mahler and Caine and involves various parts of Mahler's oeuvre being reinvented by jazz musicians and others, including a DJ (DJ Olive).[19]

The use of relatively recent popular music by Frisell is another notable point of difference from Marsalis. And yet it could also be heard as an extension of the jazz tradition: is there really any difference between a jazz musician revising recent or current popular music and the reinvention of 'Tin Pan Alley' songs in the 1940s? The use of recent popular music as a source of material has become more evident through pianist Brad Mehldau's revisions of Radiohead songs, while The Bad Plus (a jazz piano trio with the name of a rock group) have made the reinvention of popular music into a defining feature of their music. For example, The Bad Plus CD titled *Prog* (2007) includes a version of David Bowie's 'Life on Mars' (1973) along with other material, including original compositions.

If, on the specific example of *Have a Little Faith*, Frisell has extended many of the boundaries of jazz music this is a recurring aspect of his music. For example, a CD titled *Nashville* (1997) is based on the sounds of American country and western music, which has become a central preoccupation of Frisell. But, for all the eclecticism of Frisell's sources and references, and its distance from a now notional jazz tradition, this is a music that is still generally received as jazz as shaped by the marketing and reception of recordings, and the venues within which his performances often occur.[20]

DJ Spooky

Among the examples that Shipton gives of postmodern jazz is that of alto saxophonist Greg Osby who, along with Steve Coleman, was 'one of a generation of players ... who came out of the urban M-Base movement, an exciting aggregation of musicians who explored rap, hip-hop, and other urban grooves in their playing'.[21] This loose collection of then young jazz players who emerged in the 1980s, grouped around the term 'M-Base' explored the potential of yet another fusion of jazz and another music, in this case as shaped by the rhythmic energies of hip hop.

Hip hop came into view in the late 1970s as, in the words of David Toop, a 'collective term for black American urban art forms' and is applied 'specifically to a style of music that uses spoken rhyme (rap) over a rhythmic background mainly characterized by the manipulation of pre-existing recordings'.[22] For Russell Potter hip hop becomes 'one form of radical postmodernism',[23] and postmodernism is the natural location for a music and cultural practice that through its 'manipulation of pre-existing recordings' is inherently intertextual. The past, defined as 'pre-existing recordings', is now available to be selected, sampled and resituated, and the result is often fragmentary. The rhythmic energy of hip hop, in conjunction with its fragmentary surfaces, would be an obvious attraction for some jazz musicians, including those mentioned by Shipton in relation to M-Base. However, the remainder of this discussion will focus on the activities of DJ Spooky, in particular his collaborations with jazz musicians and jazz-related projects.

DJ Spooky, in the style of all hip-hop DJs, is an obviously assumed name and image, which is already a reflection of this highly constructed culture, his real name being Paul D. Miller (b.1970). DJ Spooky also comes with the subtitle of That Subliminal Kid. He describes himself as 'composer, multimedia artist and writer',[24] a description that already goes beyond hip hop into a wide range of activities. However, while the sampling and recycling of hip hop inform all these diverse activities, DJ Spooky is distanced from the street culture of hip hop through, for example, the presence of his multimedia art in major art galleries and exhibitions. This could suggest that his role might be that of a late version of Andy Warhol, blurring boundaries between art and everyday life through an aesthetic of recycling. He has also produced written texts that go some way to defining and contextualizing his many activities, often in ways that indicate an understanding of wider cultural and theoretical discourses.[25] He is also a creative individual who is drawn to the potential of collaboration with musicians from different backgrounds, including jazz. One of the most notable of DJ Spooky's encounters with jazz comes on a CD titled *Re-Bop*.

Re-Bop

Released in 2006, *Re-Bop: The Savoy Remixes* is a CD that features reinterpretations of classic bebop recordings by various hip-hop DJs and others involved in the remixing of music. Among the music that is remixed on the CD are recordings by the Modern Jazz Quartet, Duke Jordan, Curtis Fuller, Dizzy Gillespie, Charlie Parker and Miles Davis, all of whom belong to the jazz tradition that Wynton Marsalis seeks to preserve through its repetition while turning it into an object of nostalgic desire. DJ Spooky is one of the individuals who contributed to this CD. The original recording that he remixes is Charlie Parker's 'Koko' (1945), which has already been mentioned as a classic recording that radically revises an earlier song, 'Cherokee', which Marsalis repeats.

DJ Spooky's remixing of Parker's 'Koko' is featured as a starting point for Jesse Stewart's discussion of 'DJ Spooky and the Politics of Afro-Postmodernism'. Stewart summarizes Parker's transformation of Noble's original and also the remix:

> Recorded in November 1945, Parker's 'KoKo' is based on the chord changes of 'Cherokee,' a jazz standard written by Ray Noble in 1938 and made famous by Charlie Barnet's 1939 hit recording of the tune. 'KoKo' can be thought of as an abstracted version of 'Cherokee' in which the sixty-four bar harmonic form of the original is transformed through chord augmentations and an intricate melody played by Parker and trumpeter Dizzy Gillespie at an extremely fast tempo. With 'DJ Spooky's Ali Baba & 50 thieves mix' of 'KoKo,' Miller continues the process of sonic abstraction, combining looped fragments of Parker's recording with hip-hop inspired drum beats and sampled voiceovers from various sources.[26]

Stewart's description of 'Koko' reminds us of the transformational revisions of Parker's original recording. This is now subject to another level of revision through the extensive recycling of selected fragments of that recording as source material. It begins with an introductory voice (the radio DJ), then the opening moment of 'Koko' is heard but it does not seem to move; it is as if the needle is stuck, a familiar hip-hop gesture. When we do move forward in the track the rhythmic energy and direction of the original is deliberately subverted. We now hear fragmentary traces of Parker, which always seem to stop just as they have appeared to begin, against the background of a very different rhythmic shape, but it is one that is very familiar from the context of hip hop. This is a highly radical revision of the original recording that removes any real sense of how the original material might have sounded. It extends the limits of a recognizable process of revision, even in comparison to some of the other remixes on the CD, which often leave in place a more substantial repetition of the chosen original, such as, for example, the remix of the Modern Jazz Quartet's 'Movin' Nicely' with which the CD begins.

As well as engaging with jazz in the form of the remixing of a classic jazz recording, DJ Spooky has also collaborated directly with jazz musicians, most notably pianist Matthew Shipp on a recording titled *Optometry* (2002). On this recording we hear Shipp and the other musicians – William Parker (bass), Joe McPhee (tenor saxophone) and Guillermo E. Brown (drums) – play jazz music against a background of sounds generated by DJ Spooky. Shipp has been involved in other interesting collaborations, including a recording titled *Blink of an Eye* (2010), which involves

Scanner (Robin Rimbaud), who describes himself as 'traversing the experimental terrain between sound, space, image and form',[27] providing a sonic background for the jazz musicians. On this recording the group is defined as The Post Modern Jazz Quartet, which is obviously a knowing, ironic reference to the Modern Jazz Quartet, a definitive jazz presence from the 1950s.

In the collaboration between Shipp and DJ Spooky we hear the changing nature of jazz, another fusion – between jazz and hip hop – that may ask us to recollect previous points of contact and collaboration between different music and musicians. It is also a set of sounds that provokes questions about the stability and solidity of jazz as a tradition. In doing so it projects a meaningful, critical distance from the construction of a tradition that Marsalis, and others, seeks to repeat. Both DJ Spooky ('Koko') and Marsalis ('Cherokee') look to the same source but draw very different conclusions. And yet both are also contained within postmodernism, DJ Spooky arguably as an articulation of a 'postmodernism of resistance' that radically trans-forms our understanding of music, while Marsalis becomes part of 'a postmodern-ism of reaction' that seeks to conserve a tradition, an often problematic opposition that has been discussed in relation to various musical contexts at earlier stages of this book.[28]

It is fitting that it is with DJ Spooky that the many examples of postmodern music in this book draw towards an end. This does not suggest that his work is conclusive in any sense, but the issues that it generates – of race and identity as discussed by Stewart, its encounter with music of the past through the radical revision of the remixing of a seminal bebop recording and its transformation into a series of its fragmentary, disruptive surfaces – combine to present this as a, if not definitive, then certainly highly charged, realization of postmodernism in music. When placed alongside the many other different musical practices discussed in this chapter and again in relation to the earlier stages of this book it now further accentuates plurality, difference and fragmentation within a cultural context that positively celebrates such qualities.

Postscript

This book has posed questions of what postmodernism is and when it happened, presenting surveys of a carefully chosen selection of music that, it has been argued, can all in different ways be heard as examples of postmodernism in music. This brief postscript is not intended to impose a definitive conclusion to this process, which we must, I think, now accept is both unfeasible and undesirable; rather, its purpose is to suggest some ways in which the discussion may continue beyond the immediate confines of this book.

Throughout this book difference, plurality and fragmentation have been highlighted as key characteristics of postmodernism and we have considered many different musical examples that in different ways reflect these characteristics. The theoretical perspectives that have been outlined and then revisited at various stages also have a pattern of difference: Jameson's 'attempt to think the present historically', Eco's 'challenge of the past', Hutcheon's 'historiographic metafiction' and Harvey's 'new dominant ways in which we experience space and time', for example, all emerge from individual responses to, and accounts of, postmodernism and sustain their own unique positions. However, when transferred into the context of this book they can all be read as saying something really quite similar about how postmodernism, after modernism, makes meaningful, if at times fictional, engagements with the past. This underlying similarity may begin to suggest that, rather than being incredulous towards metanarratives, as Lyotard asserts, we have now begun to witness the construction of postmodernism's own metanarrative: the repeated storytelling of how postmodernism plays with fragments of the past, how different music may be intertextual in different ways but the actual process remains similar, if not the same. In effect this book has at times said some similar things about some very different sounding music.

The desire to read underlying similarities as potentially new metanarratives leads to a reconsideration of the repetition of Lyotard's incredulity. We may at some point have become incredulous towards the metanarratives of modernism in the way that Lyotard suggests, but the more texts that we read about postmodernism the more we encounter basically the same argument. We are now perhaps engaged in telling a big story about the many little stories in postmodernism. Of course, this underlying repetition does not displace the plurality, fragmentation and differences of postmodernism, but it does begin to reinforce the suggestion that, as already stated in chapter 1, postmodernism not only engages with history but has itself already become subject to its own historicizing tendencies and pressures. Jameson may still think of the 'postmodern present' but, while postmodernism may remain an effective way of defining the very recent remixing done by DJ Spooky for example, and it obviously retains some current currency as a critical term, we have moved beyond the point at which any automatically assumed correlation between postmodernism and the contemporary is unproblematic. If the idea of postmodernism has been around for some time, and the world has changed greatly since the most influential accounts of it first appeared, then perhaps we are already beginning to think of the possibility of what might happen, or already is happening, after postmodernism?

There have now already been several attempts to discuss culture after postmodernism. For example, between February and April 2009 Tate Britain, a major art museum in London, hosted an exhibition titled Altermodern. Forming part of the Tate Triennial series, this exhibition featured recent work by contemporary artists from around the world. The diversity of this work, and the many geographical locations from which it emerged, might suggest that this event formed yet another postmodern encounter, one that played with some underlying consistencies against the background of a multicultural, global perspective. But the title of the exhibition was clearly proposed as an alternative to postmodernism that intentionally, and highly self-consciously, projected a going beyond postmodernism. According to Nicolas Bourriaud, the curator of the exhibition and author of the catalogue, the term 'altermodern' serves to 'delimit the void beyond the postmodern'.[1] This statement suggests a certain absence after the debates about postmodernism, and the culture to which they referred, have been exhausted. Bourriaud's new term is intended to fill this void.

In the publicity material for the exhibition it was stated that altermodern describes 'how artists are responding to a new globalised perception. They traverse a cultural landscape saturated with signs and create new pathways between multiple formats of expression and communication.'[2] It is notable that globalization is evoked as the justification for the proposed new term, which, for many, including Jameson, intersects with postmodernism,[3] but it is now seen as beginning to signify the closure of postmodernism. Altermodern claims that the period defined as postmodernism has come to an end and that a new culture for the twenty-first century is emerging.

However, much of what Bourriaud writes in order to justify this new terminology could easily be applied to postmodernism, not just in relation to globalization, and the attempt to predict the future is not the task of critical, cultural and musicological thought. Indeed, it seems somewhat preposterous to be trying to define new terminology and proclaiming a new culture for the rest of the century at this point in time. How, or when, we begin to theorize culture, and hear music, after postmodernism, and how that might be both conceptualized and represented, may well require, rather than such easy proclamations, new theories and concepts that subject postmodernism to the kind of critical response that was once projected against modernism.

Notes

Preface

1. Leon Botstein, 'Modernism', in *The New Grove Dictionary of Music and Musicians*, 2nd edn, ed. Stanley Sadie and John Tyrrell (London: Macmillan, 2001), Vol. 16, 868–75.
2. David Harvey, *The Condition of Postmodernity: An Enquiry into the Origins of Cultural Change* (Oxford: Blackwell, 1989), chapter 2: modernism and modernity.
3. Arnold Whittall, *Exploring Twentieth-Century Music: Tradition and Innovation* (Cambridge University Press, 2003).
4. Jann Pasler, 'Postmodernism', in *The New Grove Dictionary of Music and Musicians*, 2nd edn, ed. Stanley Sadie and John Tyrrell (London: Macmillan, 2001), Vol. 20, 213–16.
5. Derek Scott, 'Postmodernism and Music', in *The Routledge Companion to Postmodernism*, ed. Stuart Sim (London and New York: Routledge, 2009), 122–32.
6. David Bennett, *Sounding Postmodernism: Sampling Australian Composers, Sound Artists and Music Critics* (Sydney: Australian Music Centre, 2008).
7. Andrew Edgar and Peter Sedgwick (eds.), *Cultural Theory: The Key Concepts*, 2nd edn (London and New York: Routledge, 2008).
8. David Beard and Kenneth Gloag, *Musicology: The Key Concepts* (London and New York: Routledge, 2005). A new edition of this book is currently in preparation, and publication is expected in 2013.

1: Introducing postmodernism

1. *Captain America: The First Avenger*, dir. Joe Johnston, reviewed by Peter Bradshaw, *The Guardian*, 29 July 2011.
2. Hari Kunzru, *Gods Without Men* (London: Hamish Hamilton, 2011), reviewed by Theo Tait, *The Guardian*, 30 July 2011.
3. Not all the literature on postmodernism takes a positive view. For various critical responses to postmodernism see, for example, Christopher Norris, *What's Wrong With Postmodernism: Critical Theory and the Ends of Philosophy* (Hemel Hempstead: Harvester Wheatsheaf, 1990).

4. Hans Bertens, *The Idea of the Postmodern: A History* (London and New York: Routledge, 1995), 3. Although there have been some attempts made to distinguish between postmodernism as an aesthetic idea and postmodernity as a historical period, for the purposes of this discussion they will be interpreted as interchangeable terms.

5. Linda Hutcheon, *A Poetics of Postmodernism: History, Theory, Fiction* (London and New York: Routledge, 1988), 3.

6. Linda Hutcheon, *The Politics of Postmodernism* (London and New York: Routledge, 1989), 1.

7. *Ibid.*

8. Jean-François Lyotard, *The Postmodern Condition: A Report on Knowledge*, trans. Geoff Bennington and Brian Massumi (Manchester University Press, 1989 [1979]).

9. Stuart Sim, 'Postmodernism and Philosophy', in *The Routledge Companion to Postmodernism*, ed. Stuart Sim (London and New York: Routledge, 2009), 7.

10. Lyotard, *The Postmodern Condition*, xxiii.

11. *Ibid.*, xxiv.

12. *Ibid.*, 60.

13. *Ibid.*

14. Jean Baudrillard, *Fatal Strategies*, trans. Philip Beitchman and W. G. J. Niesluchowski (London: Pluto Press, 1999 [1983]), 24. For a good summary of Baudrillard's career and work see Douglas Kellner, 'Introduction: Jean Baudrillard in the Fin-de-Millennium', in *Baudrillard: A Critical Reader*, ed. Douglas Kellner (Oxford: Blackwell, 1994), 1–23.

15. Victor Burgin, *The End of Art Theory: Criticism and Postmodernity* (London: Palgrave Macmillan, 1986), 163–4.

16. Linda Hutcheon, *The Politics of Postmodernism*, 2nd edn (London and New York: Routledge, 2002), 165.

17. Bertens, *The Idea of the Postmodern*, 20.

18. Fredric Jameson, *Postmodernism, or, the Cultural Logic of Late Capitalism* (London and New York: Verso, 1991).

19. *Ibid.*, ix.

20. *Ibid.*, 1.

21. David Harvey, *The Condition of Postmodernity: An Enquiry into the Origins of Cultural Change* (Oxford: Blackwell, 1989), vii.

22. *Ibid.*

23. *Ibid.*, 38.

24. Bertens, *The Idea of the Postmodern*, 3.

25. Paul Hoover, 'Introduction', in *Postmodern American Poetry: A Norton Anthology*, ed. Paul Hoover (New York and London: Norton, 1994), xxv.

26. David Brackett, '"Where's It At?": Postmodern Theory and the Contemporary Musical Field', in *Postmodern Music/Postmodern Thought*, ed. Judy Lochead and Joseph Auner (London and New York: Routledge, 2002), 208. Lyotard also argues against viewing modernism and postmodernism as historical constructs: 'neither

modernity nor so-called postmodernity can be identified and defined as clearly circumscribed historical entities, of which the latter would always come "after" the former' (Jean-François Lyotard, *The Inhuman: Reflections on Time*, trans. Geoffrey Bennington and Rachel Bowlby (Cambridge: Polity Press, 1991), 25).

27. Jameson, *Postmodernism*, 4.
28. Fredric Jameson, *Valences of the Dialectic* (London and New York: Verso, 2009), 165. Other literature provides alternative suggestions and proposed chronologies for postmodernism. See, for example, Andreas Huyssen, *After the Great Divide: Modernism, Mass Culture and Postmodernism* (London: Macmillan, 1988), 188; Steven Connor, 'Introduction', in *The Cambridge Companion to Postmodernism*, ed. Steven Connor (Cambridge University Press, 2004), 1. Judy Lochead has provided an interesting attempt to relate Connor's periodization to music and musicology; see Lochead, 'Naming: Music and the Postmodern', *New Formations* 66 (2009), 158–72.
29. Jameson, *Postmodernism*, 45–6. Jameson makes extended references to 'late capitalism' that suggest that the economic structure of a global, capital-based economy is in its late (end) stage of development as part of a wider historical periodization. However, although these issues are central in much of Jameson's work they must remain beyond the scope of this introduction. For readers who wish to pursue this issue further Ian Buchanan provides a good general survey of Jameson's work (see Ian Buchanan, *Fredric Jameson: Live Theory* (London and New York: Continuum, 2006).
30. Clearly a great deal of music that can be identified with modernism continues to be produced, with David Metzer's account of late modernist music being highly relevant (David Metzer, *Musical Modernism at the Turn of the Twenty-First Century* (Cambridge University Press, 2009)). But the presence of such music, it can be argued, only intensifies the plurality and diversity of the cultural spectrum: modernist music as a stylistic option in a postmodern context.
31. Jameson, *Postmodernism*, 1–2. I have revisited this extended quotation in a number of related publications. This process of revisiting reflects the significance I think this passage has for an understanding of postmodernism. I have commented elsewhere on what I see as the problematic nature of Jameson's characterization of the Beatles in this way and suggested alternative interpretations that position their music directly in relation to postmodernism. See my 'All You Need is Theory', *Music & Letters* 79/4 (1998), 582, and 'Situating the 1960s: Popular Music – Postmodernism – History', *Rethinking History* 5/3 (2001), 406.
32. See T. J. Clark, *Farewell to an Idea: Episodes from a History of Modernism* (New Haven, CT, and London: Yale University Press, 1999).
33. Ihab Hassan, *The Postmodern Turn: Essays in Postmodern Theory and Culture* (Columbus: Ohio State University Press, 1987), 91. Hassan's list has received extended commentary in other literature on postmodernism; see, for example, Harvey, *The Condition of Postmodernity*, 42–4.

2: Postmodern musicology – postmodern music

1. Steven Connor, 'Introduction', in *The Cambridge Companion to Postmodernism*, ed. Steven Connor (Cambridge University Press, 2004), 17. For a wider example of Connor's significant contribution to the postmodern debate see his *Postmodernist Culture: An Introduction to Theories of the Contemporary* (Oxford: Blackwell, 1989).

2. Musicology can broadly be defined as the study of music as an academic discipline. For useful surveys see Joseph Kerman, *Musicology* (published as *Contemplating Music* in the USA) (London: Fontana, 1985); Alastair Williams, *Constructing Musicology* (Aldershot: Ashgate, 2001); David Beard and Kenneth Gloag, *Musicology: The Key Concepts* (London and New York: Routledge, 2005); and Giles Hooper, *The Discourse of Musicology* (Aldershot: Ashgate, 2006).

3. Kerman, *Musicology*, 16.

4. Connor, 'Introduction', 17.

5. Kerman, *Musicology*, 17.

6. For useful, concise descriptions of each of these concepts see the relevant entries in Andrew Edgar and Peter Sedgwick, *Cultural Theory: The Key Concepts*, 2nd edn (New York and London: Routledge, 2008).

7. Nicholas Cook and Mark Everist, 'Preface', in *Rethinking Music*, ed. Nicholas Cook and Mark Everist (Oxford and New York: Oxford University Press, 1999), viii. See also Beard and Gloag, *Musicology*, xiii–xiv for further discussion of the impact of Kerman, and also Cook and Everist's description of the helpful 'myth'.

8. Beard and Gloag, *Musicology*, 122.

9. Lawrence Kramer, *Interpreting Music* (Berkeley, Los Angeles and London: University of California Press, 2011), 64. I think it is now generally recognized that the concerns of the new musicology have largely become part of a mainstream of musicological practice. Kramer himself states that 'the conceptual transformation that overtook musical scholarship during the 1990s had become more or less normative by the time the decade ended' and proposes 'critical musicology', which is a term that had been in use in Britain for some time, as a more effective description (Kramer, *Interpreting Music*, 63–4; see also Beard and Gloag, *Musicology*, 124 and 38–9).

10. For a highly imaginative and representative example of Leppert's work see his *The Sight of Sound: Music, Representation, and the History of the Body* (Berkeley, Los Angeles and London: University of California Press, 1993).

11. Lawrence Kramer, *Classical Music and Postmodern Knowledge* (Berkeley, Los Angeles and London: University of California Press, 1995), 5. For an interesting overview of this chapter, including its publishing history, see Williams, *Constructing Musicology*, 121.

12. Kramer, *Classical Music*, 5.

13. This suggestion is also made by Kramer, see *Classical Music*, 174.

14. The focus on earlier music, often from the nineteenth century, is often evident in many of Kramer's other books, while his *Musical Meaning: Toward a Critical History*

(Berkeley, Los Angeles and London: University of California Press, 2002) moves from discussions of Beethoven, Liszt and Schumann to Shostakovich and John Coltrane.

15. In this context I use 'postmodern theory' as a generalization that embraces the existing body of theoretical work on postmodernism, or that may utilize strategies consistent with postmodernism. I recognize that this generalization is problematic as it suggests some sense of homogeneity among texts that may negate difference.

16. See, for example, Susan McClary, *Modal Subjectivities: Self-Fashioning in the Italian Madrigal* (Berkeley, Los Angeles and London: University of California Press, 2004).

17. Susan McClary, *Feminine Endings: Music, Gender, and Sexuality* (Minneapolis and Oxford: University of Minnesota Press, 1991).

18. Judy Lochead, 'Naming: Music and the Postmodern', *New Formations* 66 (2009), 167.

19. Susan McClary, *Conventional Wisdom: The Content of Musical Form* (Berkeley, Los Angeles and London: University of California Press, 2000), 168.

20. Connor, 'Introduction', 17.

21. See Linda Hutcheon, *A Poetics of Postmodernism: History, Theory, Fiction* (London and New York: Routledge, 1988); and Brian McHale, *Constructing Postmodernism* (London and New York: Routledge, 1992).

22. See, for example, Jean-François Lyotard, 'Music and Postmodernity', trans. David Bennett, *New Formations* 66 (2009), 37–45.

23. Linda Hutcheon, *The Politics of Postmodernism* (London and New York: Routledge, 1989), 9.

24. McClary, *Conventional Wisdom*, 168.

25. Connor, 'Introduction', 17.

26. Judy Lochead and Joseph Auner, eds., *Postmodern Music/Postmodern Thought* (London and New York: Routledge, 2002).

27. Connor, 'Introduction', 17.

28. *Ibid.*

29. *Ibid.*

30. Fredric Jameson, *Postmodernism, or, the Cultural Logic of Late Capitalism* (London and New York: Verso, 1991), 1.

31. See also Jonathan D. Kramer, 'Beyond Unity: Toward an Understanding of Musical Postmodernism', in *Concert Music, Rock, and Jazz since 1945: Essays and Analytical Studies*, ed. Elizabeth West Marvin and Richard Hermann (University of Rochester Press, 1995), 11–33.

32. Jonathan D. Kramer, 'The Nature and Origins of Musical Postmodernism', in *Postmodern Music/Postmodern Thought*, ed. Judy Lochead and Joseph Auner (London and New York: Routledge, 2002), 16.

33. *Ibid.*

34. For a highly informative account of neoclassicism in music see Scott Messing, *Neoclassicism in Music: From the Genesis of the Concept through the Schoenberg/Stravinsky Polemic* (University of Rochester Press, 1996).

35. Jameson, *Postmodernism*, 17. Georgina Born goes as far as suggesting that neoclassicism might 'almost be considered "proto" postmodern'. The other possible musical

'proto' postmodernism within modernism is, for Born, supplied by 'a self-conscious appropriation of popular musics, both urban and folk-based, as in the work of early modernists Debussy, Satie, and Ives'. Reference to jazz music in the works of Poulenc, Milhaud and Copland, among others, is also highlighted in this context (Georgina Born, *Rationalizing Culture: IRCAM, Boulez, and the Institutionalization of the Musical Avant-Garde* (Berkeley, Los Angeles and London: University of California Press, 1995), 49). Lyotard, rather than relying exclusively on the distinction between meta- and micronarratives, argues elsewhere for a circular relationship between modernism and postmodernism that can be described as a rewriting of modernism and a close, intimate connection between the two: 'Modernity is constitutionally and ceaselessly pregnant with its postmodernity' (Jean-François Lyotard, *The Inhuman: Reflections on Time*, trans. Geoffrey Bennington and Rachel Bowlby (Cambridge: Polity Press, 1991), 25). This statement captures the fluctuating interrelationship between modernism and postmodernism. However, much of the experience of culture in the period in which Lyotard worked would seem to place natural limitations on the prevalence of such examples. It is difficult to hear the music discussed in this book as always being born out of modernism as part of a recursive pattern.

36. Kramer, 'Nature and Origins', 16.
37. Relevant works by Stravinsky in this context include *Ragtime* (1917–18), *Piano Rag Music* (1919), *Tango* (1940) and *Ebony Concerto* (1945).
38. Jameson, *Postmodernism*, 1.
39. Ihab Hassan, *The Postmodern Turn: Essays in Postmodern Theory and Culture* (Columbus: Ohio State University Press, 1987), 91–2.
40. Hutcheon, *The Politics of Postmodernism*, 1.
41. Irony features extensively in both Hutcheon's *The Politics of Postmodernism* and *The Poetics of Postmodernism* and she has devoted a book to it, although not necessarily in relation to postmodernism, titled *Irony's Edge: The Theory and Politics of Irony* (London and New York: Routledge, 1994).
42. Kramer, *Classical Music*, 227. For an outline of the mythology that has evolved around the death of Presley, see Greil Marcus, *Dead Elvis: A Chronicle of a Cultural Obsession* (London and New York: Viking, 1991).
43. For another perspective on Daugherty's *Dead Elvis* as postmodernism see Judy Lochead, 'Naming: Music and the Postmodern', 167.
44. Michael Daugherty, liner notes to *Dead Elvis* (ARGO, 458 145-2, 1998). The instrumentation consists of percussion, trumpet, trombone, clarinet, violin, double bass and bassoon (soloist).
45. *Ibid.*
46. *Ibid.*
47. David Harvey, *The Condition of Postmodernity: An Enquiry into the Origins of Cultural Change* (Oxford: Blackwell, 1989), 38.
48. See Jameson, *Postmodernism*, 1.
49. Julia Kristeva, 'Word, Dialogue and Novel', in *The Kristeva Reader*, ed. Toril Moi (Oxford: Blackwell, 1986), 34–61. For an effective introductory survey of

intertextuality within the context of literary theory see Graham Allen, *Intertextuality* (London and New York: Routledge, 2000).

50. Roland Barthes, *Image – Music – Text* (London: Fontana, 1977), 146.

51. *Ibid.*, 148.

3: From anti-modernism to postmodern nostalgia

1. David Harvey, *The Condition of Postmodernity: An Enquiry into the Origins of Cultural Change* (Oxford: Blackwell, 1989), 38.

2. Christopher Butler, *After the Wake: An Essay on the Contemporary Avant-Garde* (Oxford and New York: Oxford University Press, 1980). Any criticism of this book on the basis of what it might understand as postmodernism needs to be qualified on the basis of the obvious point that it was published in 1980, at a time when post-modernism may have been a term in use but before the full impact and development of the theoretical discourse around it.

3. *Ibid.*, 7.

4. *Ibid.* The reference to the 'critical work of René Leibowitz' is implicitly based on Leibowitz's book *Schoenberg and his School: The Contemporary Stage of the Language of Music*, trans. Dika Newlin (New York: Da Capo Press, 1970 [1949]).

5. For an outline of serialism in its various applications see Arnold Whittall, *Serialism* (Cambridge University Press, 2008).

6. David W. Bernstein, 'Cage and High Modernism', in *The Cambridge Companion to John Cage*, ed. David Nicholls (Cambridge University Press, 2002), 210.

7. *Ibid.*

8. Harvey, *The Condition of Postmodernity*, 39. Andreas Huyssen also discusses Jencks's highlighting of the potential significance of this demolition. See his *After the Great Divide: Modernism, Mass Culture and Postmodernism* (London: Macmillan, 1988), 186–7.

9. Georgina Born, *Rationalizing Culture: IRCAM, Boulez, and the Institutionalization of the Musical Avant-Garde* (Berkeley, Los Angeles and London: University of California Press, 1995), 56.

10. For a summary of the interaction between Cage and Boulez, see Bernstein, 'Cage and High Modernism', 210–13.

11. Paul Griffiths, *Modern Music and After: Directions since 1945* (Oxford and New York: Oxford Univerity Press, 1995), 264.

12. Alastair Williams, 'Cage and Postmodernism', in *The Cambridge Companion to John Cage*, ed. David Nicholls (Cambridge University Press, 2002), 228.

13. Although Nyman in his seminal account of experimental music uses this particular description of 'the first postmodernist', when it is placed in context Nyman is clearly not sympathetic to this understanding of Cage or postmodernism in general: 'Fortunately, the term postmodernism was not in vogue in 1972 and is entirely absent from this book, even though it could be, has been, argued that Cage is the first postmodernist – even though he remained an arch-modernist to the end of his

days.' Michael Nyman, *Experimental Music: Cage and Beyond*, 2nd edn (Cambridge University Press, 1999), xvi.

14. Charles Hamm, 'Privileging the Moment: Cage, Jung, Synchronicity, Postmodernism', *The Journal of Musicology* 15/2 (1997), 279.

15. For an interesting discussion of Cage's engagement with non-Western cultures, see John Corbett, 'Experimental Oriental: New Music and Other Others', in *Western Music and its Others: Difference, Representation, and Appropriation in Music*, ed. Georgina Born and David Hesmondhalgh (Berkeley, Los Angeles and London: University of California Press, 2000), 163–86.

16. Hans Bertens, *The Idea of the Postmodern: A History* (London and New York: Routledge, 1995), 20.

17. *Ibid.*, 20–1.

18. Harvey, *The Condition of Postmodernity*, 57. Harvey makes this claim through reference to a work by Rauschenberg titled *Persimmon* (1964), which uses a collage effect of many themes including a quite direct reproduction of a canonical painting by Rubens.

19. The prepared piano involves the insertion of various objects into the piano mechanism in order to alter the sound that is produced. Cage first used this in the late 1930s as a substitute for a percussion ensemble.

20. For more detailed discussion of this process see James Pritchett, 'John Cage', in *The New Grove Dictionary of Music and Musicians*, 2nd edn, ed. Stanley Sadie and John Tyrrell (London: Macmillan, 2001), Vol. 4, 797–8.

21. Richard Middleton, *Studying Popular Music* (Milton Keynes: Open University Press, 1990), 14.

22. The close proximity of these different musics is highlighted by David Clarke in his article 'Elvis and Darsmtadt, or: Twentieth Century Music and the Politics of Cultural Pluralism', *twentieth-century music* 4/1 (2007), 3–70.

23. In this context I am using the terminology of culture industry to encapsulate the economic frameworks and structures that contain, and appropriate, music and other forms of culture. In critical and cultural theory, following the work of Adorno, culture industry may be used more specifically and subject to greater theoretical understanding. For an insightful engagement with Adorno's understanding of music, including the culture industry, see Max Paddison, *Adorno, Modernism and Mass Culture: Essays on Critical Theory and Music* (London: Kahn & Averill, 1996).

24. See Born, *Rationalizing Culture* for an in-depth discussion of a specific, although later, example of this process.

25. David Brackett, '"Where's it At?": Postmodern Theory and the Contemporary Musical Field', in *Postmodern Music/Postmodern Thought*, ed. Judy Lochead and Joseph Auner (London and New York: Routledge, 2002), 217.

26. *Ibid.* Max Paddison, from a very different direction, proposes something similar through what he defines as a 'radical popular music' that has taken on a 'critical character'. Paddison mentions Frank Zappa, The Velvet Underground, John Cale,

Carla Bley, Henry Cow and the Art Bears in this context. See Paddison, *Adorno, Modernism and Mass Culture*, 100–1.

27. Fredric Jameson, *Postmodernism, or, the Cultural Logic of Late Capitalism* (London and New York: Verso, 1991), 1.

28. No discographical information is provided for the passing references to individual recordings at this specific stage of the discussion. All are readily available on greatest-hits CDs of the relevant artist and included on numerous compilations of music of the period.

29. Bruce Tucker, '"Tell Tchaikovsky the News": Postmodernism, Popular Culture, and the Emergence of Rock 'n' Roll', *Black Music Research Journal* 9/2 (1989), 278.

30. This section of the chapter is based on an unpublished paper titled 'I Remember When Rock was Young' presented at the Royal Musical Association, Music Historiography Conference, Cardiff University, September 2003 and the Symposium of the International Musicological Society, Monash University, Melbourne, July 2004.

31. Harvey, *The Condition of Postmodernity*, 38.

32. *Ibid.*, vii.

33. Such examples include hit singles in the UK charts by Roy Wood's Wizzard such as 'Ball Park Incident 'and 'See My Baby Jive', both in 1972.

34. Both recordings consist entirely of cover versions of generally well-known songs that reflect personal preferences and history of the artists.

35. Paul Longhurst, *Popular Music and Society* (Cambridge: Polity Press, 1995), 107.

36. For discussion of canon formation in popular music see Carys Wyn Jones, *The Rock Canon: Canonical Values in the Reception of Rock Albums* (Aldershot: Ashgate, 2008). Jones discusses the Beatles as the 'centre' of a canon of rock music (60–2).

37. Charlie Gillett, *The Sound of the City* (London: Souvenir Press, 1983 [1970]).

38. *Ibid.*, 411.

39. Jameson, *Postmodernism*, 19.

40. See Colin MacCabe, 'Theory and Film: Principles of Realism and Pleasure', *Screen* 17/3 (1976), 7–27; David R. Shumway, 'Rock 'n' Roll Soundtracks and the Production of Nostalgia', *Cinema Journal* 38/2 (1999), 36–51; Jeff Smith, 'Popular Songs and Comic Allusion in Contemporary Cinema', in *Soundtrack Available: Essays on Film and Popular Music*, ed. Pamela Robertson Wojcik and Arthur Knight (Durham, NC, and London: Duke University Press, 2001), 407–30.

41. The use of the Haley recording as the initial sounds of *American Graffiti* may suggest another intertextual reference, to the film *Blackboard Jungle*, in which it plays a similar role. *Blackboard Jungle* was highly successful in 1955, even if it is jazz music that is seen to symbolize the conflict between different generations. For a useful discussion of this film see Gillett, *The Sound of the City*, 14–16.

42. This retrospection is continued at the end of the film when, outside of the film's narrative structure, we are given information about what would become of some of the main characters after this point. For one character, his fate is never to leave the town, despite what we believe is about to happen in the film, an outcome that is clearly an ironic reference to Frank Capra's *It's a Wonderful Life* (1946), while one central

character will sit out the Vietnam War in Canadian exile and another is posted missing in that conflict.

43. Stephen Paul Miller, *The Seventies Now: Culture as Surveillance* (Durham, NC, and London: Duke University Press, 1999), 86–7.

44. Jameson, *Postmodernism*, 19.

4: The challenge of the past

1. Umberto Eco, *Postscript to the Name of the Rose*, trans. William Weaver (San Diego, New York and London: Harcourt Brace Jovanovich, 1984 [1983]), 67–8.

2. Umberto Eco, *The Name of the Rose*, trans. William Weaver (New York and London: Harcourt Brace Jovanovich, 1983 [1980]).

3. Brian McHale, *Constructing Postmodernism* (London and New York: Routledge, 1992), 147. This quotation from McHale comes in a chapter titled 'The (Post)-Modernism of *The Name of the Rose*', which provides a useful survey of Eco's work in this context. It is also worth noting Eco's own scepticism about some usages of postmodernism. He complains that 'I have the impression that it [postmodernism] is applied today to anything the user of the term happens to like' (Eco, *Postscript to the Name of the Rose*, 65).

4. Jean-François Lyotard, *The Postmodern Condition: A Report on Knowledge*, trans. Geoff Bennington and Brian Massumi (Manchester University Press, 1989 [1979]), xxiv.

5. Fredric Jameson, *Postmodernism, or, the Cultural Logic of Late Capitalism* (London and New York: Verso, 1991), ix.

6. David Harvey, *The Condition of Postmodernity: An Enquiry into the Origins of Cultural Change* (Oxford: Blackwell, 1989), vii.

7. *Ibid.*, 38.

8. For further discussion of Berio's relationship to serialism at this time see David Osmond-Smith, *Berio* (Oxford and New York: Oxford University Press, 1991), 16–19; and Arnold Whittall, *Music Since the First World War* (London: Dent, 1988), 247–50.

9. The description of the Mahler scherzo as the 'core text' comes from David Osmond-Smith, 'Luciano Berio', in *New Grove Dictionary of Music and Musicians*, 2nd edn, ed. Stanley Sadie and John Tyrrell (London: Macmillan, 2001), Vol. 3, 354.

10. The sources used in this work are fully discussed by David Osmond-Smith in his highly influential study *Playing on Words: A Guide to Luciano Berio's Sinfonia* (London: Royal Musical Association, 1985). The work also receives detailed commentary from David Metzer in his *Quotation and Cultural Meaning in Twentieth-Century Music* (Cambridge University Press, 2003), 128–39.

11. Jane Piper Clendinning, 'Postmodern Architecture/Postmodern Music', in *Postmodern Music/Postmodern Thought*, ed. Judy Lochead and Joseph Auner (London and New York: Routledge, 2002), 130. Of course, the identification of

Berio's *Sinfonia* as 'early' postmodernism would be dependent upon where the historical parameters are drawn.

12. Jonathan D. Kramer, 'The Nature and Origins of Musical Postmodernism', in *Postmodern Music/Postmodern Thought*, ed. Judy Lochead and Joseph Auner (London and New York: Routledge, 2002), 13–14.

13. Linda Hutcheon, *The Politics of Postmodernism* (London and New York: Routledge, 1989), 9.

14. See John Updike, *Rabbit, Run* (1960), *Rabbit Redux* (1971), *Rabbit is Rich* (1980) and *Rabbit at Rest* (1990) (all London: Penguin, 2006).

15. John Updike, *Memories of the Ford Administration* (London: Penguin, 2007 [1993]).

16. John N. Duvall, 'Troping History: Modernist Residue in Jameson's Pastiche and Hutcheon's Parody', in *Productive Postmodernism: Consuming Histories and Cultural Studies*, ed. John N. Duvall (Albany: State University of New York Press, 2002), 16.

17. Linda Hutcheon, *A Poetics of Postmodernism: History, Theory, Fiction* (New York and London: Routledge, 1988), 5.

18. *Ibid.*

19. *Ibid.*

20. John Fowles, *The French Lieutenant's Woman* (London: Vintage, 2004 [1969]).

21. Hutcheon, *A Poetics of Postmodernism*, 5.

22. This section of the chapter is loosely based on an unpublished paper titled 'Postmodern Music and the Memory of Romanticism', presented at the Music and Postmodern Cultural Theory Conference, University of Melbourne, December 2006.

23. In Paul Griffiths, *New Sounds, New Personalities: British Composers of the 1980s in Conversation with Paul Griffiths* (London: Faber, 1985), 170.

24. *Ibid.* I have previously referred to these statements by Maw, and explored their implications, in *Nicholas Maw: Odyssey* (Aldershot: Ashgate, 2008) and 'Nicholas Maw's Breakthrough: *Scenes and Arias* Reconsidered', *The Musical Times* 152 (2011), 31–57.

25. For details of the programming see Laura Kuhn, ' ISMS: New York: Horizons 83', *Perspectives of New Music* 21/1–2 (1982–3), 403. This article also provides an interesting contemporary response to this event and the constructed terminology.

26. Aspects of the reception of Maw's *Odyssey* are discussed in my book *Nicholas Maw: Odyssey*, 111–24.

27. Julian Anderson, 'Robin Holloway', in *New Grove Dictionary of Music and Musicians*, 2nd edn, ed. Stanley Sadie and John Tyrrell (London: Macmillan, 2001), Vol. 11, 633.

28. Robin Holloway, 'Composer's Note', *Scenes from Schumann* (London: Boosey and Hawkes, 1990).

29. The recording of *Fantasy-Pieces* features The Nash Ensemble conducted by Martyn Brabbins; Schumann's *Liederkreis* is performed by Toby Spence (tenor) and Ian Brown (piano) (Hyperion, CDA66930, 1998).

30. David W. Bernstein, 'Cage and High Modernism', in *The Cambridge Companion to John Cage*, ed. David Nicholls (Cambridge University Press, 2002), 210.

31. Robin Holloway, 'Modernism and After in Music', *The Cambridge Review* 110 (1989), 63.

32. *Ibid.*, 60–6.

33. *Ibid.*, 61.

34. *Ibid.*, 62.

35. *Ibid.*

36. *Ibid.*

37. *Ibid.*, 63.

38. *Ibid.*, 65.

39. *Ibid.*, 66.

5: The music of George Rochberg

1. Alexander L. Ringer, 'The Music of George Rochberg', *Musical Quarterly* 52/4 (1966), 412.

2. George Rochberg, *The Hexachord and its Relation to the Twelve-Tone Row* (Bryn Mawr, PA: Theodore Presser Co., 1955).

3. As cited in Joseph N. Straus, *Twelve-Tone Music in America* (Cambridge University Press, 2009), 75.

4. George Rochberg, *Five Lines, Four Spaces: The World of My Music* (Urbana and Chicago: University of Illinois Press, 2009), 13.

5. Christopher Lyndon-Gee, Liner notes to George Rochberg, Symphony No. 2 (Naxos, 8.559182, 2005).

6. See Rochberg's essays 'Duration in Music' (1960) and 'The Concepts of Musical Time and Space' (1963), in George Rochberg, *The Aesthetics of Survival: A Composer's View of Twentieth-Century Music* (Ann Arbor: University of Michigan Press, 2004).

7. David Harvey, *The Condition of Postmodernity: An Enquiry into the Origins of Cultural Change* (Oxford: Blackwell, 1989), vii.

8. Straus, *Twelve-Tone Music*, 77.

9. See Austin Clarkson and Steven Johnson, 'George Rochberg', in *The New Grove Dictionary of Music and Musicians*, 2nd edn, ed. Stanley Sadie and John Tyrrell (London: Macmillan, 2001), Vol. 21, 480.

10. Richard Taruskin, *Music in the Late Twentieth Century* (The Oxford History of Western Music Vol. 5) (Oxford and New York: Oxford University Press, 2010 [2005]), 415.

11. George Rochberg, Preface to *Music for the Magic Theater* (Bryn Mawr, PA: Theodore Presser Co., 1972).

12. As annotated on the score (p. 8; see Ex. 5.5).

13. Catherine Losada, 'The Process of Modulation in Musical Collage', *Music Analysis* 27/2–3 (2008), 299. See also Losada's 'Between Modernism and Postmodernism: Strands of Continuity in Collage Compositions by Rochberg, Berio and Zimmermann', *Music Theory Spectrum* 31/1 (2009), 57–100.

14. As annotated on the score (p. 45; see Ex. 5.6).

15. Rochberg, Preface.
16. See Losada, 'The Process of Modulation', 300.
17. Rochberg, *Five Lines*, 150.
18. *Ibid.*
19. See Taruskin, *Music in the Late Twentieth Century*, 415. David Metzer questions the identification of the Davis reference. This moment occurs towards the conclusion of the second movement at Fig. 51. At this point a trumpet solo emerges after the Mozart material comes to a halt and is directed to be 'played like Miles Davis – intense, felt, singing'. According to Metzer, 'The solo, however, bears little resemblance to any recording by Davis of that tune and it does not fit well the harmonic progression of the song, even by Davies's ingeniously expanded standards' (David Metzer, *Quotation and Cultural Meaning in Twentieth-Century Music* (Cambridge University Press, 2003), 122, n. 36). If it is not a direct reference to a specific Davis recording as such it can be interpreted as a then contemporary sound of the mid-1960s by way of contrast to the historical nature of the Mozart material.
20. Taruskin, *Music in the Late Twentieth Century*, 417.
21. Metzer, *Quotation and Cultural Meaning*, 114.
22. Robert Fink, 'Going Flat: Post-Hierarchical Music Theory and the Musical Surface', in *Rethinking Music*, ed. Nicholas Cook and Mark Everist (Oxford and New York: Oxford University Press, 1999), 129–30.
23. Rochberg, *Five Lines*, chapter 8, 143–64.
24. *Ibid.*, 99.
25. Mark Berry, 'Music, Postmodernism, and George Rochberg's Third String Quartet', in *Postmodern Music/Postmodern Thought*, ed. Judy Lochead and Joseph Auner (London and New York: Routledge, 2002), 243.
26. See *ibid.*, 244.
27. Taruskin, *Music in the Late Twentieth Century*, 430.
28. Berry, 'Music, Postmodernism, and George Rochberg's Third String Quartet', 244.
29. *Ibid.*, 242.
30. Fredric Jameson, *Postmodernism, or, the Cultural Logic of Late Capitalism* (London and New York: Verso, 1991), 17. For a good summary of Jameson's view of pastiche in postmodernism see Ian Buchanan, *Fredric Jameson: Live Theory* (London and New York: Continuum, 2006), 94–5; see also Losada, 'Between Modernism and Postmodernism', 60.
31. Jameson, *Postmodernism*, 17.
32. Rochberg, *Five Lines*, 100–1. The reference to the Nonesuch recording is based on the recording by the Concord String Quartet, who gave the first performance and recorded it for Nonesuch records in 1973.
33. *Ibid.*, 101.
34. *Ibid.*
35. Hal Foster, 'Postmodernism: A Preface', in *Postmodern Culture*, ed. Hal Foster (London: Pluto Press, 1985), x.
36. *Ibid.*

37. Jann Pasler, 'Postmodernism, Narrativity, and the Art of Memory', *Contemporary Music Review* 7 (1993), 17.

38. Jonathan D. Kramer, 'Beyond Unity: Toward an Understanding of Musical Postmodernism', in *Concert Music, Rock, and Jazz since 1945: Essays and Analytical Studies*, ed. Elizabeth West Marvin and Richard Hermann (University of Rochester Press, 1995), 21–2.

39. *Ibid.*, 22.

40. Although, as has been noted at earlier stages of this book, Hutcheon makes few direct references to music, in *A Poetics of Postmodernism* she positions Rochberg's music in relationship to the art of Robert Rauschenberg and, more significantly in this context, the fiction of John Fowles. See Linda Hutcheon, *A Poetics of Postmodernism: History, Theory, Fiction* (New York and London: Routledge, 1988), 11. Later in the book she refers directly to the third string quartet and describes Rochberg as a 'postmodernly parodic composer' (*A Poetics of Postmodernism*, 126).

6: The music of John Zorn

1. Hal Foster, 'Postmodernism: A Preface', in *Postmodern Culture*, ed. Hal Foster (London: Pluto Press, 1985), ix–x.

2. *Ibid.*, x.

3. Jonathan D. Kramer, 'Beyond Unity: Toward an Understanding of Musical Postmodernism', in *Concert Music, Rock, and Jazz since 1945: Essays and Analytical Studies*, ed. Elizabeth West Marvin and Richard Hermann (University of Rochester Press, 1995), 22.

4. In 2005 Zorn became artistic director of the Stone, which is described as a 'new artists' space in the East Village' and as 'a not-for-profit performance space dedicated to the experimental and avant-garde' (www.thestonenyc.com, last accessed 20 September 2011).

5. The Tzadik website gives a clear definition of its aims: 'Tzadik is dedicated to releasing the best in avant-garde and experimental music, presenting a worldwide community of contemporary musician-composers who find it difficult or impossible to release their music through more conventional channels. Tzadik believes most of all in the integrity of its artists. What you hear on Tzadik is the artists' vision undiluted' (www.tzadik.com, last accessed 20 September 2011).

6. Cited in Ajay Heble, *Landing on the Wrong Note: Jazz, Dissonance, and Critical Practice* (London and New York: Routledge, 2000), 182.

7. 'I'm not trying to fit into a certain genre that's invented by critics, postmodernism. I think "this is the way it is and I'm doing it": I'm literally just making music that I enjoy listening to.' Cited in Tom Service, 'Playing a New Game of Analysis: Performance, Postmodernism, and the Music of John Zorn' (PhD thesis, University of Southampton, 2004), 30.

8. Susan McClary, *Conventional Wisdom: The Content of Musical Form* (Berkeley, Los Angeles and London: University of California Press, 2000), 168.

9. John Zorn, Liner notes to *Spillane* (Nonesuch, 7559-79172-2, 1987).

10. McClary, *Conventional Wisdom*, 145.

11. *Ibid.*, 146. McClary's focus on the subject matter as a source of coherence in *Spillane* is partially echoed in Zorn's own assertion that this work does have a unity: '*Spillane* has a unity in the sense that each element deals with some aspect of Mickey Spillane's world'. In Cole Gange, *Soundpieces 2: Interviews with American Composers* (Metuchen, NJ: Scarecrow Press, 1993), 530. This statement combines with other reflections by Zorn on the specific question of unity to distance his own understanding of his music from some of the claims made for it in relationship to postmodernism. This point has been well made by John Brackett, see his *John Zorn: Tradition and Transgression* (Bloomington: Indiana University Press, 2008), xiii–xiv.

12. See Fredric Jameson, *Postmodernism, or, the Cultural Logic of Late Capitalism* (London and New York: Verso, 1991), 1.

13. John Zorn, 'On Carl Stalling', Liner notes to *Spillane*.

14. *Two-Lane Highway* comes between *Spillane* and *Forbidden Fruit* as the second track on the CD. It is described as being conceived and arranged by John Zorn for Albert Collins in collaboration with Collins and other musicians within what is essentially a rock band format of guitars, keyboards, bass and drums. Albert Collins as a legendary blues guitarist is the focal point of this music, with the engagement with the blues, and its influence on rock music, showing yet another dimension to the wide range of music that Zorn engages with.

15. John Zorn, Liner notes to *Forbidden Fruit* (Nonesuch, 7559-79172-2, 1987).

16. *Ibid.*

17. In other works Zorn has also reflected on the nature of the string quartet as an ensemble that has a certain history, most notably in *Cat O' Nine Tails* (1988), which contains fragmentary references to several quartets from within that history. In its rapid working through of such fragments it has notable similarities with *Spillane*, *Godard* and *Forbidden Fruit*.

18. Ellie M. Hisama, 'Postcolonialism on the Make: The Music of John Mellencamp, David Bowie, and John Zorn', in *Reading Pop: Approaches to Textual Analysis in Popular Music*, ed. Richard Middleton (Oxford and New York: Oxford University Press, 2000), 335–8.

19. Kramer, 'Beyond Unity', 22.

20. Hisama, 'Postcolonialism on the Make', 337.

21. John Corbett, 'Experimental Oriental: New Music and Other Others', in *Western Music and its Others: Difference, Representation, and Appropriation in Music*, ed. Georgina Born and David Hesmondhalgh (Berkeley, Los Angeles and London: University of California Press, 2000), 181.

22. Zorn, liner notes to *Forbidden Fruit*.

23. Hisama, 'Postcolonialism on the Make', 337.

24. Ellie M. Hisama, 'John Zorn and the Postmodern Condition', in *Locating East Asia in Western Art Music*, ed. Yayoi Uno Everett and Frederick Lau (Middletown, CT: Wesleyan University Press, 2004), 74.

25. Hisama's 'John Zorn and the Postmodern Condition' is the most direct engagement with these issues. For other insightful discussions see Susan McClary, *Conventional Wisdom*, 148–51, and John Brackett provides an extended discussion in a chapter titled 'From the Fantastic to the Dangerously Real: Reading John Zorn's Artwork', in *John Zorn: Tradition and Transgression*, 1–39.
26. Gagne, *Soundpieces 2*, 533.
27. Zorn acknowledges the importance of Coleman on his *Spy Vs Spy* recording, which involves Zorn and other musicians (Tim Berne (alto saxophone), Mark Dresser (bass), Joey Baron (drums) and Michael Vatcher (drums)) performing the music of Ornette Coleman. This recording not only uses Coleman's music but also reflects his influence on jazz and improvised music from the late 1950s onwards.
28. William Duckworth, *Talking Music: Conversations with John Cage, Philip Glass, Laurie Anderson, and Five Generations of American Experimental Composers* (New York: Da Capo Press, 1999), 446.
29. Tom Service, 'Playing a New Game of Analysis', 27–35.
30. *Ibid.*, 27.
31. Gagne, *Soundpieces 2*, 533.
32. Service, 'Playing a New Game of Analysis', 28.
33. Further consideration of the realization of such scores more generally, and the extent to which performances vary, and how they differ, would be an interesting area of future research that would connect the performance practice of this music with the availability of recordings as archive material.
34. Ann McCutchan, *The Muse that Sings: Composers Speak about the Creative Process* (Oxford and New York: Oxford University Press, 2003), 167.
35. Service, 'Playing a New Game of Analysis', 28.
36. Gagne, *Soundpieces 2*, 532.
37. For an insightful survey of the 1993 event and its wider context in terms of radical Jewish culture and the downtown music scene see Tamar Barzel, 'An Interrogation of Language: "Radical Jewish Culture" on New York City's Downtown Music Scene', *Journal of the Society for American Music* 4/2 (2010), 215–50.
38. See Barzel, 'An Interrogation of Language', 220.
39. www.tzadik.com (last accessed 20 September 2011). Many other musicians are included in Tzadik's radical Jewish culture series. One of the most notable is trumpeter Steven Bernstein. His *Diaspora Blues* features Bernstein with legendary jazz saxophonist Sam Rivers, supported by Doug Mathews (bass/bass clarinet) and Anthony Cole (drums/tenor sax). The jazz background of these musicians is clearly evident but the music is based on traditional Jewish melodies. According to the Tzadik publicity that accompanies the CD, this is an 'inspiring program of cantorial melodies associated with the great chazzan Moshe Koussevitsky, perhaps the greatest cantor of all time' (Tzadik, 02397-7164-2, 2002). Although no one recording can stand as definitive of the Tzadik series I find the musical hybridity between jazz and traditional Jewish music on this recording to be a highly effective example of the rich potential of the creative interface between these different musics.

40. Barzel, 'An Interrogation of Language', 220.
41. Heble, *Landing on the Wrong Note*, 180.
42. In using 'modern' to describe a specific jazz style, or moment, I am using it in the generally recognized description of modern jazz rather than as, at this stage, locating it directly in relation to either modernism or postmodernism.
43. Brackett, *John Zorn: Tradition and Transgression*, 118.
44. *Ibid.*
45. *Ibid.*, 118–19.
46. McCutchan, *The Muse that Sings*, 169.
47. Jonathan D. Kramer, 'The Nature and Origins of Musical Postmodernism', in *Postmodern Music/Postmodern Thought*, ed. Judy Lochead and Joseph Auner (London and New York: Routledge, 2002), 16.
48. However, I think that the distinction that Foster makes between a postmodernism of resistance and a postmodernism of reaction, and translated into music as a distinction between radical and conservative, is of limited use as a general theoretical model for postmodernism. It avoids the ambiguity that emerges from, for example, the interpretation of Rochberg's 'conservative' pastiche of the past as forcing us to radically rethink issues such as originality, authorship and the construction of the past. In its binary opposition it is also perhaps too neat and reflects the kinds of polarities that were implicit in modernist thought. For an interesting critical perspective on this claimed opposition in relation to music that we are now familiar with see Mark Berry, 'Music, Postmodernism, and George Rochberg's Third String Quartet', in *Postmodern Music/Postmodern Thought*, ed. Judy Lochead and Joseph Auner (London and New York: Routledge, 2002), 235–48.
49. McClary, *Conventional Wisdom*, 148.

7: Blurring the boundaries

1. Susan McClary, *Conventional Wisdom: The Content of Musical Form* (Berkeley, Los Angeles and London: University of California Press, 2000), 148.
2. Fredric Jameson, *Postmodernism, or, the Cultural Logic of Late Capitalism* (London and New York: Verso, 1991), 1.
3. Linda Hutcheon, *The Politics of Postmodernism* (London and New York: Routledge, 1989), 9.
4. McClary, *Conventional Wisdom*, 148.
5. These specific examples, and others, are also mentioned by Derek Scott in his 'Postmodernism and Music', in *The Routledge Companion to Postmodernism*, ed. Stuart Sim (London and New York: Routledge, 2009), 124.
6. The connections made between rock music and classical music through the development of progressive rock have been well documented. See, for example, Edward Macan, *Rocking the Classics: English Progressive Rock and the Counter Culture* (New York and Oxford: Oxford University Press, 1997).

7. The relationships between popular music and the avant-garde are contextualized through postmodernism in Bernard Gendron, *Between Montmartre and the Mudd Club: Popular Music and the Avant-Garde* (Chicago, IL, and London: University of Chicago Press, 2002).

8. Steven Connor, 'Introduction', in *The Cambridge Companion to Postmodernism*, ed. Steven Connor (Cambridge University Press, 2004), 17.

9. See McClary, *Conventional Wisdom*, 148.

10. Andreas Huyssen, *After the Great Divide: Modernism, Mass Culture and Postmodernism* (London: Macmillan, 1988), vii.

11. It is difficult to draw a meaningful distinction between mass culture and popular culture, and they are often used interchangeably. More specifically, mass culture may refer to a pre-1950s context within which popular culture was relatively homogeneous in terms of audience, and to which various theories of mass culture relate, while, under the impact of rock 'n' roll, there is a division along generational lines and the emergence of more distinctive, coexisting popular-music styles.

12. See Huyssen, *After the Great Divide*, ix. For a definitive example of the critical dismissal of mass culture and, more specifically, popular music within a pre-1950s context see Theodor Adorno, 'On Popular Music' (1941) in Adorno, *Essays on Music*, ed. Richard Leppert (Berkeley, Los Angeles and London: University of California Press, 2002), 437–69.

13. Huyssen, *After the Great Divide*, vii.

14. *Ibid.* In musical terms the gesture towards jazz, as well as specific forms of popular music, made by Stravinsky and other composers in the 1920s could be seen as examples of such strategies.

15. *Ibid.*, 197.

16. Jean-François Lyotard, *The Postmodern Condition: A Report on Knowledge*, trans. Geoff Bennington and Brian Massumi (Manchester University Press, 1989 [1979]), xxiv.

17. Huyssen, *The Great Divide*, ix.

18. As cited in Judy Lochead, 'Naming: Music and the Postmodern', *New Formations* 66 (2009), 167.

19. This point is also well made by Judy Lochead: 'But no matter how much Daugherty engages the world of popular culture, his music is still performed in concert halls by classically trained musicians, and is categorised as "classical" at "towerrecords.com"' (*ibid.*).

20. Arthur C. Danto, *After the End of Art: Contemporary Art and the Pale of History* (Princeton University Press, 1997), 13.

21. *Ibid.*

22. Jameson, *Postmodernism*, 1.

23. Other bands that have been described as 'post-rock' include Godspeed You! Black Emperor, Sigur Rós, The Sea and Cake, and Tortoise. There is no strong common link between these bands other than a shared interest in often instrumental and minimally repetitive textures.

24. I include dance in this list only because the moving shape of Zidane's body in the film suggests a certain balletic quality.

25. Connor, 'Introduction', 17.

26. Robert Fink, *Repeating Ourselves: American Minimal Music as Cultural Practice* (Berkeley, Los Angeles and London: University of California Press, 2005).

27. As cited in Keith Potter, *Four Musical Minimalists: La Monte Young, Terry Riley, Steve Reich, Philip Glass* (Cambridge University Press, 2000), 10.

28. *Ibid.*

29. For an insightful discussion of Glass's development towards the works from 1969 see Potter, *Four Musical Minimalists*, 273–86.

30. Philip Glass, *Music in Contrary Motion* (Elektra, 7559-79326-2, 1994 [1975]).

31. Potter, *Four Musical Minimalists*, 10. However, Potter's use of modernism in this context does need to be highly qualified, referring to 'radical "alternative" lines' of an experimental tradition as identified with Cage and representing 'an American reaction to the serial models of modernism offered by European composers such as Pierre Boulez and Karlheinz Stockhausen and by American serialists such as Milton Babbitt'.

32. See *ibid.*, 13.

33. Tim Page, liner notes to *Music in Contrary Motion* (Elektra, 7559-79326-2, 1994).

34. David Harvey, *The Condition of Postmodernity: An Enquiry into the Origins of Cultural Change* (Oxford: Blackwell, 1989), vii. Page describes this open form: 'The expanding figures upon which it is constructed could, theoretically, continue augmenting forever. Should an interpreter take it that far, a performance lasting hours, even days, would be possible' (Tim Page, liner notes to *Music in Contrary Motion*).

35. See Lyotard, *The Postmodern Condition*, 60.

36. Hutcheon, *The Politics of Postmodernism*, 9.

37. See Susan McClary's discussion of Glass's *Glassworks* (1982) for an interesting perspective on Glass's relationship to tonality (McClary, *Conventional Wisdom*, 142–5).

38. Philip Glass, liner notes to *Low Symphony* (Point, 438 150-2, 1993).

39. *Ibid.*

40. In Lydia Yee *et al.*, *Laurie Anderson, Trisha Brown, Gordon Matta-Clark: Pioneers of the Downtown Scene, New York 1970s* (Munich, London and New York: Prestel, 2011), 17.

41. *Ibid.*, 19.

42. *Ibid.*, 22.

43. *Ibid.*

44. Susan McClary, 'Laurie Anderson', in *New Grove Dictionary of Music and Musicians*, 2nd edn, ed. Stanley Sadie and John Tyrrell (London: Macmillan, 2001), Vol. 1, 613.

45. Susan McClary provides a useful description of the different versions of 'O Superman'. See her *Feminine Endings: Music, Gender, and Sexuality* (Minneapolis and Oxford: University of Minnesota Press, 1991), 202, n. 24.

46. McClary, *Feminine Endings*, 141.

47. McClary, 'Laurie Anderson', 614.

48. William Duckworth, *Talking Music: Conversations with John Cage, Philip Glass, Laurie Anderson, and Five Generations of American Experimental Composers* (New York: Da Capo Press, 1999), 383.

49. Paul Bley's interpretations of Carla Bley's compositions are available on a recording titled *Paul Plays Carla*, which features Paul Bley (piano) in a trio with Marc Johnson (bass) and Jeff Williams (drums).

50. This political engagement is articulated through a musical repertoire that goes back to the Spanish Civil War while also reflecting the war in Vietnam.

51. Stuart Nicholson, *Jazz-Rock: A History* (Edinburgh: Canongate, 1998), 298.

52. The recording of *Escalator over the Hill* was originally released on JCOA records in 1971 as part of the financial and artistic independence of the Jazz Composers organisation.

53. Harvey, *The Condition of Postmodernity*, vii.

8: The music of Sofia Gubaidulina (and others)

1. Alastair Williams, 'Ageing of the New: The Museum of Musical Modernism', in *The Cambridge History of Twentieth-Century Music*, ed. Nicholas Cook and Anthony Pople (Cambridge University Press, 2004), 530.

2. *Ibid.*

3. As cited in *ibid.*

4. *Ibid.*, 531.

5. *Ibid.*

6. Alfred Schnittke, Liner notes to Concerto Grosso No. 3 (BIS, CD-537, 1991).

7. This possible stylistic grouping and identification is highlighted by Judy Lochead: 'Critics and historians group her [Gubaidulina] with the Eastern European composers Arvo Pärt and Henryk Górecki, sometimes referring to them as the "Holy minimalists"' (Judy Lochead, 'Naming: Music and the Postmodern', *New Formations* 66 (2009), 166). However, the essay by Alex Ross to which Lochead refers ('Critic's Notebook: Of Mystics, Minimalists and Musical Miasmas', *New York Times*, 5 November 1993), and which is cited again in this chapter, does not directly discuss the music of Gubaidulina.

8. Paul D. Hillier, 'Arvo Pärt', in *New Grove Dictionary of Music and Musicians*, 2nd edn, ed. Stanley Sadie and John Tyrrell (London: Macmillan, 2001), Vol. 19, 165.

9. David Clarke, 'Parting Glances', *The Musical Times* 134 (1993), 684. For another interesting perspective on Pärt and postmodernism see Maria Cizmic, 'Transcending the Icon: Spirituality and Postmodernism in Arvo Pärt's *Tabula Rasa* and *Spiegel im Spiegel*', *twentieth-century music* 5/1 (2008), 45–78.

10. Clarke, 'Parting Glances', 680.

11. *Ibid.*

12. *Ibid.*

13. See Luke Howard, 'Production vs. Reception in Postmodernism: The Górecki Case', in *Postmodern Music/Postmodern Thought*, ed. Judy Lochead and Joseph Auner (London and New York: Routledge, 2002), 195–206.

14. Mikhail Epstein, 'Post-Atheism: From Apophatic Theology to "Minimal Religion"', in *Russian Postmodernism: New Perspectives on Post-Soviet Culture*, ed. Mikhail N. Epstein *et al.* (New York and Oxford: Berghahn, 1999), 345–93.

15. Alex Ross, *The Rest is Noise: Listening to the Twentieth Century* (New York: Farrar, Straus and Giroux, 2007), 530.

16. Cited in Steven Ledbetter, Liner notes to Sofia Gubaidulina, *Offertorium* (DG, 471 652-2, 1989).

17. This example is also discussed in Ledbetter, Liner notes, and Sally Macarthur, *Towards a Twenty-First-Century Feminist Politics of Music* (Farnham: Ashgate, 2010), 128–9.

18. Macarthur, *Towards*, 127. The reference is to Vladimir Jankélévich, *Music and the Ineffable*, trans. Carolyn Abbate (Princeton University Press, 2003). The ways in which Deleuze's thought may, or may not, intersect with postmodernism are beyond the scope of this introductory study. For any reader who wishes to pursue the relevance of Deleuze for music see Ronald Bogue, *Deleuze on Music, Painting and the Arts* (New York and London: Routledge, 2003).

19. As cited in Ledbetter, Liner notes to *Offertorium* and Macarthur, *Towards*, 129.

20. Ross, *The Rest is Noise*, 530.

21. Lochead, 'Naming: Music and the Postmodern', 166.

22. Alexander Genis, 'Archaic Postmodernism: The Aesthetics of Andrei Sinyavsky', in *Russian Postmodernism: New Perspectives on Post-Soviet Culture*, ed. Mikhail N. Epstein *et al.* (New York and London: Berghahn, 1999), 185–96.

23. Ross, 'Mystics, Minimalists and Musical Miasmas', 32. This is also cited in Judy Lochead, 'Naming: Music and the Postmodern', 166.

24. For a good survey of Hegel's understanding of history see Joseph McCarney, *Hegel on History* (London and New York: Routledge, 2000).

25. This argument is put forward by Fukuyama in *The End of History and the Last Man* (London: Penguin, 1993).

9: Repetitions and revisions

1. Alyn Shipton, *A New History of Jazz* (London and New York: Continuum, 2001), 873.

2. Bernard Gendron, *Between Montmartre and the Mudd Club: Popular Music and the Avant-Garde* (Chicago, IL, and London: University of Chicago Press, 2002), chapter 6 ('Moldy Figs and Modernists') and chapter 7 ('Bebop under Fire').

3. Krin Gabbard, 'The Word Jazz', in *The Cambridge Companion to Jazz*, ed. Mervyn Cooke and David Horn (Cambridge University Press, 2002), 1.

4. This influence is exerted from Marsalis's position as founding artistic director of the jazz programme at Lincoln Center, New York.

5. Robert Walser (ed.), *Keeping Time: Readings in Jazz History* (New York and Oxford: Oxford University Press, 1999), 334.

6. As cited in Shipton, *A New History of Jazz*, 878.

7. Marsalis has performed and recorded other music in the form of classical trumpet concertos but this is seen as a distinctly different musical activity.

8. This reference is to Davis's quintet of the mid-1960s, which featured Wayne Shorter (tenor saxophone), Herbie Hancock (piano), Ron Carter (bass) and Tony Williams (drums), and which is often referred to as Davis's 'second great quintet' after the first quintet recordings of the 1950s.

9. As cited in Gary Tomlinson, 'Cultural Dialogics and Jazz: A White Historian Signifies', in *Disciplining Music: Musicology and its Canons*, ed. Katherine Bergeron and Philip V. Bohlman (Chicago, IL, and London: University of Chicago Press, 1992), 79.

10. As cited in David Ake, *Jazz Cultures* (Berkeley, Los Angeles and London: University of California Press, 2002), 155.

11. *Ibid.*, 157.

12. See Ingrid Monson, *Saying Something: Jazz Improvisation and Interaction* (Chicago, IL, and London: University of Chicago Press, 1996), 97.

13. The reference to 'repetition' and 'revision' as used in this context is based on Henry Louis Gates Jr's *The Signifying Monkey: A Theory of African-American Literary Criticism* (Oxford and New York: Oxford University Press, 1988). According to Gates: 'Repetition and revision are fundamental to black artistic forms, from painting and sculpture to music and language use' (*Signifying Monkey*, xxiv). Gates's work, and this terminology, are used to telling effect by Gary Tomlinson in relation to jazz music, in particular Miles Davis's 'jazz-rock fusion', in 'Cultural Dialogics and Jazz'. The intertextual nature of jazz music is explored in some detail in relation to Miles Davis by Robert Walser in an essay titled '"Out of Notes": Signification, Interpretation, and the Problem of Miles Davis', in *Keeping Score: Music, Disciplinarity, Culture*, ed. David Schwarz *et al.* (Charlottesville and London: University Press of Virginia, 1997). Walser bases his discussion on Davis's 1964 recording of the standard 'My Funny Valentine' in comparison to an earlier recording of the song by singer Tony Bennett.

14. For a description of the details of this particular revision see Shipton, *A New History of Jazz*, 473–4.

15. Gendron, *Between Montmartre and the Mudd Club*, 143.

16. *Ibid.*, 121.

17. Gendron directly highlights this potential overlap: 'Unlike rock, which is altogether a postmodern phenomenon in its relation with the avant-garde, jazz historically has one foot in the modern era and one in postmodernism, one foot in Europe and one in America' (*ibid.*, 9).

18. See Ake, *Jazz Cultures*, 166–8.

19. See Björn Heile, 'Uri Caine's Mahler: Jazz, Tradition, and Identity', *twentieth-century music* 4/2 (2007), 229–55, for a detailed discussion of Caine's engagement with the music of Mahler.

20. The positioning of Frisell's eclectic mix of American musics as still somehow within jazz is often reinforced by the spaces within which his performances may occur. My own experience of hearing Frisell live in The Village Vanguard, New York, in April 2007 and again in May 2011 is indicative of this. The Village Vanguard is located in Greenwich Village. For decades it has been an iconic venue for jazz performance and many major jazz musicians have performed there.

21. Shipton, *A New History of Jazz*, 884.

22. David Toop, 'Hip-Hop', in *The New Grove Dictionary of Music and Musicians*, 2nd edn, ed. Stanley Sadie and John Tyrrell (London: Macmillan, 2001), Vol. 11, 542.

23. Russell A. Potter, *Spectacular Vernaculars: Hip-Hop and the Politics of Postmodernism* (Albany: State University of New York Press, 1995), 9.

24. www.djspooky.com/hype.php, last accessed 20 September 2011.

25. See, for example, Paul D. Miller, *Rhythm Science* (Cambridge, MA: The MIT Press, 2004).

26. Jesse Stewart, 'DJ Spooky and the Politics of Afro-Postmodernism', *Black Music Research Journal* 30/2 (2010), 337.

27. www.scannerdot.com/scanner.shtml, last accessed 20 September 2011.

28. Hal Foster, 'Postmodernism: A Preface', in *Postmodern Culture*, ed. Hal Foster (London: Pluto Press, 1985), ix–x.

Postscript

1. Nicolas Bourriaud. *Altermodern* (London: Tate Publishing, 2009), 11.

2. www.tate.org.uk/britain/exhibitions/altermodern/manifesto.shtm, last accessed 20 September 2011.

3. See, for example, Fredric Jameson, 'Globalization as a Philosophical Issue', in *The Cultures of Globalization*, ed. Fredric Jameson and Masao Miyoshi (Durham, NC, and London: Duke University Press, 1998), 54–77.

Bibliography

Adorno, Theodor, *Essays on Music*, ed. Richard Leppert (Berkeley, Los Angeles and London: University of California Press, 2002).

Ake, David, *Jazz Cultures* (Berkeley, Los Angeles and London: University of California Press, 2002).

Allen, Graham, *Intertextuality* (London and New York: Routledge, 2000).

Anderson, Julian, 'Robin Holloway', in *New Grove Dictionary of Music and Musicians*, 2nd edn, ed. Stanley Sadie and John Tyrrell (London: Macmillan, 2001), Vol. 11, 632–4.

Anderson, Perry, *The Origins of Postmodernity* (London and New York: Verso, 1998).

Baker, Stephen, *The Fiction of Postmodernity* (Edinburgh University Press, 2000).

Barthes, Roland, *Image – Music – Text* (London: Fontana, 1977).

Barzel, Tamar, 'An Interrogation of Language: "Radical Jewish Culture" on New York City's Downtown Scene', *Journal of the Society for American Music* 4/2 (2010), 215–50.

Bastian, Heiner (ed.), *Andy Warhol Retrospective* (London: Tate Publishing, 2001).

Baudrillard, Jean, *Fatal Strategies*, trans. Philip Beitchman and W. G. J. Niesluchowski (London: Pluto Press, 1999 [1983]).

Beard, David and Kenneth Gloag, *Musicology: The Key Concepts* (London and New York: Routledge, 2005).

Bennett, David, *Sounding Postmodernism: Sampling Australian Composers, Sound Artists and Music Critics* (Sydney: Australian Music Centre, 2008).

Bernard, Jonathan W., 'Minimalism, Postminimalism, and the Resurgence of Tonality in Recent American Music', *American Music* 21/1 (2003), 112–33.

'Tonal Traditions in Art Music since 1960', in *The Cambridge History of American Music*, ed. David Nicholls (Cambridge University Press, 1998), 535–609.

Bernstein, David W., 'Cage and High Modernism', in *The Cambridge Companion to John Cage*, ed. David Nicholls (Cambridge University Press, 2002), 186–213.

Berry, Mark, 'Music, Postmodernism, and George Rochberg's Third String Quartet', in *Postmodern Music/Postmodern Thought*, ed. Judy Lochead and Joseph Auner (London and New York: Routledge, 2002), 235–48.

Bertens, Hans, *The Idea of the Postmodern: A History* (London and New York: Routledge, 1995).

Block, Steven D., 'George Rochberg: Progressive or Master Forger?', *Perspectives of New Music* 21/1–2 (1982–3), 407–9.

Bogue, Ronald, *Deleuze on Music, Painting, and the Arts* (New York and London: Routledge, 2003).

Born, Georgina, *Rationalizing Culture: IRCAM, Boulez, and the Institutionalization of the Musical Avant-Garde* (Berkeley, Los Angeles and London: University of California Press, 1995).

Botstein, Leon, 'Modernism', in *The New Grove Dictionary of Music and Musicians*, 2nd edn, ed. Stanley Sadie and John Tyrrell (London: Macmillan, 2001), Vol. 16, 868–75.

Bourriaud, Nicolas, *Altermodern* (London: Tate Publishing, 2009).

Brackett, David, '"Where's It At?": Postmodern Theory and the Contemporary Musical Field', in *Postmodern Music/Postmodern Thought*, ed. Judy Lochead and Joseph Auner (London and New York: Routledge, 2002), 207–31.

Brackett, John, *John Zorn: Tradition and Transgression* (Bloomington: Indiana University Press, 2008).

Bradshaw, Peter, Review of *Captain America: The First Avenger*, *The Guardian*, 29 July 2011.

Bradshaw, Susan, 'Class of '45', *The Musical Times* 136 (1995), 139–41.

Brookes, William, 'Music and Society', in *The Cambridge Companion to John Cage*, ed. David Nicholls (Cambridge University Press, 2002), 214–26.

Buchanan, Ian, *Fredric Jameson: Live Theory* (London and New York: Continuum, 2006).

Burgin, Victor, *The End of Art Theory: Criticism and Postmodernity* (London: Palgrave Macmillan, 1986).

Butler, Christopher, *After the Wake: An Essay on the Contemporary Avant-Garde* (Oxford and New York: Oxford University Press, 1980).

  Postmodernism: A Very Short Introduction (Oxford and New York: Oxford University Press, 2002).

Cizmic, Maria, 'Transcending the Icon: Spirituality and Postmodernism in Arvo Pärt's *Tabula Rasa* and *Spiegel im Spiegel*', *twentieth-century music* 5/1 (2008), 45–78.

Clark, T. J., *Farewell to an Idea: Episodes from a History of Modernism* (New Haven, CT, and London: Yale University Press, 1999).

Clarke, David, 'Elvis and Darmstadt, or: Twentieth Century Music and the Politics of Cultural Pluralism', *twentieth-century music* 4/1 (2007), 3–70.

  'Parting Glances', *The Musical Times* 134 (1993), 680–4.

Clarkson, Austin and Steven Johnson, 'George Rochberg', in *The New Grove Dictionary of Music and Musicians*, 2nd edn, ed. Stanley Sadie and John Tyrrell (London: Macmillan, 2001), Vol. 21, 480–1.

Clendinning, Jane Piper, 'Postmodern Architecture/Postmodern Music', in *Postmodern Music/Postmodern Thought*, ed. Judy Lochead and Joseph Auner (London and New York: Routledge, 2002), 119–40.

Connor, Steven, 'Introduction', in *The Cambridge Companion to Postmodernism*, ed. Steven Connor (Cambridge University Press, 2004), 1–19.

  Postmodernist Culture: An Introduction to Theories of the Contemporary (Oxford: Blackwell, 1989).

Cook, Nicholas and Mark Everist, 'Preface', in *Rethinking Music*, ed. Nicholas Cook and Mark Everist (Oxford and New York: Oxford University Press, 1999), v–xii.

Corbett, John, 'Experimental Oriental: New Music and Other Others', in *Western Music and its Others: Difference, Representation, and Appropriation in Music*, ed. Georgina Born and David Hesmondhalgh (Berkeley, Los Angeles and London: University of California Press, 2000), 163–86.

Danto, Arthur C., *After the End of Art: Contemporary Art and the Pale of History* (Princeton University Press, 1997).

Daugherty, Michael, Liner notes to *Dead Elvis* (ARGO, 458 145-2, 1998).

DeKoven, Marianne, *Utopia Unlimited: The Sixties and the Emergence of the Postmodern* (Durham, NC, and London: Duke University Press, 2004).

Dell'Antonio, Andrew (ed.), *Beyond Structural Listening?: Postmodern Modes of Hearing* (Berkeley, Los Angeles and London: University of California Press, 2004).

Duckworth, William, *Talking Music: Conversations with John Cage, Philip Glass, Laurie Anderson, and Five Generations of American Experimental Composers* (New York: Da Capo Press, 1999).

Duvall, John N., 'Troping History: Modernist Residue in Jameson's Pastiche and Hutcheon's Parody', in *Productive Postmodernism: Consuming Histories and Cultural Studies*, ed. John N. Duvall (Albany: State University of New York Press, 2002), 1–22.

Eco, Umberto, *The Name of the Rose*, trans. William Weaver (New York and London: Harcourt Brace Jovanovich, 1983 [1980]).

Postscript to the Name of the Rose, trans. William Weaver (San Diego, New York and London: Harcourt Brace Jovanovich, 1984 [1983]).

Edgar, Andrew and Peter Sedgwick (eds.), *Cultural Theory: The Key Concepts*, 2nd edn (London and New York: Routledge, 2008).

Epstein, Mikhail, 'Post-Atheism: From Apophatic Theology to "Minimal Religion"', in *Russian Postmodernism: New Perspectives on Post-Soviet Culture*, ed. Mikhail N. Epstein *et al.* (New York and Oxford: Berghahn, 1999), 345–93.

Fink, Robert, 'Elvis Everywhere: Musicology and Popular Music Studies at the Twilight of the Canon', in *Rock Over the Edge: Transformations in Popular Music Culture*, ed. Roger Beebe *et al.* (Durham, NC, and London: Duke University Press, 2002), 60–109.

'Going Flat: Post-Hierarchical Music Theory and the Musical Surface', in *Rethinking Music*, ed. Nicholas Cook and Mark Everist (Oxford and New York: Oxford University Press, 1999), 102–37.

'(Post-)Minimalisms 1970–2000: The Search for a New Mainstream', in *The Cambridge History of Twentieth-Century Music*, ed. Nicholas Cook and Anthony Pople (Cambridge University Press, 2004), 539–56.

Repeating Ourselves: American Minimal Music as Cultural Practice (Berkeley, Los Angeles and London: University of California Press, 2005).

Foster, Hal, 'Postmodernism: A Preface', in *Postmodern Culture*, ed. Hal Foster (London: Pluto Press, 1985), vii–xiv.

Foster, Hal and Rosalind Krauss, Yve-Alain Bois and Benjamin H. D. Buchloh (eds.), *Art Since 1900: Modernism, Antimodernism, Postmodernism* (London: Thames & Hudson, 2004).

Fowles, John, *The French Lieutenant's Woman* (London: Vintage, 2004 [1969]).

Fukuyama, Francis, *The End of History and the Last Man* (London: Penguin, 1993).

Gabbard, Krin, 'The Word Jazz', in *The Cambridge Companion to Jazz*, ed. Mervyn Cooke and David Horn (Cambridge University Press, 2002).

Gagne, Cole, *Soundpieces 2: Interviews with American Composers* (Metuchen, NJ: Scarecrow Press, 1993).

Gates, Henry Louis Jr, *The Signifying Monkey: A Theory of African-American Literary Criticism* (Oxford and New York: Oxford University Press, 1988).

Gendron, Bernard, *Between Montmartre and the Mudd Club: Popular Music and the Avant-Garde* (Chicago, IL, and London: University of Chicago Press, 2002).

Genis, Alexander, 'Archaic Postmodernism: The Aesthetics of Andrei Sinyavsky', in *Russian Postmodernism: New Perspectives on Post-Soviet Culture*, ed. Mikhail N. Epstein *et al.* (New York and London: Berghahn, 1999), 185–96.

Gillett, Charlie, *The Sound of the City* (London: Souvenir Press, 1970 [1983, 1996]).

Glass, Philip, Liner notes to *Low Symphony* (Point, 438 150–2, 1993).

Gloag, Kenneth, 'All You Need Is Theory', *Music & Letters* 79/4 (1998), 577–83.

'I Remember When Rock Was Young', unpublished paper presented at the Royal Musical Association, Music Historiography Conference, Cardiff University, September 2003 and the Symposium of the International Musicological Society, Monash University, Melbourne, July 2004.

Nicholas Maw: Odyssey (Aldershot: Ashgate, 2008).

'Nicholas Maw's Breakthrough: *Scenes and Arias* Reconsidered', *The Musical Times* 152 (2011), 31–57.

'Postmodern Music and the Memory of Romanticism', unpublished paper presented at the Music and Postmodern Cultural Theory Conference, University of Melbourne, December 2006.

'Situating the 1960s: Popular Music – Postmodernism – History', *Rethinking History* 5/3 (2001), 397–410.

Goodwin, Andrew, 'Popular Music and Postmodern Theory', in *Cultural Theory and Popular Culture: A Reader*, ed. John Storey (Hemel Hempstead: Harvester Wheatsheaf, 1994), 414–38.

Griffiths, Paul, *Modern Music and After: Directions Since 1945* (Oxford and New York: Oxford University Press, 1995).

New Sounds, New Personalities: British Composers of the 1980s in Conversation with Paul Griffiths (London: Faber, 1985).

Habermas, Jürgen, 'Modernity: An Incomplete Project', in *Postmodern Culture*, ed. Hal Foster (London: Pluto Press, 1985), 3–15.

Hamm, Charles, 'Privileging the Moment: Cage, Jung, Synchronicity, Postmodernism', *The Journal of Musicology* 15/2 (1997), 278–89.

Harvey, David, *The Condition of Postmodernity: An Enquiry into the Origins of Cultural Change* (Oxford: Blackwell, 1989).

Hassan, Ihab, *The Postmodern Turn: Essays in Postmodern Theory and Culture* (Columbus: Ohio State University Press, 1987).

Heble, Ajay, *Landing on the Wrong Note: Jazz, Dissonance, and Critical Practice* (New York and London: Routledge, 2000).

Heile, Björn, 'Darmstadt as Other: British and American Responses to Musical Modernism', *twentieth-century music* 1/2 (2004), 161–78.

'Uri Caine's Mahler: Jazz, Tradition, and Identity', *twentieth-century music* 4/2 (2007), 229–55.

Hillier, Paul D., 'Arvo Pärt', in *New Grove Dictionary of Music and Musicians*, 2nd edn, ed. Stanley Sadie and John Tyrrell (London: Macmillan, 2001), Vol. 19, 164–7.

Hisama, Ellie M., 'John Zorn and the Postmodern Condition', in *Locating East Asia in Western Art Music*, ed. Yayoi Uno Everett and Frederick Lau (Middletown, CT: Wesleyan University Press, 2004), 72–84.

'Postcolonialism on the Make: The Music of John Mellencamp, David Bowie, and John Zorn', in *Reading Pop: Approaches to Textual Analysis in Popular Music*, ed. Richard Middleton (Oxford and New York: Oxford University Press, 2000), 329–46.

Holloway, Robin, 'Composer's Note', *Scenes from Schumann* (London: Boosey and Hawkes, 1990).

'Modernism and After in Music', *The Cambridge Review* 110 (1989), 60–6.

Hooper, Giles, *The Discourse of Musicology* (Aldershot: Ashgate, 2006).

Hoover, Paul (ed.), *Postmodern American Poetry: A Norton Anthology* (New York and London: Norton, 1994).

Howard, Luke, 'Production vs. Reception in Postmodernism: The Górecki Case', in *Postmodern Music/Postmodern Thought*, ed. Judy Lochead and Joseph Auner (London and New York: Routledge, 2002), 195–206.

Hutcheon, Linda, *Irony's Edge: The Theory and Politics of Irony* (London and New York: Routledge, 1994).

A Poetics of Postmodernism: History, Theory, Fiction (London and New York: Routledge, 1988).

The Politics of Postmodernism (London and New York: Routledge, 1989; 2nd edn, 2002).

Huyssen, Andreas, *After the Great Divide: Modernism, Mass Culture and Postmodernism* (London: Macmillan, 1988).

Jameson, Fredric, 'Globalization as a Philosophical Issue', in *The Cultures of Globalization*, ed. Fredric Jameson and Masao Miyoshi (Durham, NC, and London: Duke University Press, 1998), 54–77.

Postmodernism, or, the Cultural Logic of Late Capitalism (London and New York: Verso, 1991).

Valences of the Dialectic (London and New York: Verso, 2009).

Jankélévich, Vladimir, *Music and the Ineffable*, trans. Carolyn Abbate (Princeton University Press, 2003).

Jencks, Charles, *What is Postmodernism?* (London: Academy, 1996).

Jones, Carys Wyn, *The Rock Canon: Canonical Values in the Reception of Rock Albums* (Aldershot: Ashgate, 2008).

Kellner, Douglas, 'Introduction: Jean Baudrillard in the Fin-de-Millennium', in *Baudrillard: A Critical Reader*, ed. Douglas Kellner (Oxford: Blackwell, 1994), 1–23.

Kerman, Joseph, *Musicology* (London: Fontana, 1985).

Kramer, Jonathan D., 'Beyond Unity: Toward an Understanding of Musical Postmodernism', in *Concert Music, Rock, and Jazz since 1945: Essays and Analytical Studies*, ed. Elizabeth West Marvin and Richard Hermann (University of Rochester Press, 1995), 11–33.

  'The Nature and Origins of Musical Postmodernism', in *Postmodern Music/Postmodern Thought*, ed. Judy Lochead and Joseph Auner (London and New York: Routledge, 2002), 13–26.

Kramer, Lawrence, *Classical Music and Postmodern Knowledge* (Berkeley, Los Angeles and London: University of California Press, 1995).

  Interpreting Music (Berkeley, Los Angeles and London: University of California Press, 2011).

  Musical Meaning: Toward a Critical History (Berkeley, Los Angeles and London: University of California Press, 2002).

Kristeva, Julia, 'Word, Dialogue and Novel', in *The Kristeva Reader*, ed. Toril Moi (Oxford: Blackwell, 1986), 34–61.

Kuhn, Laura, 'ISMS: New York: Horizons 83', *Perspectives of New Music* 21/1–2 (1982–3), 402–6.

Kunzru, Hari, *Gods Without Men* (London: Hamish Hamilton, 2011).

Ledbetter, Steven, Liner notes to Sofia Gubaidulina, *Offertorium* (DG, 471 652–2, 1989).

Leibowitz, René, *Schoenberg and his School: The Contemporary Stage of the Language of Music*, trans. Dika Newlin (New York: Da Capo Press, 1970 [1949]).

Leppert, Richard, *The Sight of Sound: Music, Representation, and the History of the Body* (Berkeley, Los Angeles and London: University of California Press, 1993).

Linton, Michael, Liner notes to George Rochberg, String Quartets Nos. 3–6, Concord String Quartet (New World Records, 80551–2, 1999).

Lochead, Judy, 'Naming: Music and the Postmodern', *New Formations* 66 (2009), 158–72.

Lochead, Judy and Joseph Auner, eds., *Postmodern Music/Postmodern Thought* (London and New York: Routledge, 2002).

Longhurst, Paul, *Popular Music and Society* (Cambridge: Polity Press, 1995).

Losada, Catherine, 'Between Modernism and Postmodernism: Strands of Continuity in Collage Compositions by Rochberg, Berio and Zimmermann', *Music Theory Spectrum* 31/1 (2009), 57–100.

  'The Process of Modulation in Musical Collage', *Music Analysis* 27/2–3 (2008), 295–336.

Lyndon-Gee, Christopher, Liner notes to George Rochberg, Symphony No. 2 (Naxos: 8.559182, 2005).

Lyotard, Jean-François, *The Inhuman: Reflections on Time*, trans. Geoffrey Bennington and Rachel Bowlby (Cambridge: Polity Press, 1991).

  'Music and Postmodernity', trans. David Bennett, *New Formations* 66 (2009 [1996]), 37–45.

The Postmodern Condition: A Report on Knowledge, trans. Geoff Bennington and Brian Massumi (Manchester University Press, 1989 [1979]).

Macan, Edward, *Rocking the Classics: English Progressive Rock and the Counter Culture* (New York and Oxford: Oxford University Press, 1997).

Macarthur, Sally, *Towards a Twenty-First-Century Feminist Politics of Music* (Farnham: Ashgate, 2010).

MacCabe, Colin, 'Theory and Film: Principles of Realism and Pleasure', *Screen* 17/3 (1976), 7–27.

McCarney, Joseph, *Hegel on History* (London and New York: Routledge, 2000).

McClary, Susan, *Conventional Wisdom: The Content of Musical Form* (Berkeley, Los Angeles and London: University of California Press, 2000).

Feminine Endings: Music, Gender, and Sexuality (Minneapolis and Oxford: University of Minnesota Press, 1991).

'Laurie Anderson', in *New Grove Dictionary of Music and Musicians*, 2nd edn, ed. Stanley Sadie and John Tyrrell (London: Macmillan, 2001), Vol. 1, 613–14.

Modal Subjectivities: Self-Fashioning in the Italian Madrigal (Berkeley, Los Angeles and London: University of California Press, 2004).

'More PoMo Than Thou: The Status of Cultural Meanings in Music', *New Formations* 66 (2009), 28–36.

McCutchan, Ann, *The Muse that Sings: Composers Speak about the Creative Process* (Oxford and New York: Oxford University Press, 2003).

McHale, Brian, *Constructing Postmodernism* (London and New York: Routledge, 1992).

Postmodernist Fiction (London and New York: Routledge, 1989).

Marcus, Greil, *Dead Elvis: A Chronicle of a Cultural Obsession* (London and New York: Viking, 1991).

Marwick, Arthur, *The Sixties: Cultural Revolution in Britain, France, Italy, and the United States c. 1958–74* (Oxford and New York: Oxford University Press, 1998).

Messing, Scott, *Neoclassicism in Music: From the Genesis of the Concept through the Schoenberg/Stravinsky Polemic* (University of Rochester Press, 1996).

Metzer, David, *Musical Modernism at the Turn of the Twenty-First Century* (Cambridge University Press, 2009).

Quotation and Cultural Meaning in Twentieth-Century Music (Cambridge University Press, 2003).

Meyer, Leonard B., *Music, the Arts, and Ideas: Patterns and Predictions in Twentieth-Century Culture* (Chicago, IL, and London: University of Chicago Press, 1994 [1967]).

Middleton, Richard, *Studying Popular Music* (Milton Keynes: Open University Press, 1990).

Miller, Paul D. [DJ Spooky], *Rhythm Science* (Cambridge, MA: The MIT Press, 2004).

Miller, Stephen Paul, *The Seventies Now: Culture as Surveillance* (Durham, NC, and London: Duke University Press, 1999).

Monson, Ingrid, *Saying Something: Jazz Improvisation and Interaction* (Chicago, IL, and London: University of Chicago Press, 1996).

Nicholson, Stuart, *Jazz-Rock: A History* (Edinburgh: Canongate, 1998).

Nicol, Bran, *The Cambridge Introduction to Postmodern Fiction* (Cambridge University Press, 2009).

Norris, Christopher, *What's Wrong With Postmodernism: Critical Theory and the Ends of Philosophy* (Hemel Hempstead: Harvester Wheatsheaf, 1990).

Nyman, Michael, *Experimental Music: Cage and Beyond*, 2nd edn (Cambridge University Press, 1999).

Osmond-Smith, David, *Berio* (Oxford and New York: Oxford University Press, 1991).

'Luciano Berio', in *New Grove Dictionary of Music and Musicians*, 2nd edn, ed. Stanley Sadie and John Tyrrell (London: Macmillan, 2001), Vol. 3, 350–8.

Playing on Words: A Guide to Luciano Berio's Sinfonia (London: Royal Musical Association, 1985).

Paddison, Max, *Adorno, Modernism and Mass Culture: Essays on Critical Theory and Music* (London: Kahn & Averill, 1996).

'Postmodernism and the Survival of the Avant-Garde', in *Contemporary Music: Theoretical and Philosophical Perspectives*, ed. Max Paddison and Irène Deliège (Farnham: Ashgate, 2010), 205–28.

Page, Tim, Liner notes to Philip Glass, *Music in Contrary Motion* (Elektra, 7559-79326-2, 1994).

Pasler, Jann, 'Postmodernism', in *The New Grove Dictionary of Music and Musicians*, 2nd edn, ed. Stanley Sadie and John Tyrrell (London: Macmillan, 2001), Vol. 20, 213–16.

'Postmodernism, Narrativity, and the Art of Memory', *Contemporary Music Review* 7 (1993), 3–32.

Paterson, Alexis, 'The Minimal Kaleidoscope: Exploring Minimal Music through the Lens of Postmodernity' (PhD thesis, Cardiff University, 2010).

Potter, Keith, *Four Musical Minimalists: La Monte Young, Terry Riley, Steve Reich, Philip Glass* (Cambridge University Press, 2000).

Potter, Russell A., *Spectacular Vernaculars: Hip-Hop and the Politics of Postmodernism* (Albany: State University of New York Press, 1995).

Pritchett, James, 'John Cage', in *The New Grove Dictionary of Music and Musicians*, 2nd edn, ed. Stanley Sadie and John Tyrrell (London: Macmillan, 2001), Vol. 4, 796–804.

The Music of John Cage (Cambridge University Press, 1993).

Ramsey, Guthrie P., Jr, *Race Music: Black Cultures from Bebop to Hip-Hop* (Berkeley, Los Angeles and London: University of California Press, 2003).

Reise, Jay, 'Rochberg the Progressive', *Perspectives of New Music* 19/1–2 (1980–1), 395–407.

Ringer, Alexander L., 'The Music of George Rochberg', *Musical Quarterly* 52/4 (1966), 409–30.

Rochberg, George, *The Aesthetics of Survival: A Composer's View of Twentieth-Century Music* (Ann Arbor: University of Michigan Press, 2004).

Five Lines, Four Spaces: The World of My Music (Urbana and Chicago: University of Illinois Press, 2009).

The Hexachord and its Relation to the Twelve-Tone Row (Bryn Mawr, PA: Theodore Presser Co., 1955).

Preface to *Music for the Magic Theater* (Bryn Mawr, PA: Theodore Presser Co., 1972).

Ross, Alex, 'Critics Notebook: Of Mystics, Minimalists and Musical Miasmas', *New York Times*, 5 November 1993.

The Rest is Noise: Listening to the Twentieth Century (New York: Farrar, Straus and Giroux, 2007).

Schnittke, Alfred, Liner notes to Concerto Grosso No. 3 (BIS, CD-537, 1991).

Scott, Derek, 'Postmodernism and Music', in *The Routledge Companion to Postmodernism*, ed. Stuart Sim (London and New York: Routledge, 2009), 122–32.

Service, Tom, 'Playing a New Game of Analysis: Performance, Postmodernism, and the Music of John Zorn' (PhD thesis, University of Southampton, 2004).

Shipton, Alyn, *A New History of Jazz* (London and New York: Continuum, 2001).

Shumway, David R., 'Rock 'n' Roll Soundtracks and the Production of Nostalgia', *Cinema Journal* 38/2 (1999), 36–51.

Sim, Stuart, 'Postmodernism and Philosophy', in *The Routledge Companion to Postmodernism*, ed. Stuart Sim (London and New York: Routledge, 2009), 3–12.

Smith, Jeff, 'Popular Songs and Comic Allusion in Contemporary Cinema', in *Soundtrack Available: Essays on Film and Popular Music*, ed. Pamela Robertson Wojcik and Arthur Knight (Durham, NC, and London: Duke University Press, 2001), 407–30.

Stewart, Jesse, 'DJ Spooky and the Politics of Afro-Postmodernism', *Black Music Research Journal* 30/2 (2010), 337–61.

Straus, Joseph N., *Twelve-Tone Music in America* (Cambridge University Press, 2009).

Strickland, Edward, 'Philip Glass', in *The New Grove Dictionary of Music and Musicians*, 2nd edn, ed. Stanley Sadie and John Tyrrell (London: Macmillan, 2001), Vol. 9, 932–6.

Subotnik, Rose Rosengard, *Deconstructive Variations: Music and Reason in Western Society* (Minneapolis and London: University of Minnesota Press, 1996).

Tait, Theo, review of Hari Kunzru, *Gods Without Men* (London: Hamish Hamilton, 2011), *The Guardian*, 30 July 2011.

Taruskin, Richard, *Music in the Late Twentieth Century* (The Oxford History of Western Music, Vol. 5) (Oxford and New York: Oxford University Press, 2010 [2005]).

Tomlinson, Gary, 'Cultural Dialogics and Jazz: A White Historian Signifies', in *Disciplining Music: Musicology and its Canons*, ed. Katherine Bergeron and Philip V. Bohlman (Chicago, IL, and London: University of Chicago Press, 1992).

Toop, David, 'Hip-Hop', in *The New Grove Dictionary of Music and Musicians*, 2nd edn, ed. Stanley Sadie and John Tyrrell (London: Macmillan, 2001), Vol. 11, 542–3.

Tucker, Bruce, '"Tell Tchaikovsky the News": Postmodernism, Popular Culture, and the Emergence of Rock 'n' Roll', *Black Music Research Journal* 9/2 (1989), 271–95.

Updike, John, *Memories of the Ford Administration* (London: Penguin, 2007 [1993]).

Rabbit at Rest (London: Penguin, 2006 [1990]).

Rabbit is Rich (London: Penguin, 2006 [1980]).

Rabbit Redux (London: Penguin, 2006 [1971]).

Rabbit, Run (London: Penguin, 2006 [1960]).

Walser, Robert, '"Out of Notes": Signification, Interpretation, and the Problem of Miles Davis', in *Keeping Score: Music, Disciplinarity, Culture*, ed. David Schwarz *et al.* (Charlottesville and London: University Press of Virginia, 1997), 147–68.

Walser, Robert (ed.), *Keeping Time: Readings in Jazz History* (New York and Oxford: Oxford University Press, 1999).

Watkins, Glenn, Liner notes to George Rochberg, *Music for the Magic Theater* (New World Records, 80462–2, 1994).

Pyramids at the Louvre: Music, Culture, and Collage from Stravinsky to the Postmodernists (Cambridge, MA, and London: Harvard University Press, 1994).

Whittall, Arnold, *Exploring Twentieth-Century Music: Tradition and Innovation* (Cambridge University Press, 2003).

Music Since the First World War (London: Dent, 1988).

Serialism (Cambridge University Press, 2008).

Williams, Alastair, 'Ageing of the New: The Museum of Musical Modernism', in *The Cambridge History of Twentieth-Century Music*, ed. Nicholas Cook and Anthony Pople (Cambridge University Press, 2004), 506–38.

'Cage and Postmodernism', in *The Cambridge Companion to John Cage*, ed. David Nicholls (Cambridge University Press, 2002), 227–41.

Constructing Musicology (Aldershot: Ashgate, 2001).

Worton, Michael and Judith Still (eds.), *Intertextuality: Theories and Practices* (Manchester and New York: Manchester University Press, 1990).

Yee, Lydia *et al.*, *Laurie Anderson, Trisha Brown, Gordon Matta-Clark: Pioneers of the Downtown Scene, New York 1970s* (Munich, London and New York: Prestel, 2011).

Zorn, John, Liner notes to *Forbidden Fruit* (Nonesuch, 7559-79172-2, 1987).

Liner notes to *Spillane* (Nonesuch, 7559-79172-2, 1987).

Websites

www.djspooky.com
www.michaeldaugherty.net
www.scannerdot.com
www.tate.org.uk
www.tzadik.com

Recordings

Anderson, Laurie, *Big Science* (Warner Bros., 7599–23674–2, 1982).

Bad Plus, The, *Prog* (do the math records, 08602517268326, 2007).

Bernstein, Steven, *Diaspora Blues* (Tzadik, 02397–7164–2, 2002).

Bley, Carla, *Escalator over the Hill* (ECM, 839 311–2, 1998 [1971]).

Bley, Paul, *Paul Plays Carla* (Steeplechase, SCCD, 31303, 1992).

Bowie, David, *Low* (Virgin, 21907, 1999 [1977]).

    Pin Ups (Virgin, 21903, 1999 [1973]).

Costello, Elvis, *The Juliet Letters* (Warner Bros., 9362–45180–2, 1992).

Crispell, Marilyn, *Amaryllis* (ECM, 1742 013 4000–2, 2001).

Daugherty, Michael, *American Icons* (ARGO, 145–2, 1998).

Davis, Miles, *Bitches Brew* (Columbia, 65351, 1997 [1970]).

    In a Silent Way (Columbia, 9117, 1996 [1969]).

    Miles in the Sky (Columbia, 66584, 1998 [1968]).

    On the Corner (Columbia, 65343, 1997 [1972]).

Dion and the Belmonts, *Reunion: Live at Madison Square Garden 1972* (Rhino, RS 70228, 1989 [1972]).

Emerson, Lake and Palmer, *Pictures at an Exhibition* (EMI, CD 342, 1996 [1972]).

Ferry, Bryan, *These Foolish Things* (Virgin, 47598, 2000 [1973]).

Frisell, Bill, *Have a Little Faith* (Nonesuch, 79302–3, 1992).

    Nashville (Nonesuch, 79415–2, 1997).

Glass, Philip, *Low Symphony* (Point, 438 150–2, 1993).

    Music in Contrary Motion (Elektra, 7559–79326–2, 1994 [1975]).

    Songs from Liquid Days (CBS, MK 39564, 1986).

Gubaidulina, Sofia, *Offertorium* (DG, 471 625–2, 1989).

Haden, Charlie, *Liberation Music Orchestra* (Impulse, IMP 11882, 1996 [1969]).

Holloway, Robin, *Fantasy-Pieces* (Hyperion, CDA66930, 1998).

John, Elton, *Greatest Hits 1970–2002* (Mercury, CD 063–450–2/063–451–2, 2002).

Kronos Quartet, *Kronos Quartet* ('Purple Haze') (Nonesuch, 79111, 1986).

McLean, Don, *American Pie* (EMI, CDP 7–46555–2, 1988 [1971]).

Mahler, Gustav and Uri Caine, *Urlicht/Primal Light* (Winter & Winter, 910 004–2, 1997).

Marsalis, Wynton, *Standard Time Vol. 1* (CBS, CK 40461, 1987).

    Standard Time Vol. 2: Intimacy Calling (CBS, CK 47346, 1991).

Oliver, King, *Louis Armstrong and King Oliver* (Milestone, MCD-47017–2, 1992 [1926]).

Parker, Charlie, *Ornithology: Classic Recordings 1945–1947* (Naxos CD 8.120571, 2001).

Rochberg, George, String Quartets Nos. 3–6, Concord String Quartet (New World Records, 80551-2, 1999 [1973]).

Scanner with the Post Modern Jazz Quartet, *Blink of an Eye* (Thirsty Ear, TH 57195, 2010).

Shipp, Matthew and DJ Spooky, *Optometry* (Thirsty Ear, TH 57121.2, 2002).

Various, *41 Original Hits from the Sound Track of American Graffiti* (MCA, MCLDD 19150, 2007 [1973]).

Various, *Re-Bop: The Savoy Remixes* (Savoy Jazz World Wide, SVY 17598, 2006).

Zorn, John, *Aporias* (Tzadik, TZ 7085, 2003).

   The Big Gundown (Tzadik, TZ 7328, 2000).

   Spillane (also includes *Forbidden Fruit* and *Two-Lane Highway*) (Nonesuch, 7559-79172-2, 1987).

   Spy Vs. Spy (Elektra, 7559-60844-3, 1989).

Zorn, John and Masada, *Masada First Live 1993* (Tzadik, TZ 7387, 2002).

Zorn, John and Naked City, *Naked City* (Nonesuch, 7559-79238-2, 1990).

   Naked City Live Vol. 1: Knitting Factory 1989 (Tzadik, TZ 7336, 2002).

Films

American Graffiti (1973), dir. George Lucas.

Brazil (1985), dir. Terry Gilliam.

Captain America: The First Avenger (2011), dir. Joe Johnston.

The French Lieutenant's Woman (1981), dir. Karel Reisz.

It's a Wonderful Life (1946), dir. Frank Capra.

The Naked City (1948), dir. Jules Dassin.

Psycho (1960), dir. Alfred Hitchcock.

Sleeping with the Enemy (1991), dir. Joseph Ruben.

That'll Be the Day (1973), dir. Claude Whatham.

Zidane (2006), dir. Douglas Gordon and Philippe Parreno.

Index

Cambridge Introductions to Music

'Cambridge University Press is to be congratulated for formulating the idea of an "Introductions to Music" series.' Nicholas Jones, *The Musical Times*

Each book in this series focuses on a topic fundamental to the study of music at undergraduate and graduate level. The introductions will also appeal to readers who want to broaden their understanding of the music they enjoy.

- Contain features which highlight and summarize key information
- Provide helpful guidance on specialized musical terminology
- Thorough guides to further reading assist the reader in investigating the topic in more depth

Books in the series

Gregorian Chant   David Hiley

Music Technology   Julio D'Escrivan

Opera   Robert Cannon

Postmodernism in Music   Kenneth Gloag

Serialism   Arnold Whittall

The Sonata   Thomas Schmidt-Beste

The Song Cycle   Laura Tunbridge